J. E. Ayars

The People's Hand-Book of the Bible ..

J. E. Ayars

The People's Hand-Book of the Bible ..

ISBN/EAN: 9783337171711

Printed in Europe, USA, Canada, Australia, Japan

Cover: Foto ©Lupo / pixelio.de

More available books at **www.hansebooks.com**

THE PEOPLE'S
HAND-BOOK OF THE BIBLE,

AN INTRODUCTION

TO THE

STUDY OF THE HOLY SCRIPTURES.

ON THE BASIS AND PLAN OF J ANGUS D D

As Compared with the Best Standard Authorities on Evidences and Principles of Right Interpretation of the Bible.

PREPARED IN THE

LIGHT OF THE REVISED VERSION OF 1880-4, OXFORD EDITION.

𝔚ith 𝔑ew, 𝔄dditional and 𝔍llustrative 𝔐atter, both 𝔒riginal and from the 𝔅est 𝔄ncient and 𝔐odern 𝔄uthors.

By J E AYARS

GRADUATE OF FIRST CLASS OF 1858, GARRETT BIBLICAL INST.

"Thy word is a *lamp* unto my feet and a *light* unto my path " Ps 119 : 105.

" Every scribe who hath been made a disciple (instructed) to the kingdom of heaven, is like . . . unto a householder, who bringeth forth out of his treasure things new and old " MATT 13 : 52.

PHILADELPHIA :
METHODIST EPISCOPAL BOOK ROOM,
NO. 1018 ARCH STREET.
[*Electrotyped.*]

COPYRIGHT, 1896,
By J. E. Ayars, for JESUS.

EXAMINED and approved on behalf of the COMMITTEE OF PUBLICATION, Philada. Conference Tr. Soc'y of the Methodist Episcopal Church.
By Charles Roads, D.D.

TO the MEMORY of the late JOHN DEMPSTER D D, (spoken of as "the tin peddler," and only convert at a camp meeting in N Hampshire, and whose name is a household word throughout New England), founder and PRESIDENT of the first BIBLICAL school at CONCORD N H, and first President of the GARRET BIBLICAL INSTITUTE my *alma mater*, at EVANSTON ILL, by whose example—faith, learning, devotion to CHRIST, burning words, I was impressed and brought to the knowledge of the TRUTH more than by any other.

And to MY MATERNAL GRANDFATHER

JOS JONES, of precious memory, *natus* Ireland 3. 12. 1769, who came from Dublin to America in 1815, preserved of GOD Ps 91, through the troubles between the protestants and papists, and that night he was called out of his house by armed men to be killed;

Whose gracious looks, words and manner, in memory linger as real as childhood's golden dreams, in his calls, and also at his *beautiful* farm near Cinnaminson N J; whence, from the breakfast table, he so peacefully was removed to the "supper of the LAMB" Jan 22 1842.

He was familiar with Mr Wesley's ministry, and an earnest exhorter.

And to my UNCLE

JOS JONES, *natus* 1799, late President of the Commercial Bank of Pa, who inherited the virtues of my grandfather, and whose business talent, common sense, learning, piety and benevolence raised him to an honorable place in Philadelphia, who fell on sleep Feb 12 '76, whose *great kindness*, letters, books and counsel, have endeared him to me as my best earthly friend.

And to my COUSIN

J ALFRED JONES, *natus* 7. 15. 1840, whose heroic spirit (a son of affliction from childhood), many offices and brotherly kindness had endeared him to me on so brief acquaintance, and whose sudden and unexpected death Dec 23 '91, did for weeks

"All my life-joy overcast,"

whose remains, with this branch of kindred, from which I inherited my early religious inspirations, rests in the

JONES' LOT

N LAUREL HILL CEMETERY,

till the resurrection of the just.

And to his SISTER

MRS E B E, whose patronage and favor is hereby most humbly and devoutly acknowledged in its publication, is

This VOLUME lovingly inscribed

By the AUTHOR.

PREFACE.

> WHEN at the first, I took my pen in hand
> Thus for to write, I did not understand
> That I at all should make a book
>   In such a mode. BUNYAN.

THE idea and plan—the germ of this work, was suggested by letters on the OLD and N TESTAMENTS to one dear to me, in whose salvation after thirty years, GOD gave me great joy, and who was providentially dependent on this ministry principally, for her furtherance and joy of faith.

These letters* (by request monthly), covering a period of four years, were composed through gleam and gloom of change of season, in delicate health, (being to my mother in age and feebleness), with that godly jealousy and painstaking, which one feels in his own spiritual state and GOD's glory; feeling my dependence on JESUS for strength and the HOLY SPIRIT for guidance.

This filial duty and interest shown, the MASTER has honored as done to himself, blessing my own soul also; opening my mind to understand the SCRIPTURES, and to behold him in his person, character and work as the SON OF GOD, "THE DIVINE MAN," as never before. At times, I shouted his praise while bending over my pleasant task. And tears of the joy of faith, have filled my eyes along in the course of this vol. The love of CHRIST and souls has inspired and

---

* *Vide* Pt III c VI

warmed the heart in this work of faith, in the hope that others may have the gift of God stirred up in *them*, also.

A book, in importance next to the HOLY SCRIPTURES—a better legacy than gold and silver to leave after one, was also a cherished desire.

And it is "with desire I have desired"—in reliance on and prayer for the blessing of the AUTHOR of the BOOK it aims to illustrate, both on the reader, and as to the favor it may find with those who desire a clearer revelation through their BIBLE, to be spared to see the MS taken out of obscurity and put "on a candlestick."

As in the letters, no time nor labor was spared, so in the preparation of this VOL. The threefold object in them—

> To inspire a greater reverence and love for the WORD,
> Make both it and the plan of salvation clearer,
> "Stir up the gift of God which is in thee,"

has been kept in view from first to last.

The work is on the basis and plan of the one which stands at the head of its class—The BIBLE HAND-BOOK by Dr Angus, LONDON, REL TR SOCY 1857. It is *unequalled* by any other, but too voluminous and erudite (being for students of divinity), for the common people.

And the reader will be pleased to learn that the piety and catholic spirit of our author—such a blessing to my own soul, and which we have aimed to transfuse throughout this work, are equal to his learning.

As Mr Wesley anticipated the light of the REVISED VERSION in his "NOTES," so has Angus in his work (issued before the R V), anticipated in part, the advance of Biblical science; e g, in *exegesis* of the obscure portions and mistranslations in the AUTHORIZED VERSION, he agrees with the R V in most cases.

While this is true, it is also true that the appearance of the NEW VERSION adopted for our text, must add to the interest of such a work, *above* any previous one.

The substance of ANGUS is reproduced in a simplified form, supplemented with *much* new, additional and illustrative matter from our *best* standard authors, ancient and modern.

The writer is conscious, not only of regard for the truth, but also of having used the means for accuracy, as in quotations, references, the chronological and historical portions etc. While the departments on evidences, and principles of interpretation—laws governing the intelligent study of the WORD, it is believed will be found complete, and up to the highest and latest standards.

Every reference and proof text has been once more examined and compared with its place in the BIBLE, while the pages have been going through the press, and before being committed to the "immortal custody" of it and the "plates."*

As it was our plan to produce a thought field rather, or seed plot, the concise style—the style in which the SPIRIT has given us our BIBLE, was necessary. It is hoped the simple, inornate diction, though in contrast with the *popular* style, will be no objection, but a real recommendation to the reader.

* So inaccurate has this portion in Angus been found, that we hereby record the hope and request, that on this account, and for other known mistakes etc throughout, there be no new edition of that work published, without a revision, and abridgement also.

TOPICAL INDEX.

INTRODUCTION—A J KYNETT D D, LL D 11

Part I.

CHAPTER.   *INTRODUCTORY TO THE BIBLE.*   PAGE.

I. EVIDENCES OF REVELATION 18
    SEC. 1. GENUINENESS DEFINED AND PROVED 18
    "   2. ORIGINAL HEBREW AND VARIOUS READINGS 21
    "   3. THE GREEK—N T AND SEPT 23
    "   4. AGE AND CHARACTER OF MSS 24
    "   5. HEBREW TEXT 26
II. GENUINENESS CONTINUED 27
    SEC. 1. ANCIENT VERSIONS 27
    "   2. VARIOUS READINGS 28
    "   3. AUTHORIZED VERSION 32
    "   4. REVISED VERSION 38
III. AUTHENTICITY AND AUTHORITY 42
    SEC. 1. THE BIBLE THE ONLY INSPIRED TEACHER 42
    "   2. INSPIRATION 45
    "   3. THE CANON 48
    "   4. PRESERVATION OF THE BOOKS 49
    "   5. APOCRYPHA 50
IV. EXTERNAL EVIDENCES 51
    SEC. 1. HISTORICAL 51
    "   2. MIRACLES 55
    "   3. PROPHECY 58
V. INTERNAL EVIDENCES 64
    SEC. 1. MORAL 64
    "   2. LITERARY 72
    "   3. SPIRITUAL 73
VI. THE BIBLE—PECULIARITIES OF 78
    SEC. 1. A REVELATION OF GOD AND MAN 78
    "   2. A REVELATION OF SPIRITUAL TRUTH 79
    "   3. GRADUAL AND PROGRESSIVE 82
    "   4. UNITY OF THE BIBLE 85
    "   5. NOT SYSTEMATIC 88

Part II.

INDUCTIVE STUDY.

I. INTERPRETATION OF SCRIPTURE 91
    SEC. 1. NECESSITY OF CARE IN STUDYING THE SCRIPTURES . . 91
    "   2. TROPICAL WORDS, ALLEGORY, TYPE, SYMBOL 94
    "   3. ON THE SPIRIT OF SEARCHING THE SCRIPTURES . . . 96
II. RULES OF INTERPRETATION 99
    SEC. 1. SENSE OF THE WORDS 99
    "   2. CONNECTION 102
    "   3. CONTEXT 103
    "   4. SCOPE 106
    "   5. COMPARING SCRIPTURE WITH SCRIPTURE 107

TOPICAL INDEX.

CHAPTER.	PAGE.
III. INTERPRETATION CONTINUED. EXTERNAL HELPS	111
SEC. 1. OPINIONS AND IDEAS	111
" 2. HISTORY	113
" 3. ECCLESIASTICAL HISTORY	114
" 4. CHRONOLOGY	115
" 5. NATURAL HISTORY	120
IV. INTERPRETATION CONTINUED	122
SEC. 1. MANNERS AND CUSTOMS	122
" 2. REVENUE AND TAX	125
" 3. COINS AND MEASURES	126
" 4. TIME, MODES OF RECKONING, ETC.	126
V. INTERPRETATION CONTINUED	128
SEC. 1. GEOGRAPHY,	128
Hebron, Jericho, Gilgal, Shiloh, Beersheba, Bethlehem, Shechem, Samaria.	130
SEC. 2. PALESTINE	134
VI. INTERPRETATION CONTINUED	136
SEC. 1. JERUSALEM, ZION, MORIAH, ACRA, BEZETHA, GETHSEMANE, HINNOM.	136
" 2. PHYSICAL GEOGRAPHY	146
VII. ALLEGORIES, SYMBOLS, TYPES, PARABLES, INTERPRETATION OF	149
VIII. PROPHECY, INTERPRETATION OF	154

PART III.

I. SYSTEMATIC AND INFERENTIAL STUDY	164
SEC. 1. DOCTRINES	164
" 2. PRECEPTS	168
" 3. MORAL AND POSITIVE PRECEPTS	170
II. SYSTEMATIC AND INFERENTIAL STUDY	172
SEC. 1. PROMISES	172
" 2. EXAMPLES	177
III. QUOTATIONS OUT OF THE OLD IN THE N T, CLASSIFIED AND EXAMINED WITH REFERENCE TO THE TEXT, TRUTHS AND EVIDENCES OF SCRIPTURE, AND PRINCIPLES OF INTERPRETATION	185
IV. ORIGIN, NATURE AND USE OF SCRIPTURE DIFFICULTIES	188
SEC. 1. ORIGIN. CLASS I ENUMERATED. ARE MATTERS OF INTERPRETATION ONLY. EXAMPLES	188
" 2. CLASS II ENUMERATED. DIFFICULTIES IN THE SENSE. USE AND LESSONS	197
V. STATE OF THE JEWS FROM THE EXILE TO CHRIST, AS ILLUSTRATIVE OF GOD'S MORAL GOVERNMENT, FROM THEIR OWN SCRIPTURES AND HISTORY	210
SEC. 1. THE EXILE, WITH NOTICE OF THE PROPHETS AND BOOKS IN ORDER, BELONGING TO THIS PERIOD	210
" 2. FROM THE RESTORATION TO MALACHI—139 YRS. CLOSE OF THE CANON	222
" 3. THE JEWS FROM MAL TO CHRIST—CIVIL HISTORY	239
" 4. FROM MALACHI TO CHRIST—MORAL HISTORY	248
VI. LETTERS	254
ADVENT AND NATIVITY OF CHRIST	254
LIFE OF JESUS UNTIL "HE BEGAN TO TEACH"	257
THE FOUR GOSPELS	262
THE EVANGELISTS IN THEIR MUTUAL RELATION TO THE GOSPELS	265

RESUMÉ.

INTRODUCTION.

A. J. KYNETT, D.D., LL.D.

AT no time in the history of the world has there been more thorough and critical study of the Holy Scriptures than now; and never before has there been so great popular interest in the problems and difficulties developed by Biblical research. This is true of both friends and foes of the Bible. The results of the so-called higher criticism, filters down through current literature into popular thought and conversation. Questions never before thought of are raised, and difficulties entirely new, are suggested. The interests of truth demand prompt and satisfactory answers. Nor should these answers be confined to voluminous, scholastic books; they should be accessible to the multitude of busy thinkers and workers, whose time is largely pre-occupied with other things. Ours is a busy, hurrying age. What is spoken, or read, or done, must conform to this spirit. Even in our great newspapers, secular and religious, the old-time editorials are largely giving place to concise, pungent paragraphs.

It is especially necessary, that any system of popular instruction in the Holy Scriptures, should be available to parents and Sunday-school teachers, on whom the children and youth depend for Biblical knowledge. Without this, Sunday-school instruction will of necessity, be superficial and unsatisfactory; and our young people, emerging from our Sunday-schools, will on the first attack of intelligent and determined skepticism, be thrown into confusion and perhaps defeat.

THE PEOPLE'S HAND-BOOK OF THE BIBLE will, therefore, supply a real need. It is the condensed product of many years of devout and careful study of the Bible and Biblical literature. The author has happily chosen, as a basis for his plan, the well known work of Joseph Angus, D.D., which is, in its sphere, without a rival. But the PEOPLE'S HAND-BOOK OF THE BIBLE is no mere copy. Our author has condensed, improved and simplified, making his work what the title expresses—THE PEOPLE'S HAND-BOOK OF THE BIBLE. The best authorities on evidences and principles of interpretation have been consulted with great care, so that the student of this book will have before him, in small compass, the equivalent of prolonged research in the archives of Biblical literature and theology. The topical index will suggest the wide scope and thorough treatment of the subject, and the body of the work will reveal the ability and scholarship of the author, and his familiarity with the results of the latest Biblical science.

For the sacred text, the author has adopted the Revised Version. While conceding the unequalled English diction of King James' Bible, he maintains that the later revision is the better translation, that many obscure expressions are made clear, and even holds the opinion that the New Version will gradually supplant the Old. All will agree that the Revised Version is a great help to a correct understanding of the original Scriptures. The concise and simple style of the author will prove of great advantage to the ordinary reader, as no difficulty will be found in understanding *exactly what he means.*

A marked feature of this work is, the apt quotations in illustration and proof of his positions, taken from the best authors, ancient and modern. Above all, it will be found throughout that the "Holy One," "of whom Moses in the law and the prophets did write," is constantly in the *foreground.* All lovers of the Lord Jesus will find themselves in hearty sympathy with the spirit and faith of the writer.

This book should be in every family, and in the hands of all Sunday-school teachers, who are so often called upon promptly to meet difficulties and solve questions unthought of before. It will prove an invaluable companion to our English Bible, a well-ordered, spiritual armory, in which weapons, offensive and defensive, are so arranged as to be promptly available as occasion may require. The author has condensed into this treatise his life, and tenders it as his legacy to the Christian Church.

PHILADELPHIA, June, 1891.

PART I.
INTRODUCTORY TO THE BIBLE.

Scarcely can we fix our eye on a single passage of this BOOK, that has not afforded comfort and encouragement to thousands.—DR. PAYSON, BIBLE AB ALL PRICE.

> This lamp from off the everlasting throne,
> Mercy took down, and in the night of time
> Stood, casting on the dark her gracious bow.—POLLOK.

THIS BOOK OF GOD, "the god of books" as one calls it, opens with GENESIS—"creation" of the worlds, about six thousand years ago, and ends with REVELATION A D 100.

Create in ver 1, means out of nothing, when time began. The six days work refer to the *re*-formation—reconstruction of our earth.

On the meaning of "day" there are two views; some reading it as literal, others as an indefinite period of time. "One day is with the LORD as a thousand years, and a thousand years as one day" II PET 3: 8.

While it was as easy to create, i e prepare in six days as six milleniums, there are evidences both in nature and revelation, in favor of reading "day" as an age.

2 As the BIBLE is the oldest, so it is the only record dating back to the beginning, shedding on our minds light as to the great FIRST CAUSE, formation of the universe, of man, providence etc.

GOD has preserved his own truth through the ages of change, waste and death; the fires and floods of persecution of devils and men, like his only begotten SON, who during infancy, must be kept alive by the ministry of angels.

Even as a literary production, it has been the admiration of mankind. It is the only reliable account of the origin of matter and mind, of the nations and GOD's government to the time modern history begins. The BIBLE is worth more—contains says Sir Wm Jones, purer doctrines of morality and religion, more important history and biography, sublimer strains of poetry and eloquence, than all other books.

3 Herodotus the Father of history (wrote abt 445 B C), and Josephus (37-93 A D), are the most trustworthy ancient authors that have survived the ordeal of time. Herodotus gives us a history of a few of the nations between 713-479. And this mere sketch is from oral tradition and unauthentic sources mostly. From the creation then—for 3300 yrs, there is scarce a ray of light outside the BIBLE to illume the darkness of our world.

The Iliad and Odyssey of Homer (from 1000-900 B C), regarded by the Greeks as authentic, is all that is known about the heroic age of that remarkable people. All uninspired ancient histories and biographies have perished.

Had the BIBLE been a cunningly devised fable, it too would have passed away. What a comment is this on Is 40: 6-8, quoted I PET 1: 25, a voice out of the Old and N Testaments——

"All flesh is grass, and all the goodliness—'the glory thereof,' is as the flower of the field. . . . But the WORD of our GOD shall stand forever!"

4 Again, the BIBLE is the only book that grows not old, but renews its youth from generation to generation. The secret of its preservation and influence is, it contains in itself the indestructible germs of life And blessed thought!

"The POWER that gave it still supplies
The gracious light and heat."

5 What the sun—that fount of light and heat is to this planet—the source of vegetable and animal life, this book is to man intellectual, religious and social.

For example the Greeks, the most enlightened of the heathen, taught that the worlds came by chance, matter is eternal, and deified fate. Claudius Ptolemaus 150 A D, the most renowned astronomer and geographer perhaps of any age, taught and was followed till Copernicus (1532) discovered—"revived the true solar system," that this earth is at rest, and the sun, moon and stars revolved round it. It was also a popular belief that our planet is flat, rested on the head of a (the old) serpent, which in turn was supported on the back of a tortoise etc.

The light of nature, and teaching of their wisest, purest reformers as Socrates, Plato and Confucius, was cold and inefficient as a rule of faith and practice.

The doctrine of one living and true GOD, creation and fall of man, the devil, providence, promise—coming and atonement of CHRIST, immortality, resurrection and general judgment, were either unknown or imperfectly understood. And what the gentiles knew of GOD, his work and ways, was the lingering, waning light of revelation, the traditions of their golden age in EDEN.

The religion of the Greeks and Romans allowed fornication, revenge, suicide; and their gods were of like appetites, desires and passions. The beings worshipped were, so to speak, the reflection of the vices and virtues of the worshipper.

Of the other nations, we have but an idea of their sin, misery and degradation. There are to day tribes in Africa who eat their kind, and millions who worship GOD in the character of a devil! Paul's picture ROM 1, is not overdrawn.

The pagan compared to the Christian world, is like the part of the globe the sun shines on, to that immersed in its shadow.

6 Man in innocency had the law of his MAKER written in his heart. He saw GOD in his works, walked and talked with him. Reason (if he had to depend on that faculty), was then a guiding, unerring light. When he lost the HOLY SPIRIT and became "earthly, sensual, devilish," reason was darkened. GEN 3, I COR 2: 14.

Faith in its nature and office, is right reason, never contrary, and was required after man's apostacy, for his guiding light. Faith implies ignorance, sin, dependence. **Sin** did not obliterate the idea of GOD. The sense of one SUPREME is innate. And atheism, the lowest form of unbelief, is unnatural, a credulity **born of** sin. Ps 14: 1. So WATSON'S INSTS.

7 *Ex nihilo nihil fit*—out of nothing nothing comes, is **an** axiom—**self evident truth.** The mind is constituted to ascribe every effect **to a** cause.

It is observable that inspired writers assume the existence of GOD, uncreated, self **existent,** creator and ruler of all. **Moses** opens "In **the beginning** GOD created the heaven and the earth"

The *à posteriori*—from effect to cause, and *à priori*—from cause to effect arguments, have both been used to prove as against atheism, there **is a** GOD. The first **is the** one depended **on by** theologians, **and is** the one employed by **the** HOLY SPIRIT.——"The heavens declare the glory of GOD" Ps 19. "**The invisible** things of him . . . **are understood by the things** that are made, even his **eternal power and** GODHEAD" ROM 1.

The **marks of** design in our world suggests a designer. The sun, moon and stars numberless in space, **their order** (heaven's first **law**), the two mysterious forces—centripetal and centrifugal motions, holding them in their orbits, urging on from age to age, proclaim

"The hand that made us is divine."

Also best **means to** ends, with simplicity of means, **teach** infinite wisdom in the AUTHOR. WATSON'S INSTS.

God in creation thus displays
His wisdom and his might. MONTGOMERY.

SEC. 2

1 The **BIBLE** consists of 66 books and letters, 39 of which are in the O T.

TESTAMENT means covenant, the name given by GOD to indicate the relation between himself and his people. Covenant or appointment at **first** meant relation, but afterwards was applied to the books themselves. GEN 21: 27, 32, EX 24: 7.

By the Jews the O T was called the LAW, PROPHETS and HAGIOGRAPHA (Gr *hagios* holy, *grapha* writings), which is composed of the PSALMS, PROVERBS, ECCLESIASTES, CANTICA; all which they called PSALMS, from the first book.

In the N T, the books are called SCRIPTURE JNO 10: 35, SCRIPTURES, LUKE 24: 27, and WORD OF GOD LUKE 11: 27, 28. Also ORACLES OF GOD. ACTS 7: 38.

Oracle is also the name given to the place where the will of GOD was revealed I KGS 8: 6, II CHRON 4: 20, Ps 28: 2.

The primitive church from the time of Origen 185–213, named the BOOKS collectively the CANON (*kan'un*), a Greek word meaning straight, rod; thence tropically—figuratively law, rule GAL 6: 16, PHIL 3: 16.

BIBLE is from Greek βιβλος* book; and hence *par* excellence, *the* BOOK.

Of all names THE WORD OF GOD is the most impressive and complete, justifying the faith of the feeblest, and suggesting the utterance of the infinite wisdom and love.

2 Our aim—"the Sabbath and port of our labors," is to make more clear and impressive the BIBLE itself. Therefore both writer and reader are cautioned against using such a help to SCRIPTURE as an end—confounding it with the study of the WORD itself. The road we are about to travel may be attractive; but the end—"the wells of salvation"—and "living bread," are more excellent than the means thereto. And the thirsty, hungering seeker after the truth as it is in JESUS, will not rest satisfied with the discovery—the ravishing glimpses, but will quench his thirst at the fountain head, and satisfy his immortal soul longings to the full.

In other view, he will not be content to stand before, to contemplate the TEMPLE OF TRUTH in all its imposing grandeur and proportions, but will strive to enter—seek admission to the *sanctum sanctorum*, to worship in spirit and

* Given by Chrysostom 4th Cy.

truth, and be in touch with the pure, the beautiful and good there, and possess also of her hidden treasures.

Let no one deceive himself, for it is only the obedient, the loving, humble; those who "seek her as silver and search for her as hid treasures, that shall understand the fear of the LORD and find the knowledge of God " PROV 2: 4, 5.

> BEHOLDEST thou yonder on the crystal sea
> Beneath the throne of GOD, an image fair,
> And in her hand a mirror large and bright?
> Tis TRUTH, immutable, eternal TRUTH,
> In figure emblematical expressed.
>
> Before it Virtue stands, and smiling,
> Sees in her reflected soul no spot.
>
> The sons of heaven, archangel, seraph, saint,
> There daily read their own essential worth;
> And as they read, take place among the just,
> Or high, or low, each as his value seems.
>   *   *   *   *   *   *   *   *
> The BIBLE holds this mirrors place on earth.   POLLOK.

CHAPTER I.

EVIDENCES OF REVELATION.

THE evidences of the integrity of the Christian faith are tenfold more various, copious and conclusive than of any other ancient writings. ISAAC TAYLOR.

SEC 1 GENUINENESS DEFINED AND PROVED.

IF a MS of every book of the BIBLE in the author's own writing were extant, every copy agreeing therewith would be genuine. There are no such autographs now in existence. But there are circumstances attending their preservation and transmission, which prove their genuineness.

When a MS varies from the one its author wrote, it is said to be corrupt. When not the one by its author, it is said to be forged or spurious.

There is a printed copy of the Hebrew BIBLE dated 1488,

in Exeter College Oxford; and one in the Royal Library Berlin of 1494, from which Luther made his translation. There are copies of the N T dated Basil 1516, edited by Erasmus. Copies also in Greek and Latin dated Alcala or Complutum Spain, 1514. These copies agree with one another and our own editions. And these two editions form the basis of the received text. The 1st edition of said text was printed by Elzevir in 1624. Erasmus had advantage of editions of Stevens Paris 1546, and of Beza Geneva 1565.

Dr. Kennicott collated 630 MSS for his critical edition of the Heb BIBLE. De Rossi 734 more. And more than 600 MSS have been examined for our late editions of the N T—AUTH VERSION.

In the Greek and Roman classics—their best authors, 20, even 10 MSS, are sufficient for an accurate text. There are 15 MSS of Herodotus extant, oldest only of 10th cy. How much greater are the evidences in this respect, in favor of the SCRIPTURES!

Most MSS of the HEB. SCRIPTURES may reach back as far as the 10th cy. There are some of the 8th and 9th cys.

A MS. of Virgil in the Vatican claims antiquity of the 4th cy. But most MSS of the classic writers belong to the 10th and 15th cys. In antiquity as in numbers also, are the evidences in favor of the SCRIPTURES.

2 As we go back towards the times when written, another kind and confirmatory evidence is at hand—the quotations and references of the Christian Fathers and Jewish Rabbins.

Quotations from and references to the Classics—Homer, Socrates, Plato; Herodotus, Cicero, Virgil, may prove their antiquity, but are of such a nature, i e, imperfectly rendered, as to leave them of no critical value as to the originals.

The inspired writings were copied verbatim, with conscientious care, so that not "one jot or one tittle" might fail.

We have the commentaries and writings of about 180 of the Fathers and ecclesiastical writers, including Irenæus,

Clement and Theophilus of the 2nd, Origen of the 3rd, Chrysostom, Augustine and Jerome of the 4th cys. These authorities reach back to St. John. The works of these contain quotations from the four GOSPELS, ACTS, EPISTLES and REVELATION so full and exact, that collected together, they would give us the whole N. T. What a proof of the genuineness of the gospel!

3 The *Targums*—translations, versions of Onkelos about 60 B C, give us the PENTATEUCH in Chaldaic Heb. That of Jonathan about the time of CHRIST, gives us the PROPHETS and HISTORICAL BOOKS. In the 4th cy Joseph the Blind wrote one, the *Hagiographa*. Still later versions were made. These translations, 10 in all, are witnesses of the genuineness of the HEB BIBLE for nearly 2000 years past.

The PESH'ITO—literal, version of the OLD and N TESTS in Syriac, made it is probable in the 1st cy. This version was used by the Christians in Syria and in the churches. Being quite literal (as its name implies), it has been of inestimable value in determining the original text. The VULGATE translated by Jerome about 385, is a fair translation, and adopted by the Latin Church.

The SEPTUAGINT (so called from its 70 or 72 translators), is the most ancient on the O T. It was made at Alexandria about 285, in the time of Ptolemy Lagus or Philadelphus.* The LXX (as it is often called), was well done, and is oftener quoted by our LORD and his apostles than the HEB. It was in high repute with both Jews and Christians It is often spoken of by writers of the 2nd cy.

The above is but a sample of the varied and cumulative

---

* Under these first two Ptolemies, Egypt was raised to the height of her prosperity. They were the patrons of religion, learning and the fine arts. They founded the celebrated library of Alexandria, built the Pharos (one of the "seven wonders of the world"), restored the Suez Canal, built cities, etc. The second continued the reforms by his father, finished the canal, encouraged commerce. His court surpassed any of his age, and was illustrated by such minds as Theocritus. WORCESTER'S UNIV. HISTORY. c. XIX. SEC. 3.

evidence of the uncorruptness of our BIBLE. The libraries of Europe and the world have been ransacked, but nothing discovered to set aside, or cast doubt on, any important doctrine or portion.

And as to such persons as JESUS, Matthew, Mark, Luke and John, and such works as are ascribed to them, history and the whole world wrote, and knew, and talked about them at the time.

Is not such a result—to know our BIBLE does not differ from that of the primitive church—that we have the word of GOD as truly as they, ample reward for the time and labor bestowed? It is our duty, for GOD challenges us to examine the foundations of our hope, and to prove him in his WORD, and rewards them that honor him therein.

To give the reader a more definite idea, examples of various readings are added—

ROMS. 7: 6. For "that being dead wherein we were held," read "having died to that wherein we were holden." 11: 6. Omit the last half. 16: 5. Read "first fruits of Asia," not "Achaia."
GAL 4: 26. For "mother of us all" read "which is our mother." 5: 19. Omit "adultery."
ACTS 8: 37. Omit 9: 6. Omit first part. See R V.
PHIL 4: 13. For "through CHRIST" read "in him."
I TIM 3: 16. "GOD manifest" read "He who was manifested."
REV 8: 13. For "angel" read "eagle."

Of the 7959 verses in the N T, there are 10 or 12 which affect the sense, not the doctrines but number of proof passages.

1314 various readings have been found in the O T. Of these, 566 were adopted in the A V. 147 of the whole affect the sense, not the doctrines. Generally they correct a date or complete the sense.

SEC 2 ORIGINAL HEBREW AND VARIOUS READINGS.

The history of these—an outline, comes in here as related to and on the knowledge of which, genuineness depends.

The Hebrew—the language of nearly all the O T, was that of the Israelites in the days of their independence.

There is evidence that it was the language of the Canaanites and Phœnicians. There is no mention of any difference, and the names of persons, places, etc., as Abimelech, Melchizedek, Salem, are pure Heb. It seems also that the Hebrew of Abraham's time was cognate—kindred with the original, as the names in the first chs. of GENESIS show, being *significant* also of the persons and things applied to.

2 It is divided into three periods. The first was in the days of Moses, and as found in the PENTATEUCH. Here are words and phrases not found elsewhere, which soon become obsolete, or used in a different sense.

In the post-Mosaic period a change is noticed. New words are introduced, old ones forgotten, and forms not found in Moses, on to the time of David, who writes with great purity and elegance. To this period belong, in order, the book of JUDGES, RUTH, SAMUEL, writings of Solomon, JONAH, AMOS and HOSEA. ISAIAH, MICAH, NAHUM, HABAKKUK and OBADIAH are pure, in good style, though in the first and second is admixture of a foreign element. All these belong to the golden age of the language.

ZEPHANIAH, JEREMIAH, DANIEL and EZEKIEL fall into the third period, and exhibit intercourse with foreign tongues, as do the writings in and after the exile—EZRA, ESTHER and NEHEMIAH, who use words and phrases not found in the early prophets. (EZRA and DANIEL are part in Chaldee.) The later prophets—HAGGAI, ZECHARIAH and MALACHI, write a purer idiom,* the Heb having during the exile, become a written rather than spoken tongue; and in *writing* it, was not necessary to use the words in common parlance.

"Added to his people" is in the PENT. "Sleep with his fathers," in later books. "People" in the 1st is applied to the Jews. In the PROPHETS, the word is more extended.

It is on the knowledge and use of the original tongues, that the superiority of our modern lexicographers chiefly depends. ANGUS.

* Expression peculiar to a language.

Sec 3 Greek N T and Septuagint.

There was a controversy in the 16th cy. between Erasmus and Stevens, the former asserting the N T was written in Greek, with Hebrew words and phrases; the latter, that the text is pure Greek. The question was thought important *theologically, in evidence,* and *interpretation* of the N T.

The parties forgot that the question is a matter of fact, simply. The book is Hellenistic Greek—Greek mixed with Heb words and ideas, principally. The books are by Jews who spoke Greek, with modes of thinking formed on Heb originals. Hence evidence of the truth of the record. Hence also, a rule of interpreting, though the chief means to the sense of words and expressions is in the BIBLE *itself*.

The Hellenists (from *Hellas* Greece), consisted at first of different tribes, the Dorians and Ionians being chief. The Doric dialect was 1st in time and influence. It is rough and broad sounding, as in Pindar and Theocritus.

The Ionic comes next in time, was soft and smooth, was first in Attica, then in Asia Minor after the Ionians migrated thither. It is represented by Herodotus and Anacreon.

The Attic was formed after the Ionians left Attica, and rates between the Doric and Ionic. The chief authors are in Attic—Thucydides, Plato, Zenophon, Demosthenes, Euripides.

After Philip conquered Greece B C 338, these dialects were blended and Hellenic formed, with Attic for its base.

After Alexander's death (B C 324), the people of Macedon and Alexandria became first in literature and power, and through them, Macedonian and Alexandrian idioms became common in Greece, especially in Egypt and the East.

At Alexandria many Jews lived. Here the SEPT was written by Jews whose tongue was Alexandrian Greek. Hence the Hebraisms in it. And this is the language of our N T, as modified by Jews in Palestine and Alexandria. Hence words in Aramean, Latin, Persian, Egyptian, in their orthography, form, inflexion and gender. **Hence words and phrases Jewish and Christian——**

Aramean is seen MARK 5: 41, *Talitha cumi*, 14: 36, *Abba*, 3:17, *Boanerges*. *Latin* MATT 10: 29, farthing   *Persian* MATT 27: 32, *Cyrene*.   Egyptian MATT 27: 59, *sindoni*—linen.   Heb 17: 27, *Shekel*, R V.

SEC 4 AGE AND CHARACTER OF MSS.

Some have date and other confirmatory marks on them. Dates are not found on them before the 10th cy.

2 TRADITIONAL or known history. The CODEX ALEX A, was given by Cyril, Patriarch of Constantinople to Charles I, with tradition on it in Arabic, that it was written by Thecla an Egyptian princess after the Council of Nice 325, which is supported by internal evidence.

3 PROOF often must come from the material, letters, style etc. Some MSS were of skins tanned, dyed etc. An entire part of SCRIPTURE as the PENT, was usually on one roll* of skins. Next comes parchment from *Pergamena* (Pergamos), where first "perfected." Most SCRIPTURES earlier than the 6th cy, are on parchment.

Tables of wood or stone † called *codices*, were also used. Hence *Codex*—MS on any material. As laws were often on durable materials, a system came to be called *code*. They were written on with an iron needle—stylus, whence comes our "style."

For ages till the 9th cy, papyrus—from the flag of Egypt, was popular. Then paper from the cotton plant, resembling Chinese paper, came into use. In the 10th cy linen was utilized to make paper.

Herodotus mentions the skins of goats and sheep dressed, in use among the Ionians. Pausanias says he saw the works of Hesiod engraved on lead. Pliny says papyrus was in use before the Trojan war **1184**. Books of cotton cloth are mentioned by Livy.

By the material, antiquarians are aided in estimating the

* JER 36: 2, ZECH 5: 1.
† EX 32: 15, DEUT 6: 9, IS 8: 1, LUKE 1: 63 "tablet."

age of MSS. The earliest Greek writings whose date is known, were found in Pompei and Herculanæum, destroyed Aug 24 A D 79. The writing runs from side to side, in uncial—capital letters, without division of words, sentences or accents, and few pause marks. They are older than any MS of the N. T. In Vienna there is a MS of the 5th cy. In manner, style &c, it agrees with the above.

In early times the N T was in 3 parts:—GOSPELS, ACTS and EPISTLES, and REVELATION. In the 3rd cy the GOSPELS were divided into two kinds of chs. In 315–40, Eusebius published his "Canons."

In 360 Chrysostom speaks of some MSS on finest parchment, in gold and silver letters. In 458 Euthalius gave the letters of Paul, with contents of chs. In 490, he divided ACTS and letters into sections, introduced accents, (adopted in the 8th cy), and a system of lining, and the subscriptions now at the end of the EPISTLES.* In the 7th cy, the uncial style began to be compressed and inclined. In the 8th cy, more changes, as punctuating, were added. In the 9th, notes of interrogation and comma. In the 10th, the cursive—running, hasty style came in place of the uncial, and in the 13th cy, Cardinal Hugo divided the N T into chs.

It is from such data, experts have been able to decide with much accuracy the age, and also relative character of MSS. For example, one with verses and chs is supposed to be not earlier than the 12th cy.

The Reformation had quickened the spiritual pulse of Europe, and in 1657, the examination of the SCRIPTURES began with renewed vigor. In 1675 Dr Fell chose Dr Mill to complete a revision of MSS. Mill spent 30 yrs on MSS and works of the Fathers. Bengel in 1734 added his reseaches, followed by Wetstein in 1751. Griesbach 1796–1806, improved on Wetstein. Meantime Matthaei of Moscow edited the Constantinopolitan recension,— revision, enumeration.

Griesbach discovered with others, MSS are divisible into 3 classes—Alexandrian, Constantinopolitan and Western,

* In A. V.

each having a different set of readings. The MASORETIC has but one recension.

This discovery changed the grounds of evidence from the No of MSS to the No of families, though some hold antiquity rather, to be a better test.

Sec 5 Hebrew Text.

In the 6th and 7th cys at Tiberias, existing Heb. MSS were collated and a correct text—the MASORETIC, formed. When the Mohamedans came, many Jews took refuge in Spain, Italy and Germany, taking the MASORETIC with them. Copies of this they multiplied as the people's wants required.

In 1650 Cappellus, and after him Bp Walton, began to correct the errors and lack of Buxtorf,* and to form a critical apparatus. In 1667 Athias a Rabbi, in 1690 Jablonski, in 1705 Van der Hoogt, in 1709 Opitz at Kiel, in 1720 Michaelis at Halle, in 1746–53 Houbigant Paris, and Kennicott; in 1784–8, De Rossi, Parma, (in 1793 Kennicott and De Rossi were published at Leipsic, and by Jahn Vienna 1806), and Boothroyd in 1810–16, all published editions of the MASORETIC.

It is in the light of such progress, that we have evidence of the comparative worth of the version of 1880–4 over that of 1611. "Others have labored, and ye have entered into their labor." We ought to be as thankful as we are dependent, for such grace of GOD.

In the 10th cy the Jews at Babylon had one set of readings and those at Tiberias another—the Eastern and Western families. Bp Walton has given the difference between the two—220 letters in all. Certain copies were long celebrated for their accuracy.——That the Jews agree with Christians in the letter of the Old, and Romanists with protestants in that of the N T, is evidence of their genuineness.

* See Rev Ver Ch II Sec 4.

CHAPTER II.

GENUINENESS CONTINUED.

Sec 1 Ancient Versions.

THERE is a story by Aristeas (who tells us he was in the good graces of Ptolemy Philadelphus), that the SEPT was by 72 Jews (6 of every tribe), sent to Alexandria by Eleazar, and finished in 72 days. It was one in Origen's *Hexapla*—six columned, BIBLE. This column had been copied by Eusebius before the *Hexapla* was destroyed, (it is thought by the Saracens at the sacking of Cesaræa 653.) It was printed by Montfaucon Paris, 1714. Of versions of it, the *Old Italic* as Jerome testifies, is best, ascribed by Eichhorn to the 1st cy.

In 382 Jerome revised it, but it began to fall into disfavor with the Jews, as it was appealed to by the Christians. Jerome then prepared a version from the HEB, finished 405, and honored 604 by Gregory the Gt, as the VULGATE.* Pope Sixtus and Clement's eds (with papal authority), contain many errors.

History says, Ethiopia was converted abt 330 and the SCRIPTURES given them soon after; and in the 3rd or 4th cy, to the Egyptians.

The Gothic version (4 GOSPELS), by Ulphilas Bp of the Moeso Goths 4th cy, is in the library at Upsal Sweden. It is in silver letters.

About 706 Adhelm Bp of Sherborn, gave the PSALMS in Anglo Saxon, as did Egbert Bp of Holy Island the GOSPELS. Bede rendered portions, and King Alfred began the PSALMS, but died (900) before finishing. Ælfric translated the PENT and historical books also, from the VULGATE, and even Luther made use of it.

The old SAMARITAN PENT referred to by Eusebius and Cyril, was supposed to have been lost. But a copy was

---

* From *Vulgatus*—usual, common.

sent from Constantinople to **Paris in** the 17th cy. Usher and Kennicott obtained copies. It is thought to be a recension from the HEB, made in the days of Rehoboam.

The PESHITO was probably by Jewish Christians, those who " were sent to Palestine by Jude and Abgarus King of Edessa."

Philoxenius Bp of Maberg Syria, translated the N T about 508. The best MS of it, now at Oxford, belonged to the martyr Ridley.

In forming the *textus receptus*—received text, it follows therefore that the SEPT, VULGATE, SAM and PESHITO, are authority for the original HEBREW.

For fuller information see ANGUS.

SEC 2 VARIOUS READINGS.

Of Hebrew as said, 1368, and of Greek, more than 600 MSS have been examined.

The SCRIPTURES have been copied many times, by different persons, in different countries, under different circumstances and influences, through the generations and ages. Before printing 1440, the danger of mistake was greater than now. It would not be human not to err in a point, a letter, a word somewhere and sometimes. Sometimes the writer copied from the MS before him, sometimes by amanuensis. His eye in the 1st and ear in the second mode, might deceive. A MS partly effaced, a misunderstanding of the MS from which he copied, would lead to misinterpretation of abbreviations, or inaccurately dividing the words (the old MSS had no pause marks), and other causes, as will be shown, were at work. The editions of Sixtus and Clement have many errors. Papal infallibility made mistakes.

In the face of such facts, the wonder is that our inheritance has come down to us with so few blemishes from the hand of man, and is evidence of the sleepless vigilance with which the church, and above all, watchful PROVIDENCE has guarded the heavenly TREASURE.

As ancient Heb letters resembled one another even more than now, and different words, in *sound* also, it was natural that various readings should happen.

The following are some of the causes.

SIMILARITY OF FORM OR SOUND.

Gen 14: 5, The Heb, Sam and Sept read "with them"—*behem* בהם. Read *becham* בחם in Ham.

TRANSPOSITION.

As Salmai for Shalmai, Neh 7: 48, Ez. 2: 46. Almug for Algum I Kgs 10: 11, II Chron 9: 11.

SIMILARITY OF ENDING—letters and words.

Matt 28: 9, Went to tell his disciples is the same in Greek as bring his disciples word v. 8, A V, com with R V.

SYNONYMOUS EXPRESSIONS.

"He spoke" for "he said," II Kgs 1: 10. "They found" for "they saw," Gr *euron* for *eidon*, Matt 2: 11.

Copyists knew other tongues, and this would give diversity in orthography. Also many ancient MSS were without stops and divisions of words.

"Unto death" Ps 48: 14, some MSS and the LXX read "for ever." See also Ps 25: 17 might be made to read "enlarge the troubles of my heart."

ABBREVIATIONS MISUNDERSTOOD.

" י (J) is Heb for Jehovah. It means also *my*. Hence an occasional mistake. In the LXX "fury of the Lord" Jer 6: 11, is translated "my fury." The Jews would not pronounce Jehovah, but wrote and read *Adonai* or *Elohim*, as in their MSS.

The Hebrews never divided a word nor left a vacant space at the end of a line, but filled it with some letter, or the initial of the next word, which of course was repeated in the next line.

e g, "For them" Is 35: 1, omit as in R V. The Heb is written and read from right to left.

VARIOUS READINGS.

MARGINAL READINGS seem to have found their way into the text, in places.

The various readings thus far may be called accidental. **Others** were intentional either from good or bad motives. A Greek copyist not used to oriental idioms, and thinking **a** Hebraism **a** violation of grammar, would correct it, not considering it to be a proof of genuineness. Sometimes **he would** correct one evangelist by another, or fill the shorter account from the longer.

In some copies **a** mistake is retained throughout a book.

The Heb for *a boy* is put twenty one times in the PENT for *a girl* —*na-ar* for *na-ara*, which is found but once DEUT 22: 19. All the **versions** and MASORA direct us to read it as feminine.

THE ALEXANDRIAN FAMILY SEEMS TO CHANGE words **to make better grammar,** the Western, to make better sense.

TO SUIT THE PARALLEL, OR THE TEXT QUOTED FROM.

LUKE 4: 18, "heal the broken **hearted**" **not in R V.** Probably found its way into A V from Is 61 through the SEPT.

MATT 12: 35, "out * * * of the heart," not in R V, is probably from LUKE 6: 45.

TO SERVE A PARTY OR FAVOR THE TRUTH.

DEUT 27: 4, "Ebal" **the** Samaritans changed to Gerizim, and so built their temple there.

JUDGES 18: 30, Manassah **is** for Moses, to save the honor of his family. So Solomon Jarchi acknowledges. R V, Moses.

CARELESSNESS.

I CHRON 6: 28, for Vashni read Joel, as in R V.

The various readings amount to some thousands, not one of which affects a single doctrine of SCRIPTURE. Bp Lowth found 50 in Isaiah.

The comparative value of various readings is by critics, estimated by the following rules:—

VARIOUS READINGS. 31

1 When MSS, versions and quotations agree, the *external evidence* is complete; and when the reading thus fixed, nature of the language, sense, historical facts and parallel passages agree, the *internal evidence* is complete.

2 It is generally in proportion to age, fewness of transcriptions, number in the family and preservation.

A SCRIPTURE is received when supported by the oldest MSS, versions, quotations and parallel passages.

EPH 5: 9, Most read "fruit of the SPIRIT." The VULGATE, Syriac and R V, " of the light."

When a text is corrupt, a parallel passage may fix the true reading.

II KGS 25: 3, for ninth of the month A. V, read of the fourth month JER 52: 6. So R. V.

Of two readings equally probable, the fuller is usually the right one, unless there be reason to suspect an interpolation, then this rule is reversed.

ACTS 8: 37, omitted in R. V, may be an interpolation of ROM 10: 9. LUKE 23: 17 is not in R. V. MARK 16: 9 to the end, the oldest two Greek and other authorities omit. Also most ancient authorities omit JOHN 7: 53, 8: 1–11. SEE R. V.

Of two readings, one classical the other oriental, or one easy and the other difficult, the latter is most probable.

Of two readings, that is chosen, best agreeing with the style of the writer, design etc.

JOHN 6: 69 "Son of the living God" is preferable to Griesbach and R V—HOLY ONE OF GOD. So Wesley and Strong. So prophets is preferable to "prophet Isaiah" MARK 1: 2. Is and Mal both speak of JOHN. Is 52: 15 * * * "sprinkle many nations" may mean atone for, purify. Many nations shall *admire*, SEPT, CLARKE. R V adds "startle" in marg.

To illustrate the above rules, let us take 1 JOHN 5: 7.

It is in the Clementine edition of the VULGATE, Complutensian,

Erasmus 3rd edition, and thence found its way into Stevens, Beza and Elzevir's text.

1 No Greek MSS before the 15th cy have it, nor 174 of the cursive MSS.

2 It is wanting in the ancient versions except the Latin, most MSS of the VULGATE, and in none earlier than the 9th cy, the SYRIAC, and other versions.

3 The Fathers do not quote it, though 6–9 v they do.

4 Nor best eds of the Greek Test, 1st and 2d of Erasmus, Matthæi, Griesbach, Lach, Scholz, Tisch, Hahn, though Mills and Bengel do.

In its favor it is in some Greek MSS, in 1st Berlin and 4 others. But the 1st is a forgery, one of the others has it in the margin and the others belong to the 15th cy or later.

2 It is in some old Latin versions.

3 Is said to be quoted by Tertullian and Cyprian, but the 6 and 8 vs may be meant.

SEC 3 AUTHORIZED VERSION

In the light of such evidence, we are satisfied that we have the WORD as if fresh from the hand of its divine ORIGINAL, save those imperfections—finger marks from the hand of man, in its passage through.

The committee in the days of the Commonwealth* on improving the BIBLE, reported back THE BEST OF ANY TRANSLATION IN THE WORLD. Of all European translations, says Dr A Clarke, this is the most accurate and faithful. The translators have seized the very spirit of the original and expressed it with pathos and energy. Dr Doddridge bears similar testimony.

While this was the decision of the most competent authorities *then*, time with its increasing light, had brought out errors and faults along,—mistranslations etc (See Sec 7), enough to require a revision. Of this, it may now be said *truly*, THE BEST OF ANY TRANSLATION IN THE WORLD.

The following are some of the causes objectionable, with an example or so (there are about 150 in Angus), added.

---

* Beginning with the death of Charles I 1649 and accession of Cromwell.

Inaccurate Translation.

Exs. In Acts 7: 45, Heb 4: 8, Joshua is for Jesus.
Ex 3: 22, borrowed should read *asked* of the Egyptns.
II Sam 12: 31, under saws is *to* saws. The original means to servile work.
Gen 4: 15, for set a mark on Cain—gave a *sign* or *assurance.*
I Kgs 18: 43, for go seven times read, he said, Go again seven times.

Inadequate translation—not giving the full force.

II Thess 1: 12, for grace of our God and Lord Jesus Christ, read "grace of our God and the Lord Jesus Christ."
I Cor 4: 5, read " Shall each man have his praise from God."

Neglect of the idiom.

I Cor 4: 4, read "I know nothing *against* myself."
II Pet 2: 5, for Noah the eighth person, read "Noah with seven others."

Verbs in wrong tenses.

Some of the imprecations in the O T are also predictive.
John 13: 2, contradicts vs 26 and 28. The Greek is, supper *being come*—"during supper" R V.

Translating oriental numbers wrong.

I Sam 6: 19, The Lord smote 50070 men. Beth-shemesh was a small town. Jud 12: 6, 42000 Ephraimites were slain. A little while before, that tribe had but 32500 people. By a notation in use among the Arabians, the first literally read, is seventy men, fifties and a thousand—1170. The second, there fell 40 and 2000—2040. Angus, Taylor, Clarke. R V agrees with A V. "The numbers in Josephus are very corrupt."

Same words translated *by different words.*

Ps 132: 6, for fields of the wood, read *of Jearim*, as in I Chron 13: 5—"Kirjath (city of) Jearim." Matt 25: 46, read "eternal" in both clauses.

Different words *rendered by the same word.*

"Conversation" is the rendering of two words, meaning—1 citizenship as in Phil 1: 27, 3: 20. 2 in every other place manner of life, behavior.
"Hell" again, means 1 invisible state, place of departed spirits,

simply. MATT 11: 23, 16: 18. 2 place of eternal punishment as in MATT 5: 22, 29, 30. The Greek gives two different words—*hades*, *gehenna*.

OBSOLETE WORDS. See R V CH II SEC. 4.

Want of uniformity in translating.

Ps 19: 4, "line" is "sound" ROM 10: 18.
JER 31: 32, I was a husband to them, is "I regarded them not" HEB 8: 9.

WORDS UNTRANSLATED.

Maranatha, Sabaoth, Higgaion. Selah may have been "a musical mark."

Marginal readings may enlighten, or give another sense the original is capable of. They might be multiplied with profit.

Italics are words added to express the sense; sometimes happily, sometimes not.

Ps 109: 4, "I *give myself unto* prayer." 133: 3, "As the dew of Hermon, *and as the dew* that descended upon the mountains of Zion." Without the italics the connexion would be false, Zion being over 100 m south of Hermon.

But in MATT 20: 23, they represent CHRIST as not having power to reward in heaven. Read "to sit on my right hand * * * is not mine to give, but *it is for them* for whom it hath been prepared of my FATHER" R V.

The analysis of chapters, the titles and subscriptions to books in the N. T. (omitted in R V), are no part of revelation. The order of the BOOKS is not divine, nor are they bound in their historical connexion—order in which written. The first BIBLE (VULGATE) chaptered, was by Cardinal Hugo (died 1263), or Langton Abp of Canterbury, 1227. The first HEBREW SCRIPTURES chaptered was by Mordecai Nathan 1445. In 1661 Athias divided this into verses, as Robert Stevens 1537, the N T, in a journey (*inter equitandum*), from Paris to Lyons.

These divisions are imperfect, and even when not inaccurate, tend to break and obscure the sense. The revisers have in the NEW VERSION, corrected this fault, the paragraph showing where every subject begins; though for "convenience of reference," chapter and verse are left as in A V.

Exs. The humiliation and glory of Messiah Is 53, begins 52: 13, and the verses before belong to ch 51. Jer 3: 6, begins a distinct prophecy, on to ch 7. Col. 4: 1, belongs to ch 3. John 8: 1, belongs to ch 7. The last 2 verses of Acts 4 belong to c. 5.

If the showings of this Section discount the reverence and zeal for the A V, they will not, for the Bible; while they suggest the relative value of the New over the Old version.

Note. The two prefaces and appendixes in the R. V, more fully suggest this.

These corrections serve 1, to answer objections. 2 Clear up difficulties and reconcile contradictions. 3 They give us an idea of the difference between the version of 1611 and the original text.

The Bible is the result of repeated revisions. In the preface to the Bishop's Bible (1568), reference is made to early Saxon versions. And there are extant portions by Bede,*

Alfred the Gt and Ælfric of Canterbury. Early Saxon MSS are preserved in the libraries of the British Museum and Corpus Christi College, Cambridge.

The first complete English translation was by John Wycliffe, 1380. It was regarded with suspicion, and a bill was brought into the House of Lords to suppress it. John O Gaunt defeated this. In 1408, it was decreed that no

---

* Styled "The Venerable Bede," monk of Jarrow, *natus*, Moncton Eng, abt 666, is styled by Burke the "Father of English learning." Of the eight chief writers who flourished between 650 and the 10th cy, Bede excelled. He gathered around him at Jarrow about 600 pupils. * * * His last act was to give John's gospel called by some the "Heart of Christ," to the world. The last chapter and verse were translated on his dying couch as the evening shadows were gathering around, by "his boys"—his pupils. Then sitting on the floor of his cell singing Glory to the Father, Son and Holy Spirit, he died with his head in the hands of his loving, sorrowing pupils. Chrn Adv.

one should translate SCRIPTURE into English, and no book of this kind be read. This led to great persecution, but it is believed there were many copies in circulation.

The first printed edition was by Tyndale, the N T 1526 and the BIBLE in part, 1532. Tonstal Bp of London and Sir Thos Moore, took pains to buy up and burn the impressions. One result of this was, to enable the translator to publish an improved edition.

After Tyndale, who suffered as a martyr—taken out of prison, strangled and burnt, Miles Coverdale revised the whole and dedicated it to Henry VIII 1535. In 1537 John Rogers who had aided Tyndale and was at Antwerp, reprinted an edition from Tyndale and Coverdale. This was published under the assumed name of Thos Matthews. A revision was made 1539 by Richard Taverner.

The GREAT BIBLE appeared in 1539. It was Coverdale's revised under Bp Cranmer. For the edition of 1540, Cranmer wrote a preface, hence it was called CRANMER'S BIBLE.

During the reign of Mary, was published the GENEVA BIBLE. Coverdale and others who had taken refuge in Geneva, edited it and added marginal annotations.

Abp Parker obtained authority from Queen Elizabeth to revise the existing translations, and with the aid of Bishops and others, published 1568, the BISHOP'S BIBLE. It contains short annotations. Editions of this from 1589 like the Genevan, were divided into verses. This was printed in 1572 in larger form with prefaces, under the name of MATTHEW PARKER'S BIBLE. It was used in the churches 40 yrs, though the GENEVAN may have been used more in families. The *Rhemish* N T published at Rheims 1582 and Douay O T at Douay 1609-10, are the English BIBLE of the Romanists.

In 1603 King James appointed 54 of the most learned and pious of his realm to make a revision of the translation. Forty seven met, and in 4 years—from 1607-11, the task was completed The text became what is known as the AUTHORIZED ENGLISH VERSION and won its way on its own merits, into all English speaking countries.

The preservation of the SCRIPTURES is regarded by Jew and Christian as miraculous. "The words of the LORD are pure words; as silver tried in a furnace of earth, purified seven times. Thou shalt keep them O LORD, thou shalt preserve them from this time forever!" **Ps 12.**

How else e g, could they have come through the Dark Ages—from the 6th to the 16th cy till the Reformation,

> "Through the church's long eclipse,
> When from priest or pastor's lips
> Truth divine was never heard,"

when Christian Rome, the papacy, then at its height, ruled over man's moral agency, claimed authority over the conscience, "took away the key of knowledge," persecuted unto death the little flock, as the Waldenses, Albigenses and Huguenots, and destroyed their SCRIPTURES wherever found? Surely the words of Bryant are illustrated in the history of this BOOK:

> TRUTH crushed to earth shall rise again,
> The eternal years of GOD are hers;
> While error wounded, writhes in pain,
> And dies among her worshippers.

What grace, what wisdom is it that we have a written revelation and not tradition only! Not many BIBLES but one * * * Apart from any intention even, to vitiate a divine message, oral tradition must have suffered from the state of those to whom addressed. Such is the influence of man's moral condition on his reason, emotions, will, that in the lapse of ages, rise and fall of nations, and corruption of the church, an unwritten revelation must have undergone essential changes. Every truth not considered of present importance, or repugnant to the carnal mind, would have been dropped out of the part handed down to the next generation, until we should have left us such a BIBLE as neither reason nor faith could receive; while men would contend not so much for the meaning of the TEACHER's words, as the words themselves—"the letter that killeth."

What mercy to a world deteriorating and falsifying

everything holy and true, every ordinance of GOD, that whatever has grown old with age, has in it the germs of renewing its youth! Whatever has been lost from the memory of the church, is not lost irrecoverably. We have the seeds of restored knowledge—the very " word of GOD which liveth and abideth " forever.

As each truth of SCRIPTURE was made known, GOD gave proofs whence it came and wherefore sent * * * Awe, submission and a sense of the divinity, were impressed on the mind.—Adam heard GOD in the garden, Moses saw him in a flame of fire in the bush, John in the SPIRIT on Patmos, saw and heard " one like unto the SON of man."—A complete written revelation is inconsistent with miraculous or sensible evidence. SEE MIRACLES. And hence the danger lest the every day appearance of the BIBLE, its familiar tone etc, should deceive or lead us to treat it as an uninspired volume ANGUS.

Let us remember that our faith is bought and sealed with the blood of JESUS on Calvary, tried through Jewish and pagan persecution, purified in the *auto da fees* of Spain, and fires of Smithfield in England's daybreak—the times when the truth as it is in JESUS was heresy, and to be heard praying or singing even, was a crime to be punished by the HOLY INQUISITION!—For every ray of light and drop of joy in this dark, sin cursed world, we are dependent mediately on this BOOK of life—the HOLY BIBLE.

SEC 4 REVISED VERSION

The Anglo-American, the first denominational and interdenominational revision of the SCRIPTURES, is regarded by many as a sign of the times—the progress of the GOSPEL. That barriers are being burned away and " middle walls " broken down. Also, as a means of giving a fresh start to the word of the LORD on its mission among the nations, looking forward to CHRIST'S coming in millenial times.

There had long been a growing conviction among BIBLE scholars of the need, not of a re-translation so much, as a revision of the A V. *That* was as shown, but a revision of previous succesive versions.

The O T was begun 6. 30. 1870, and finished 6. 20. 1884. The N T 6. 22. 1870, and published May 81. The three centres of the English Company* were Oxford, Cambridge, Westminster. The preface reports to both TESTAMENTS are subscribed

JERUSALEM CHAMBER, WESTMINSTER ABBEY.

The American company met in the Bible House N Y, co-operating with the English. It was represented by such masters of the Heb and Greek as Philip Schaff DD, President, and James Strong LLD. The original number in both companies was 101, out of the most learned and pious of different denominations.

In the appendixes to the OLD and N TESTAMENTS are the words, renderings etc preferred by the American, and at their request, recorded by the English Co. These two appendixes contain about one thousand variations from the English, add great interest, and will ever be referred to by the reader with profit.

We give exs——

For HOLY GHOST read uniformly, HOLY SPIRIT.
" wot, wist, hale—know, knew, drag.
" Seethe, sod, sodden—boil, boiled.
Omit " S " (i e Saint) from the GOSPELS and top of page.

Incidentally, these tables also illustrate how much difference in climate, social relations, customs etc, between the two nations, have to do with forming people's ideas and words, even in translating our BIBLE.

The object of this revision was to bring the Old version up to the present standard of scholarship—to the advance in Heb and Greek philology (science of origin, construction and history of lang), BIBLE geography, history, archæology (from Gr *archa* ancient) etc.

* Dr Angus was one of them.

1 There were many words and phrases in use in 1611, which have dropped out or changed their meaning.

Exs. LUKE 17:7 "by and by," ACTS 21:15 "carriages," 28:13 "fetched a compass," now rendered straightway, baggage, made a circuit.

2 The sense was not always interpreted accurately. The Heb and Greek article was not always translated right. The means of finding the age of a MS also, is superior to 1611, when the daughter of Zion in Britain was loosing the bands of sin and popery from her neck.

3 New Heb and Greek MSS had come to light, some even of the 4th and 5th cys, and writings of the Fathers of the 1st and 2nd cys. "Comparative philology in 1611 was rudimentary. BUXTORF's HEB GRAMMAR for example, was the best James' revisers had, and meager at that."

Our revisers had also the aid of such BIBLE critics as Griesbach, Wetstein, Lachmann, Tischendorf, Bengel, Alford.—Biblical science was then in its morning, now at its noon. In Germany, Luther's translation it has been found necessary to revise. So in Holland, Sweden and Denmark.

Exs in interpretation.—II TIM 4:14 for "the LORD reward him" read "will render to him." ROM 4:19 omit "not" and read, Abraham "considered his own body, now as good as dead." Ps 19:3, read "There is no speech nor language. Their voice cannot be heard."

In the R V, the long, imperfect, misleading headings of chs and subjects at top of the page, do not appear. The chs are indicated by 1, 2, 3 on the left margin. A perfect system of paragraphing adopted, poetic SCRIPTURES are in metrical form etc; and the whole so to speak, made to look more like inspired men wrote the different books.

The people henceforth, owe a debt of love and gratitude to the GIVER of "every perfect boon," like, or next to that called for in the gift and coming of his only SON—the "light of the world," for a BIBLE in accuracy, literary merit and mechanical form, ahead of any age or nation;

and to the two companies our heartfelt thanks are due, and on their behalf, for their part in supplying the "unspeakable gift."

And if what F W Faber (who went over to the church of Rome) says—" Who will say that the beauty and marvellous English of the protestant BIBLE, is not one of the strongholds of heresy in this land? It is like music never to be forgotten—the church bells the convert knows not how to forego. Its felicities seem like things rather than words. It is a part of the national mind, the anchor of national seriousness. It is worshipped and idolized. The memory of the dead passes into it. The potent traditions of childhood are stereotyped in its verses. The griefs and trials of a man are hid underneath its words. It is representative of his best moments, and all about him of soft and gentle, pure, penitent and good, speaking to him out of his BIBLE. It is his sacred thing controversy has never dimmed, doubt never soiled," be so true of the OLD, even better things are predicated of the NEW VERSION. And like that of 270 yrs before, it too will win, on its own merits, its way into all lands.

> Upon the GOSPEL's sacred page
> The gathered beams of ages shine;
> And, as it hastens, every age
> But makes its brightness more divine.
> SIR J BOWRING.

CHAPTER III.

AUTHENTICITY AND AUTHORITY.

Sec 1

If those facts (origin, nature and progress of religion), are not established, nothing in the history of mankind can be believed. CH JUS BUSHE.

If some of these BOOKS were disputed at first and then adopted, they are confirmed by the trial. GAMBIER.

THE BIBLE AN INSPIRED, AND THE ONLY INSPIRED TEACHER.

IN speaking of the genuineness of the SCRIPTURES, nothing has been said of their authority. What they are and claim to be, must be sought in the BOOKS themselves. A little attention will satisfy us of the following—

1 THEY SPEAK OF THE MISSION OF JESUS AS DIVINE.

He professes to be a teacher sent from GOD, and from the first declares he is to give his life for the redemption of the world.

JNO 8: 42, 7: 16.

He wrought miracles, spoke as never man spoke, and showed acquaintance with the thoughts of the heart and future events.

JOHN 6: 64, 16: 30, MATT 20: 17–19.

His enemies could not resist the spirit and wisdom with which he spoke, nor account for his works on any other grounds.

MARK 6: 1–3, JOHN 7: 15.

His life private and public, was self denying, disinterested, beneficent.

JOHN 4: 34, 7: 18.

He was put to death for making himself the SON of GOD, a charge he did not deny. He sealed his TESTAMENT on the Cross, and confirmed everything by rising from the dead and ascending to the right hand of GOD.

LUKE 22: 70, JOHN 20: 17.

2 THEY SPEAK OF THE CALL AND WORK of his apostles as divine. Of the eight whose writings we have, Matthew, Peter, James, John and Jude, were of the number he commissioned to establish his kingdom and authority,

"By all the works that I have done,
By all the wonders ye shall do,"

sending the promise of his FATHER upon them.

MATT 10, LUKE 9: 6.

They proved their calling by following their LORD, by word and deed, making many converts.

ACTS 4: 16, 5: 29, 2: 41.

3 LUKE AND MARK WERE COMPANIONS of the apostles. Mark was a convert of Peter I: 5: 13. LUKE was the friend and companion of Paul COL. 4: 14, II TIM. 4: 11.

Papias 110, Justin (d 164), Irenæus 180, and Origen, speak of Mark's GOSPEL as divine and sanctioned by Peter.

Luke and Paul itinerated together, were 2 yrs in Palestine, and with each other in Rome.

ACTS 21: 17, 28: 16, II TIM 4: 11.

Irenæus, Tertullian and Origen tell us Luke's GOSPEL is inspired, was read by all Christians and sanctioned by Paul.

Paul was called by JESUS ACTS 9, and proved his call by miracles, imparting of gifts etc, as the chiefest of the apostles.

ACTS 26: 12-17, 9: 13-17, GAL 1: 1-12.

4 THEIR WRITINGS were composed by CHRIST'S command. Their writings agree with their preaching and embody their teachings in a permanent form. Their writings were received by the first Christians as of equal authority with

their preaching. They were regarded as sacred as the HEB SCRIPTURES JAS 4: 5, 2: 8.

5 THE Jewish SCRIPTURES and religion are spoken of in the N T as divine. CHRIST and his apostles assume the O T to be divine; the call of Abraham and Moses, the moral law, ritual and civil enactments of Moses as of GOD, and Christianity the completion of Judaism, and as foretold by the prophets.

JOHN 4: 22, 19: 36, MATT 15: 4, 22: 31, ACTS 3: 13, ROM 7: 22, 9: 4.

The O T writers acknowledge what they spoke and wrote was from GOD.

MATT 5: 17, 26: 54-6, ACTS 10: 43, DEUT 18: 18, JER 1· 6.

They speak of the O T books according to their names —LAW, PROPHETS and PSALMS, as authoritative.

MATT 22: 31, 43, JOHN 10. 35, HEB 3: 7.

Admitting CHRIST to be the SON of GOD, it follows that the BIBLE is of GOD. It claims also to be the sole authority, not *a* rule, but *the* rule of man's faith and practice. To understand the SCRIPTURES we employ reason, the views of Biblical scholars, and an honest and good heart.

The public reading of the SCRIPTURES in the tongue of the people, is commanded——

DEUT 31: 11-13, JOSH 8: 33, I THESS 5: 27, COL 4: 16.

The private reading of the SCRIPTURES is enjoined——

DEUT 11: 18-20, ROM 15: 4, I TIM 3: 15.

The exercise of one's own judgment is taught, and is essential to the progress of pure religion.

PHIL 1: 9, 10, COL 1: 9.

All doctrines must be brought to the test of SCRIPTURE.

IS 8: 20, I JOHN 4: 1.

Our LORD and his apostles (to them who had the O T), always appealed to its authority.

INSPIRATION. 45

From the days of Moses, GOD commanded to commit all SCRIPTURE to writing.

Ex 17: 14, DEUT 31: 19.

Nothing may be added or taken from it.

DEUT 4: 2, REV 22: 18.

Oral tradition is condemned.

Is 29: 13, MATT 15: 2-4.

These are some of the truths received by protestants as opposed to Romanism, some of which are held the more sacred because fought and bled for by the Waldenses, through the Reformatiom and Renaissance, and to the days of Victor Emmanuel, as "the faith * * * delivered to the saints" JUDE 3.

SEC 2 INSPIRATION.

As authority depends on inspiration, they are interchangeable terms, and authority is sometimes treated under this head.

We will now take up the mode and degrees of inspiration.

The unconverted Jews and heathen it seems, believed the voluntary action of the writer was suspended while under the divine impulse.

From the Fathers, we gather that the first Christians believed the writer generally exercised his voluntary powers. When the authority of the Pope was called in question, the theory was examined. The fact was admitted, but the doctrine best accounting for it was left an open question.

There are two views. 1 The ideas and words were both dictated. 2 The ideas were given, but the words were left to the discrimination of the writer. This its advocates think, will best account for differences in quotations, references to other SCRIPTURES, diversities of style etc.

Some again have taught that fundamental truths are inspired, but arguments, illustrations etc, are of the writer.

Such a theory degrades and brings SCRIPTURE into disrepute.

Others, that those portions whose tendency is moral and religious are inspired, but the rest not.

Dr Doddridge and many modern theologians, teach three different kinds of inspiration—

1 Revealing things unknown.

2 Providing against mistakes in doctrines, precepts etc, known.

3 Authorizing writings of uninspired men.

Some take another view, different mostly in the manner of stating; i e, Holy men wrote under inspiration, and were kept from mistake in things known and unknown.

All SCRIPTURE is by inspiration of GOD, and new truths are revealed. Or, as Thos Scott expresses it, inspiration discovers new truth and superintends the communication of the old. This distinction is well stated.

It may be added, the gift in the writer was consistent with diligent research, expression of the same thought in different words,* such differences in their accounts as might arise from their different standpoints; quotations from uninspired authors,† use of uninspired documents, peculiarity in style, matter and manner from diversity of mind, moral character, education etc.

The reader has observed the differences, in Isaiah and Ezekiel, John and Paul. How does the historic, evangelical, deep-toned, simple, pathetic numbers of the fire crowned "son of Amoz," contrast with the authoritative, dashing, figurative, "whirlwind, cloud and fire"—obscurer style of "Ezekiel the priest, the son of Buzi!" And how different the impression we get from the "SPIRITUAL or DIVINE GOSPEL," than the classic, episodial, impetuous, logical style of him who had been brought up at the feet of

* To this class belong quotations from the O T which are out of the LXX, or Heb, and *sense* often, rather than words. See PT. III. c. III.

† JOSH 10: 13, NUMB 21: 14, JUDE 9, 14, 15.

Gamaliel, "caught up even to the third heaven," and ravished with the sights and sounds there, his soul ever after seemed struggling to give utterance to!

An exact knowledge of the truth was accompanied in the writer with an exactly regular series of arguments, a precise expression of the meaning, and genuine vigor of suitable affections. In the words we may observe the utmost depth and utmost ease. All the elegancies of human composure sink into nothing before it. GOD speaks, not as man, but as GOD. His thoughts are deep and of inexhaustible virtue. And the language of his messengers also, is exact in the highest degree; for the words given, accurately answered the impression made on their minds. Hence as Luther says, DIVINITY is but the grammar of the language of the HOLY SPIRIT. To understand this, we should note the emphasis on every word, the holy affections expressed thereby, and tempers shown by the writer. But how little is this attended to! WESLEY'S PREF to N T.

Add to the above, that the writer was sometimes uncertain of the import or application of his message, and we have the main facts on this subject.—"The secret things belong unto the Lord * * * the things that are revealed, belong unto us and to our children" DEUT 29: 29.

The prophet was GOD'S mouth-piece and amanuensis. DEMPSTER.

OBS. 1 There seem to be in the books, degrees of inspiration comparable to that which impresses us in the "gifts, grace and usefulness" of living ministers. We read David and Isaiah in the Old, and John and Paul in the N T, feeling ourselves in communion with minds having a deeper baptism, than in the historical writers, for example.

So, some are more impressed and profited by the GOSPELS, as being the very words and acts of the TEACHER, than the ACTS and LETTERS.

2 As O T inspiration terminated, and has its realization in CHRIST and his teachings, its light and power losing itself so to speak, in ante-millenial day, so there is a sense in which every Christian may feel he has of the prophetic gift. SEE PT. II c VIII, Con.

Duty and privilege call on us to be filled with the SPIRIT.

This is in a different view, like having the "mind in you which was also in CHRIST JESUS" PHIL. 2: 5.

But while we sing

"O for that flame of living fire
Which shone so bright in saints of old,"

let us not be enthusiasts, but use the SCRIPTURAL—"old time" way, as suggested MATT 13: 12, LUKE 24: 49.

SEC 3 THE CANON

THE BOOKS approved by the early church as inspired, were called canonical, and the whole the CANON. Hence on the authority of any BOOK, it has sometimes been asked simply, Is it canonical?

The BOOKS are canonical because **divine, and** not divine because canonical. The subject comes in here between genuineness and authority, because it involves the facts of both.

We begin with the N T. There were many GOSPELS and memoirs of our LORD in the apostolic times, but only four were adopted. MARK and LUKE were written under the care of Peter and Paul. John is recorded to have attested the first three, and having them before him, when he added his own.

There are 13 LETTERS bearing Paul's name, other disciples being witness. Most were by amanuenses, who in turn became witnesses. These LETTERS were dispatched through messengers. Nine were addressed to different churches.

Ignatius, Polycarp, Clement and Peter II 3: 16, testify that these are inspired, and were read, with the O T in the churches and by all Christians. Peter applies the name SCRIPTURE to all of Paul's LETTERS; and the name, though found 50 times in the N T, is never applied but to the canonical books.

All the BOOKS of the O T, four GOSPELS, ACTS, 13 LETTERS of Paul, I JOHN and I PETER, were received from the first. The other seven were subjected to a rigid examination and then adopted, the ordeal only making their genuineness more certain; i e, to the minds of such as had not the means of knowing.

Spurious letters were abroad in the name of Peter, John, James and Jude. It was therefore necessary that the successors of the apostles should examine the MSS to satisfy some. The question was not about their inspiration, but whether by the four writers whose names they bore. At the end of the 4th cy, the last one was adopted.

Between 200 and 400 A D, 15 catalogues of the SCRIPTURES were published. The PESHITO as said, and early Latin versions come in here, as evidence for the whole N. T.

Canonicity is co-ordinate with divine authority, rests on the same evidences, and is introduced only as a collateral proof—another view from another standpoint. Let us remember (and as we are about to show), the chief evidence is found in the BOOKS themselves.

As the authority of the O T is confirmed by the New, so its canonicity. CHRIST received and used the Heb SCRIPTURES as delivered. There are 263 quotations out of nearly every BOOK, and over 350 references and allusions in the N T. SEE PT III c III.

The O T CANON in CHRIST'S day was as now. Josephus and Philo testify to this. Jos tells us the BOOKS he gives were received by all Jews and that they would contend for them to the death.

The following among many testimonies are added. The N T speaks of all under the head of the LAW, PROPHETS and PSALMS. The LXX has every BOOK. The son of Sirach 130 B C, Philo 41 A D, and Josephus, speak of all; besides Greek and Latin Fathers without number.

SEC 4 PRESERVATION OF THE BOOKS.

The five BOOKS of Moses were put into the ark of the Tabernacle and preserved during the 40 yrs wandering in the wilderness, and afterwards in Jerusalem.* The successive writings from Joshua to David were preserved in the same sanctuary. Solomon when he built the temple, placed

* Deut 31: 9, 26, I Sam 10 : 25.

all in it, enriching them with his own. After Solomon, Jonah, Joel, Amos, Hosea, Isaiah, Micah, Nahum, Zeph, Jeremiah, Hab and Obadiah during the 1st temple, arose and added their writings. On the destruction of the temple, the books are lost sight of to us. Daniel in Babylon speaks of that of JEREMIAH and other prophets 9: 2, 10.

Under the Restoration (about 80 yrs after the return), Ezra is said to have gathered and compiled the MSS to his time, to which were added his own, with ESTHER, NEHEMIAH and MALACHI.

The existence of the GREAT SYNAGOGUE is spoken of by Jewish writers. It consisted of Ezra, Nehemiah, Malachi, ending with Simon the Just; and the editing and canonizing of the Heb SCRIPTURES is ascribed to this body. The SEPT as said, proves their canonicity to 285. SEE PT III c V SEC 2.

We will end this lesson with ART V of our CREED

* * "In the name of HOLY SCRIPTURE, we do understand those canonical BOOKS of the OLD and NEW TESTAMENTS, of whose authority was never any doubt in the church."

SEC 5 APOCRYPHA.

External evidence is against these books. They are not in any catalogue of the 1st 4 cys, nor received till the council of Trent 1545. Philo does not name, and Josephus excludes them. The Jews did not adopt them. JESUS and his apostles do not quote therefrom.

Internal evidence is against them. The writers do not claim inspiration, and some virtually disown it. The books contain things at variance with history, are self contradictory, and opposed in places, to the precepts of the BIBLE.

The WISDOM OF SOLOMON, ECCLESIASTICUS, I and II MACCABEES,* are first in order of merit, religious and historical.

BARUCH, SONG OF THE THREE HOLY CHILDREN and PRAYER of MANASSEH, rate next in value. I and II ESDRAS, TOBIT, JUDITH, ESTHER, SUSANNAH, the IDOL

*PT III c V SEC III.

BEL and the DRAGON, rate last. They show evidences of credulity and disregard for truth.

These books are of use however, as illustrating the progress of knowledge among the Jews, their government, religious character, taste; while some explain ancient prophecies and their fulfilment.

CHAPTER IV.

EXTERNAL EVIDENCES.

SEC 1 HISTORICAL.

History has but a fraction of the evidence there is in support of the GOSPEL story. ANGUS.

HAVING shown SCRIPTURE to be genuine, and that from the earliest times the parts were received as written by the names they bear, also that the truth of the record—its authenticity, is implied in its genuineness, we proceed to speak of a branch of evidence noticed CH I, from authors sacred and profane.

The books were referred to, copied and received as history while their writers were yet living. That Palestine was under the Roman yoke, that in Herod's reign, CHRIST was born, professed to be from GOD, wrought miracles, taught and illustrated a morality unknown to the gentiles and even the Jews; had followers, was crucified under Pontius Pilate, that believing him risen from the dead, many turned to him, that in a few years his disciples were in all lands; and in a word, whatever might be thought of his divinity, these things were deemed true, even by those who rejected their spiritual significance.

During the first 4 cys, we have more than 100 ecclesiastical writers speaking of these things. Jerome 392, refers to about fifty. These authors belong to the Greek, Latin, Syrian and other tongues. They represent the Christian and heathen world from the Euphrates to the Pyrenees, from Germany to the Sahara. The whole or parts of these annals, are extant. They agree in quoting SCRIPTURE as authentic, speak of it as a book and divine. Heretics and heathen admitted the facts. Infidels founded their denial on the facts.

Justin Martyr 165, and Tertullian 200, inform us that CHRIST was worshipped as GOD, and that Christians in some places were in the majority.

Heathen and Jewish writers without reference to the N T, confirm in a general way, or illustrate the life of our LORD. Josephus, Tacitus 100 in his history, Suetonius in his Biographical Sketches 117, Juvenal in his Satires 128, and Pliny in his LETTERS 103, tell the sacred story *

This knowledge puts us back to the days of our LORD—carries us in spirit to the time when JESUS walked in Palestine, filled with the HOLY SPIRIT and power, going "about doing good, and healing all that were oppressed of the devil." The days when he spoke those

"Wonderful words of life"

which brought life and immortality to light. And still

"More wonderful they seem"

after 1800 yrs, and will, till they have filled the whole earth.

What memories are roused up! What inspiration of "words that shook the world," and lingered on ear and heart during the life of them that heard the TEACHER! What revelations of GOD, heaven and hell—openings, and views into the world to come—through the vail and *hades*, he made!

This evidence brings us in the spirit to a scene in the TEACHER's early ministries near Capernaum, MARK 1: 19—the call of the beloved disciple (who followed his LORD whithersoever he went), as described in a poem on his departure at Ephesus—

* SEE PALEYS EVS CH II.

> Some seventy years ago
> I was a fisher by the sacred sea.
> It was at sunset. How the tranquil tide
> Bathed dreamily the pebbles! How the light
> Crept up the distant hills!
>
> * * * * * * * * * *
>
> And then he came and called me. Then I gazed
> For the first time on that sweet face. Those eyes
> Out of which as from a window, shone
> Divinity, looked on my inmost soul
> And lighted it forever. Then his words
> Broke on the silence of my heart and made
> The whole world musical. * * *
> O what holy walks we had! * * *
>
> ST. JOHN THE AGED.

The person, looks, words and doings of JESUS have been the inspiration of believers, of the most pathetic tributes of tongue and pen to love and sorrow, the keynote of the loftiest flights of eloquence, of poetic and historic fame, through the centuries. In

> "That was a happy, happy day in the olden time,
> When the LORD to Bethany came,"

we have the scenes of Bethany reproduced—lessons of faith, devotion, of love, reminiscences of the human and divine.

> When we sing
> "What means this eager, anxious throng," in
> "JESUS OF NAZARETH PASSETH BY,"

we have awakened in us a sense of the fame of JESUS, an idea of his power over men in his day.

And some like the writer, have been filled with rapturous awe and love, as the opened eyes of faith have beheld JESUS walking; making us feel that *we* ought to "walk even as he walked." Such a view of the MASTER'S sacred footsteps, as he moved along from place to place, making the wilderness and solitary place glad, and desert rejoice and blossom as the rose, is eloquent with divinity—the wisdom, love and power of the SON of GOD.

> "And from his love's exhaustless spring,
>   Joys like a river come
> To make the desert bloom and sing,
>   O'er which we travel home."

While we believe those who saw and heard MESSIAH, happy above any before them, it is nevertheless true that we have varied, accumulative evidences that the believing Jew and early Christian even, had not, when the "SUN of righteousness" had only risen. It is not those darker times in the "land of ancient story"—the days and place of our SAVIOR'S rejection and crucifixion, we are to think of as so favored as our own GOSPEL day. As both the AUTHOR and plan of redemption are a mystery, so also the highest blessedness of knowing and having the companionship of JESUS, must be by FAITH. While in a human form, it seems the divinity was to a great degree, hidden from mortal view.

It may be observed that the "OLD OLD STORY" is repeated and come down to us through the ages, in universal history. "Their sound went into all the earth, and their words to the ends of the world." ROM 10: 18.

In accordance with our plan, we will take up each BIBLE help or topic in its natural, historic order. Although it is in the very nature of the purer, higher forms of spiritual truth, to be dry and distasteful to the gross and worldly mind, to the heavenly minded, the inquirer after truth—the *true riches*, the evidences of REVELATION are both interesting and profitable; a means of grace, and which like the path of the righteous, "shineth more and more to the perfect day." PROV. 4: 18.

From the being and attributes of GOD, it is reasonable that he would not leave man in ignorance of his will, our duty and means of happiness. Also, that a REVELATION from him, oral or written, would be in agreement with nature and our relations to him. This is called *presumptive* evidence, and is nowhere so ably treated as in BUTLER'S ANALOGY. Evidence which rests on REVELATION is called *positive*.

EVIDENCES CLASSIFIED. In God are attributes of power, knowledge, holiness, love; and we accordingly divide and classify evidences under the head of *miraculous, prophetic, moral* and *spiritual*. Furthermore, a messenger from GOD must have credentials, and also evidences in his message. The first is *external*, the second internal. Prophecy has both kinds of proof; first in the prediction, then the fulfilment, found in the BIBLE or history.

The internal evidence again, is twofold: 1 *Moral*—relating to the character of GOD, the writers, and whole BIBLE teaching—appealing to the *conscience*. 2 *Spiritual*—consisting in the wisdom and harmony of revealed truth, as consistent with the character and purpose of GOD, and adapted to our every need—appealing to the intellect and heart. We shall adhere to the above order.

SEC 2 MIRACLES

MIRACLE is an event out of and above the order or laws of nature. WATSON.

BEFORE a NEW TESTAMENT, miracles are necessary to confirm it. The works of CHRIST, particularly his resurrection and ascension, gave his word the seal of divinity. They also confounded his enemies, convinced unbelievers, confirmed his friends. They were more necessary in the dawn than in the day-time. Also, but for "signs and wonders," some would not believe.*

In a rudimentary, transition state, they were more common. The MASTER appeals to them; "If I do not the works of my FATHER, believe me not." JOHN 10: 37. "Go * * tell John what things ye have seen and heard," LUKE 7: 22.

It is believed that our LORD wrought *many thousand* works of mercy not related. Hundreds it is probable, were re-

* It seems proper to notice here (as this subject may also suggest), the value or importance given the words—teaching of our LORD, above even his miracles. While we accept this, it is also true that his "miracles and finished work" on Calvary, resurrection and ascension, were necessary to and part in, our redemption. The word creative GEN 1, Ps 33: 6, and saving JOHN 6: 63, HEB 4: 12—the word of GOD, is also for a criterion and test of man's obedience of faith —discipleship.

stored to perfect health body and mind, in many places and on many occasions.

He also gave of his plenary power to his apostles, the 70 and many others. What majesty and grace—authority, wisdom, power, shine through his commission and charge to the twelve, related MATT 10, and what powers does he impart!

After he was taken up, he gave his apostles pentecostal power to preach and impart gifts to all they laid hands on. These signs and wonders were wrought openly, were satisfactory to all, and turned many to the LORD. JOHN 7 : 31, 3 : 2. The record of them ought to be and is, saving faith. JOHN 6 : 14, 2 : 11, 20 : 30.

The age of miracles is not past, as some would have us believe. JESUS is the SAVIOUR of the body, as of the spirit, *to-day.*

"The Great Physician now is near"

to heal and save every one of his members in affliction, according to his faith MATT 21 : 22, MARK 16 : 17, 18.

HISTORY tells us that Matthew finished his course by the sword in Ethiopia, Mark at Alexandria, after being dragged through the streets; Luke was hanged on an olive tree in Greece, John was thrown into a cauldron of boiling oil and banished to Patmos. Peter was crucified at Rome head downwards, James was beheaded at Jerusalem; James the Less was thrown from a pinnacle of the temple and beaten to death. Philip was hanged against a pillar in Phrygia, Bartholomew was flayed alive; Andrew bound to a cross, preached to his enemies till death. Thomas was run through at Coromandel India, Jude was shot to death with arrows; Matthias stoned and beheaded. Barnabas stoned to death by Jews at Salonica, Paul beheaded at Rome by Nero.

Does this world furnish such examples, such miracles of sincerity and devotion?

But the objector asks, Did CHRIST not deceive? or Was he not deceived himself? Ans. To believe that JESUS was an impostor or enthusiast, is to suppose a greater miracle than the BIBLE contains. For if JESUS be not divine, we have a Jew, a peasant, changing the faith of this world, weaving into his life story the prophecies of the O T, and a morality in advance of his times, as different from the traditions of his people, as it was superior to the Gentile philosophy; enduring reproach, and teaching his followers to submit to persecution and death; in proof, not of opinions, but of his resurrection from the dead. These "unlearned" men going forth, persuading the Greeks and Romans to cast away their gods, give up their religion and customs, and receive instead, a Jew who had been crucified between two thieves; and yet all impostors, all enthusiasts!!

The BIBLE itself is greater than any miracle it relates, and the SON of GOD more wonderful than anything in support of his claims. The believer feels this in every fiber. Rob me of miracles and prophecy, you have not deprived me of JESUS. * * * The morning star pales and fades at sunrise. CHRIST'S presence is a glory to which all else is dim. MANY INF PRFS.

We can but allude to the stupendous signs recorded in the O T—the burning bush, 10 plagues of Egypt, opening of the Red Sea, destruction of Pharaoh, the pillar of cloud and fire, manna and "spiritual rock that followed" Israel 40 yrs, fall of Jericho, sun and moon at Joshua's word standing still till he had destroyed the Canaanites. The miracles of the Old and N Tests would require a volume, but the subject may be examined in brief in LESLIE'S SHORT METHOD with DEISTS, a 20 p tract. These infallible marks are 1, Such as the senses could judge of. 2, Done in public. 3, Monuments preserved and actions in commemoration. 4, These instituted at the time and observed thenceforward to the end of a dispensation, or their purpose be fulfilled. The first two prevent deception *at the time*, and the last two *in future ages*. For example, the reader will observe how Leslie's rules meet in circumcision and the passover, baptism and LORD'S Supper.

IN CON. But for unbelief, it follows that there had been scarce need of signs and wonders. Man as said, in union with his MAKER, saw GOD. There are Christians who see him in the ordinary as well as the extraordinary events; in secondary or occasional, as well as in first causes. What a lesson of faith in GOD and rebuke to skepticism is taught in the words of JESUS JOHN 20: 29, to his doubting apostle Thomas!—"because thou hast seen me thou hast believed; blessed are they that have not seen and yet have believed"!

If you will put yourself in connexion with that PRESENCE with unveiled eye, and wait till bathed in the glory of that LIGHT, * * * you will need no starry miracles to assure you that he is the SUN OF RIGHTEOUSNESS. MANY INF PRFS.

SEC 3 PROPHECY.

PROPHECY goes hand in hand with Providence as twin sisters. It suggests that back of the "capricious" changes in the world, there is ONE controlling all events. * * * The caprice is resolved into a consistent plan and purpose. The discord is due to our partial view. We have a providence with its prevision, provision and presidence, permissive and decreeing. * * * Prophecy also outlines the future, showing us glimpses of GOD as for the right. It brings the past and future together in the present. MANY INF PRFS.

Prophecies are miracles **of** knowledge. That which is to the senses—tangible, has its evidence *per se*. The evidence of prophecy is gradual and cumulative.—"At first a rill receiving tributary streams, which swell to a river, whose flood sweeps all before it."

PROPHECY implies—
    1 Divine prescience and an inspired **teacher**
    2 Event foretold
    3 Fulfilment not intentional by man.

OBS. The most famed oracles—Jupiter at Dodono and Apollo at Delphi, are not worthy of comparison with the Heb prophets, and fail in the above marks at every point.

Their utterances were known to **be** ambiguous, obscure and convertible, so that when the first interpretation failed, the priests were ready with another. SEE EXS and ILLUSTS c II PROPHECY, in MANY INF PRFS, from the *Sibylline* books in the case of Maxentius against Constantine, and from the Delphian Oracle to Crœsus, against Cyrus of Persia.

Apollo, the most skilful in the secrets of futurity, and most resorted to, antedating the Trojan war, was so mysterious in his responses as to get the name of *loxia*—crooked, obscure. They were through a female—*pythia*, seated on a tripod, over a vapor cavern in the temple, her mind being in an enthused, mesmeric state.

This Oracle had its origin in the discovery of a cavern on the slope of Parnassus, whence issued a vapor which produced a phrenzied state of mind, especially on the female. These two circumstances the priests conspired to make subservient to their religion, and so built this temple on the spot. CLEVELAND'S GRECIAN ANTS, ORACLES.

Every stage has its predictions fuller and clearer. Enoch tells of a coming judgment. JUDE 14v. Noah of the flood. After that, charter of the seasons is renewed, and the world not to be again destroyed by a flood. In Abraham, the covenant of Canaan and CHRIST, and to his seed a country, and all nations blessed in him; the Egyptian bondage and deliverance. Jacob foretells the history of Israel in his 12 sons Gen 49.

During the 215 yrs in Egypt, the gift was withheld, but renewed at the giving of the LAW, foretelling " a prophet," dignity of Judah, and destinies of GOD's people to the end of time, and in a typical way, the coming of MESSIAH.

400 yrs silence follow the giving of the LAW, and 400 from Malachi to CHRIST.

It was revived in Samuel, foretelling the consequences of a king to backslidden Israel and death of Saul; of David and his reign, of Solomon; afterwards, the division of the kingdom under Rehoboam; breaking of the idol altar at Bethel, the dispersion of the 10 tribes, with here and there references to CHRIST and his kingdom.

Elijah and Elisha figure in these, the days of the two kingdoms, nearly to Jonah 850, with whom the prophets may be said to begin. Amos tells of the destruction of Samaria and 10 tribes, as also Is 7 : 6–8. Is 37, tells of the captivity of Judah by Babylon, and deliverance of Hezekiah from Sennacherib, whose army was then around Jerusalem. The 70 yrs captivity was shown JER 29, and reasons EZEK 24, results JER 30, Is 27, and means of restoration " Is 13, 44 c." Nations scarce formed, a king

(Cyrus) yet unborn, are named, and the story sounds more like history than prediction Is 7 : 6–8, 39 : 2–6, 37 c.

During this period, is noised a change in their covenant, and the future of the chief of the nations. In the captivity, we have the prophecies of Daniel, Ezekiel and Obadiah. After the return, the prophets Haggai, Zechariah and Malachi, cheered the builders of the temple, and speak yet more clearly of the coming of MESSIAH.

Thus is shown how prophecy begins and ends in the O T, preparation for the advent of our LORD.

In this connexion of prophecy with its chief object, it is worthy of notice that before Pentecost, CHRIST had but a few who had received his teachings. But after 1800 yrs, a large proportion of mankind is Christian, and all other religions show signs of decay.

OBS. From the time the "star in the east" led the *Magi* to pay divine honors to the ONE "born KING of the Jews," and the day JESUS began to "utter the things hidden from the foundation of the world," and stood in the person of his apostle in the midst of Areopagus in Athens, the respect for and faith in their gods, oracles and divination, began to wane with the heathen, till " in the reign of Constantine the Gt, when the name of even Apollo fell into contempt." CLEVELAND'S GRN ANTS.

Thus are we notified of the plan—through the "seed of the woman" GEN 3 : 15; then to and through Abraham and his family 22 : 18, and one chosen out of the people to be the AUTHOR. He was to be despised, rejected and killed, but rise into everlasting renown Is 9 : 6, 11 : 1, 53 c. His human and divine nature are spoken of as from Isaac, not Ishmael; Jacob, not Esau; Judah, not Reuben the first born, nor Levi father of the priesthood; but from David the youngest of Jesse. GEN 49 : 10, I SAM 16 : 11, JER 23 : 5. Time and place of birth MIC 5 : 2; a prophet, priest and king Ps 110, Is 61 : 1; beginning and place of his ministry, miracles, sufferings, resurrection, ascension, pentecost, and kingdom increasing Is 53.

These are samples of more than 100 predictions, besides typical and allusive SCRIPTURES of him.

Most of these were made known more than 600 yrs before he appeared, some looking improbable and contradictory. Such a series of predictions relating to the person and kingdom of our LORD, could emanate only from ONE who "worketh all things after the counsel of his will."

Note that while no man, not even Moses, MESSIAH is the *theme* of all. So that at his coming, he had his signs before and along with him. It was in the form and for the purpose, as GOD foretold "by the mouth of his holy prophets * * since the world began." Luke 1: 70.

The other nations are spoken of. Noah is shown the destiny of his sons—Canaan a servant of servants, Japheth enlarged and in the tents of Shem—Europe master of Asia. To Abraham, the judgment of Mizraim and the Canaanites, of Sodom and Gomorrah. Balaam spoke of the Hebs, Christianity, the Amalekites, Kenites and Assyrians. Moses tells of the Roman power 800 yrs before it rose.

Ishmael was to be "as a wild ass among men, his hand was to be against every man and every man's hand against him, and dwell in the presence (mar coasts), of his brethren" GEN 16: 12. To this day, this race is unsubdued, though Sesostris, Cyrus, the Roms and Turks have tried to conquer them in turn.

The overthrow of Persia, Babylon, Tyre and Egypt by Alexander DAN 11, EZEK 28, 29; the conquests by the Saracens and Turks, the nations to escape, or fall by them; history of Edom, Moab, Philistia and Ammon, are sketched in such a way, as to prove that each must have been present to the vision of the prophet DAN 11, JER 48, 49, EZEK 25.

These were given in the decadence of the Jews, were intended to rebuke pride, to console, instruct, to lead to that kingdom which cannot be moved. In Babylon, Daniel numbered and weighed the kingdoms of the world, and spoke of the dominion of the "ANCIENT of days." 7: 9, 13, 22.

It may be added that every answered prayer, promise realized, act of honored faith, blessing of obedience, is prophecy fulfilled. While the typical persons and events of the dispensation, further swell the evidence, till we have a series so full and clear, as not to be accounted for but by the inspiration of the ALMIGHTY.

Compare Ps 22 and Is 53 with the GOSPELS; or the predictions of the PENT—DEUT 28: 64–5, LEV 26: 32–3, concerning the Jews, referred to by NFH 1: 8, 9c, and repeated in part by AMOS, JEREMIAH and EZEKIEL. The PENT has been in hostile keeping over 2500 yrs, and all the predictions were known and quoted by other writers over 2000 yrs ago. Their relation (priority) in time, to fulfilment, is therefore sure.

When the promise was to Abraham, he was childless, and in 200 yrs increased to only 70. Their greatness was foretold by Balaam and Moses, when the heathen were combining to destroy them. Isaiah told of their captivity when in power. Jeremiah of the restoration, after the 10 tribes were taken and Judah in Babylonia.

After the destruction of Jerusalem by Titus, the land was trodden down by the gentiles. For 1800 yrs the Jews have been without a prince, government, temple, priesthood or sacrifice,* dispersed among, though unmixed with, the nations, a proverb and a by-word still. To make the lesson morally complete, their LAW remains, and they guard the prophecies their case fulfils, a "reproach and taunt," but an "instruction" among the nations EZEK 5: 15.

Again, Jeremiah and Obadiah speak of Israel and Edom. Both families were from Isaac. Utter desolation of the family and country of Esau was predicted JER 49: 7–22, OBAD 8. Thirty ruined cities within 3 days journey of the Red Sea, attest their former greatness. Edom lies *en route* to India. But as foretold, travellers are afraid to pass through it Is 34: 10. Even the Arabs are afraid to enter, or conduct travellers through it OBAD 8. It is a vast expanse of sand, drifted up from the Red Sea, and the wretched inhabitants regard the ruins as the abode of spirits.

* After CHRIST's offering on the cross, the passover ceased. And it is said that no Jew now knows from what tribe he is descended.

EXTERNAL EVIDENCES—PROPHECY. 63

160 yrs before Babylon fell, Isaiah calls Cyrus by name, telling him it was his surname, not given by man 44, 45, summons a people from Elam (Persia), and Media, tells how **Cyrus** will get into the capital—by the diversion of the Euphrates, opening of the two leaved gates, and city surprised in the night of Belshazzar's impious feast.

100 yrs after Isaiah, Jeremiah prophesied the desolation of this "glory of kingdoms" and "praise of the whole earth," and both said it should never be inhabited, but become a lair for "wild beasts of the desert * * and their houses full of doleful creatures, and ostriches shall dwell there, and satyrs shall dance there. And wolves * * and jackals in the pleasant palaces" Is 13: 20-22, 14: 23, JER 51.

A century later, **these utterances** began to be fulfilled. Nebuchadnezzar conquered Judea, and in Herodotus 250 and Zenophon 350 yrs after Isaiah, we have historical proof of these predictions. Herodotus states, Cyrus assumed that name on his accession to the throne BK I 114. Zenophon describes his army, **naming the** Persians and Medes CYROP V. ciii. 38. Both give account of the siege, lapse of the Euphrates, capture of the city and death of the king.

Strabo says the city is a vast ruin. Lucian, that Babylon will soon, like Nineveh, be sought for and not found. Pausanias, Nothing is left but the walls. Jerome, that in his time it was a receptacle for beasts; and modern travellers, with R K Porter, testify similarly. "It is little better than a swamp says one, and I could not help reflecting how the prophecies have been fulfilled."

Nineveh founded by Asshur, was 60 m around, mighty in wealth and power. "I AM" said she, and "there is none beside me" ZEPH 2: 15. Jonah was sent to foretell her judgment. Nahum afterwards repeated the message. 100 yrs later—50 before she fell, Zephaniah told of her desolation His account as compared with Diodorus Siculus, is so literal as to seem like history. Lucian (d 312 A D), who lived in that region, tells us Babylon had perished.

Such is the end of the wicked, "cursed be the man who

trusteth in man." "Who hath showed this from ancient time? Who hath declared it of old? Have not I the LORD? and there is no GOD else beside me, a just GOD and a SAVIOR" Is 45: 21.

CHAPTER V.

INTERNAL EVIDENCES.

SEC 1 MORAL EVIDENCE.

Even miracles and prophecy would not convince, without agreement between our moral sense and teachings of this BOOK. * * * * * This evidence of co-relation is an argument worthy to fill volumes. INF PRFS.

WE now take up what is called the moral evidence of the BIBLE. This comes before the spiritual, as a book on ethics would naturally come before one on religious experience.

While the chief object of internal evidence is to prove the SCRIPTURES divine, it may be observed also that man is not competent beforehand, to decide what a revelation should be; yet he *is*, to judge whether its internal marks be such as the wisdom of this world would produce. While all may judge of this, it implies a knowledge of the ways of man and also of the BIBLE, rightly to appreciate it. If not of GOD, what a cunningly devised fable this BOOK must be!

1 Contrary to every other religion, it makes holiness (wholeness, soundness, health), the *alpha* and *omega* of its teachings.

Mohammed gives the highest heaven to men who fight and fall for his faith. The Hindoo ideal is a ritual service. Jewish tradition taught that all Jews are saved. The SCRIPTURES bring everybody before a BEING of infinite purity, and teach that nothing we can say or do will answer in place of the love of GOD and our neighbor. CHRIST

INTERNAL EVIDENCES—MORAL.

says he will disown them who preach him, if they know him not MATT 7: 21-3.

OBS. It is in such persons, that we have illustrated JER 17 : 9, "The heart is deceitful above all things;" and words of JESUS MATT 6: 23, that the very light of some is darkness; and of Paul, that some are more ready to believe a lie than the truth, that they may be damned. Our desperate sickness (JER 17 : 9), is also seen in a class of Christians who take up with an outward righteousness for CHRIST'S, to satisfy conscience, not having the mind that is Christ, which implies the *death of self, and faith "working through love."*

2 This morality was not known to the heathen, nor discovered by reason, nor such as man approved. When CHRIST came, the Romans were proud of military glory, the Greeks of their wisdom. A Pharisaic temper had divided the Jews into sects, jealous of one another, but all united in hating their masters the Romans, and gentiles at large. An enthusiast would have become a partizan, and an imposter flattered each sect at the expense of the rest, or the Jews at the expense of the Roms. JESUS came independent, reproving the errors of all, condemning every sect, courting favor of none; teaching good for evil, humility, forgiveness, to love enemies, and that every race and station is on a level with GOD; doctrines acceptable to none, yet repeated and enforced on all.

If it be said that men are ready to commend a purer morality than they practice, it may be answered that if the Jewish fishermen had studied philosophy, they could have taught a purer morality than people practiced. But they were "ignorant," yet their precepts go beyond what was practiced and approved.

3 Add to this another fact, on which Paley has enlarged —that SCRIPTURE regulates the thoughts, purposes, and refers all our acts to GOD'S will. Bad men would not have taught this, and good men would not have deceived.

4 Another feature of SCRIPTURE morality is, it everywhere teaches that sin is an evil against GOD, and also that it is GOD *alone* who is honored and not his agent. The first is inconsistent with heathen philosophy, and the second with

the natural heart. "This" as Cicero says, "is the common principle of philosophers, that the deity is never displeased, nor inflicts injury on man."

Sin is the "evil thing and a bitter," because *dishonoring to* GOD. Hence the destruction of the Amalekites, Ex 17: 16 (marg.) of Sennacherib II Kgs 19: 22-37, Belshazzar DAN 5: 23, abandonment of the gentiles to a reprobate mind ROM 1: 21, 28.

The object of the writers is to *honor*—lead our thoughts to GOD. The false teacher (Simon) ACTS 8: 9, gives out that *he* is some great one. See DEUT 1: 31, 2: 33, 4: 32-38, Ex 18: 8, JOSH 23: 3, I CHRON 29: 11, 14, how Moses, Joshua and David speak of themselves.

We are taught also that GOD is in nature Ps 19, 104, JER 5: 24. That the rise, progress and fall of nations is GOD in history. DAN 4: 35, JER 25: 9, Is 44: 28.

It is thus, that faith in him is taught as the ground of our obedience, and of our well being and success in a ruined, disorganized world. To GOD-ward, faith is a confession of our sin, weakness, lack of merit or good works. Nevertheless, it is our faith in GOD that is to unite to him, and make us finitely omnipotent, a doctrine as philosophical as it is practical. ROM 3: 27, EPH 2: 8, 9, I COR 1: 29-31, JNO 11: 40, PHIL 4: 13.

The candor of the writers is inconsistent with enthusiasm or imposture. Moses denounces the rebellion of Israel DEUT 9: 24, records the sins of the Patriarchs GEN 12: 11-13, of his grandfather Levi 49: 5-7, his brother Aaron and his sons Ex 32, LEV 10, and his own NUMB 20.

The evangelists notice their own faults and of the apostles MATT 26: 31-56, JNO 10: 6, and record the humiliation of their LORD. The apostles tell of the disorders in their own churches I COR 1: 10-17. Thus the very simplicity of the writers convinces us, that their object was by manifestation of the truth, to commend themselves "to every man's conscience in the sight of GOD" BP LOWTH.

But no analysis can give a just idea of the moral beauty and sublimity of the BIBLE. It must be compared in the bulk with other teaching. Men have praised *maxims of virtue*, or appealed to the *moral sentiments* of our nature, or sought to promote holiness by *systems of morals*. But all these are defective. Their maxims are mere dictates of prudence, without authority or influence. Our moral sentiments are retiring and evanescent, easily corrupted by the passions in whose neighborhood they dwell, are feeblest when most wanted; and systems of morals, like all processes of reasoning, depend on the perfection of our faculties, are disputable, and not motives sufficient to holy living. They are, moreover, defective in not taking into account our fall and provision for our recovery. SCRIPTURE teaches us to depend on these helps, opens with the story of our sin, and foresight of its own end; brings man into harmony with GOD and himself, enlightens and educates the conscience, subjects instincts to reason, reason to love and to GOD. Its teachings are as saving as its revelations are unearthly and sublime.

SEE also PIERSON on MOR BEAUTY and SUBLIMITY of the BIB. CHS VII, VIII.

The character of our LORD (CH III SEC 1) is a proof of the divine origin of this BOOK. It is an evidence rather to be *felt* than described, and will convict in proportion to the spirituality of the reader. Pure minds like Nathaniel (Bartholomew), "in whom is no guile," will feel it most, and will with him exclaim, "RABBI, thou art the SON OF GOD, thou art KING of Israel"! PT III c II Exs.

Three things are obvious. 1 The story of JESUS is free from panegyric. 2 His person, life and work are unstudied, written by "unlearned and ignorant men." 3 His life is unimpeached even by his enemies. His apostles notice this as a fact admitted and notorious. And if his life had not agreed with his teaching, it would have been noticed and condemned.

That his *holiness* was admitted, will appear from JNO 8: 46; MATT 27: 23-4; LUKE 23: 13-15; ACTS 3: 13, 14.
His *benevolence* and *compassion* in JNO 4, LUKE 9: 55, 10: 30-7; MARK 7: 26, 10: 13-21; LUKE 13: 16, 14: 12, 22: 50-1.

His *kindness* and *affection* MATT 14: 27-31, LUKE 19: 5, 22: 61.
His *meekness* and *humility* MATT 9: 28, 18: 22, 5: 1-12; LUKE 22: 24; JNO 13: 4. His *moral courage, firmness* and *resignation.* MATT 26: 39-46; MARK 10: 32; LUKE 4: 23, 13: 31; JNO 11: 7, 18: 4. His hatred of hypocrisy and courting favor. MATT 6: 1-18, 10: 16-39, 22: 18; MARK 12: 38-40; LUKE 11: 44. *Moderation* and absence of *austerity.* LUKE 5: 29-35; JNO 2: 1; MARK 12: 17

In our REDEEMER, says an eminent writer, we see a character which departs in every way from the models of the most enlightened heathen, even of the Jewish types of excellence; at variance with all that custom, education, patriotism and religion had consecrated as most beautiful. His four biographers, recording different facts, exhibit the same conception of him, but differing from anything they had ever seen or heard. And while he borrows nothing from even GOD's chosen race—nothing in common with established laws of perfection, he is nevertheless to every man and every nation, the type of moral excellence.

"For eighteen centuries, CHRIST's teaching has been the leaven to pervade and lever to uplift society."

We notice *three* of the many things in our LORD for instance, which impress us—

1. HIS AUTHORITY. "**Ye have heard** * * said * * * thou shalt not kill; but *I* say unto you" etc. "When JESUS had ended these words, the multitudes were astonished at his teaching; for he taught them as one having authority and not as their scribes." SER. on the MOUNT. While he sanctions Moses and the prophets, he intimates he is greater —that he is not only the subject and end, but their AUTHOR. "*I* am the resurrection and life. He that believeth on me, though he die, yet shall he live." "I am the light of the world" JNO 11: 25, 8: 12. To the high priest— "Henceforth (hereafter), ye shall see the SON of man sitting at the right hand of power, and coming on the clouds of heaven" MATT 26: 64. To Pilate—"Thou wouldest have no power (authority) except * * given thee from above" JNO 19: 11. How supreme are his words MATT. 28: 18, 19, after his humiliation!—"All power hath been

given me in heaven and on earth. Go * * * make disciples of all the nations."

Plato *thought* that the soul is immortal. Cicero says "There is a presage in the minds of men of a future existence, and the idea takes deepest root in the most exalted souls." JESUS brings life and immortality to light, and gives us the pledge of ours by himself rising from the dead. "He dissects the very character of GOD, and refutes what was false in the faith of the church. With the calmness of divinity, he wipes away the daubing from the face of GOD's LAW—the glosses of its teachers, and makes it again to be seen in its original simplicity." "Never man so spoke." Man's teaching is finite, CHRIST's infinite.

"From heaven he came, of heaven he spoke,
 To heaven he led his follower's way;
 Dark clouds of gloomy night he broke,
 Unveiling an immortal day."

"The whole drift of his teaching, like a mighty glacier, began to grind and plough the very structure of society into new form. But instead of attacking the gigantic wrongs, he put beneath the social life the all conquering law of *faith and love*. He knew these, like Archimedes' lever, would move the world."

2. OMNISCIENCE and PRESCIENCE. JESUS, as the incarnate WORD, the expression of the infinite MIND, showed acquaintance with the heart and things to come. His Sermon on the Mount in the beginning, filled the hearers with a sense of his divinity. His style and matter were original. He gave new words and ideas, he reconstructed and gave a new sense to our language. See PT II, C I SEC 1. He was never at a loss for the *best* word or act for every one, friend or foe, and on every occasion. He not only justified his words and acts to his craftiest foes from their SCRIPTURES and reason, but turned their arms against themselves. His tongue was sharper than the Damascus sword in the heart of the King's enemies. His teaching was *radical*, striking the root of the tree, to make its fruit good, the life holy by

regeneration of the heart. His words are vital—spirit and life. The GOSPELS—his words and works, are the germ, the seed plot of the N T dispensation, " till he come." They are the savor of life to his friends, but of death to his enemies.

The mind is filled with adoring wonder and admiration at the authority, wisdom and power displayed on the last three days MATT 21-3, of his active ministry, till he left (Tuesday), their " house * * *desolate*." It was under the high pressure of mind and body, in the face of the gathering storm ready to burst upon him; and the work on heart and hands to perfect—(to make an end of Judaism—spoiling principalities and powers, in order to set up his own authority and kingdom over all nations, and perfect our redemption), that we see him rising with the occasion, and shining forth above any archangel.

After answering the priests and elders, Pharisees and Herodians, Sadducees and lawyer with such skill as to deprive them even of the power to ask him any more questions, interlusively adding the discourses predictive of their rejection of him, GOD's rejection of them etc, having cleared his way through devils and men, on Tuesday his "field day," he steps forth (in their "holy temple," in the face of those thirsting for his blood) and begins to unmask the pretensions of his foes from the high priest down, opening up and laying bare their hypocrisy and murderous intent; and in seven woes, tells them of the awful judgments of GOD about to fall upon them. Then, as with a heart of infinite pity, he closes with a last lament over their city and temple his words had doomed! * * * Next on the Mt of Olives, he circumstantially tells his disciples of the siege of Jerusalem, and opens the vision upon the secret counsels of heaven to the end of the ages, and his second coming to judgment.

3. UNIVERSALITY. All nations were to serve him, and "the isles wait for his LAW." His example and precepts were to be for all time. One of his titles is IMMANUEL. He calls himself the "SON of man," significant of his relation,

sympathy and work. Paul calls him the second Adam—as our federal, representative head. He patronizes no sect or nationality, but claims, seeks to bring together and unite all in one universal brotherhood; by putting his LAW in men's hearts, to rule over them. Other reformers, even Moses, legislated for one people, or church, or dispensation; but the TEACHER fills out our ideal of moral beauty forever.*

GOD sent his SON to recast, and summon to obedience every nation. W. E. GLADSTONE.

We will close with a brief notice of its effects on individuals and society in the first age. That the doctrines of the BIBLE like its precepts, contain urgent motives to holiness, is admitted. We read of their workings in ACTS and the EPISTLES. Paul tells us incidentally, what the preaching had done in Corinth and at Ephesus, Peter in Pontus and Galatia.

Similar appeals are found in the early apologists. Clement of Rome 100, in his Epistle to the Corinthians says, Who did ever live among you who did not admire your piety and hospitality? You are humble, content with daily bread as from GOD, hear his word and walk in love. J Martyr 165, (a converted Platonic philosopher), in his Apology,—We who delighted in adultery, now practice chastity; we who practiced magic, now trust in GOD; we who loved gain, now cast what we have in common and give to the poor. You, says Minucius Felix to an opponent, punish wickedness committed; we believe it sin to indulge an evil thought. The prisons are crowded with

* THE DIVINE PERSON, PT II of MANY INF. PROOFS, A. T. PIERSON DD, in this connection, is most instructive and impressive. This book is rich in matter, illustrations, style etc, and no one can read it and not have his faith and love for JESUS and the BIBLE increased.

IMAGO CHRISTI by J. STALKER, GLASGOW SCOTLAND, like MUSICA ECCLESIASTICA—CHRN PATTERN, impresses us with the feeling that its author has a personal acquaintance with CHRIST, its subject. In some vital respects, IMAGO is superior to KEMPIS.

your party, but not one Christian, except an apostate or confessor, is there. Tertullian 220, Origen in his reply to Celsus 246, Lactantius, preceptor of Constantine 325, repeat these appeals. And even Julian the Apostate holds up Christians for imitation of pagans, for their **love to** strangers, enemies, and sanctity of life.

In Greece, the grossest impurities had been encouraged by Lycurgus and Solon. At Rome, they were openly practiced and approved. * * * Seneca and Plutarch, the elder Pliny and Quinctilian, applaud self murder. * * * Human sacrifice and exposure of children were even enforced. But when the GOSPEL came, it discouraged and destroyed these sins. It was not civilization that did it, for they were kept up by nations superior to Christians in refinement. ANGUS.

In Constantinople and Rome there was not a hospital or charitable home. After the GOSPEL came, the former had more than thirty for orphans, strangers, sick, aged and poor, and the latter 25. "Truth and candor," **says** Gibbon, "**must** own that the conversion of these nations brought temporal benefits, prevented the extinction of letters, mitigated **the fierceness of** the times, sheltered the poor, and preserved **or revived the peace and** order in society."*

SEC 2 LITERARY EVIDENCE.

There **is a** branch **of** evidence now in order, called LITERARY—the unity **and harmony** throughout, **of** revealed truth.

On the **agreement between the** *doctrines* **and** peculiarities **of** SCRIPTURE **and facts of** *nature,* the ANALOGY of BP BUTLER **is unrivalled.**

On coincidences **between the** parts of the *record* itself, Paley and Birks have written well.

On the agreement between the *two economies,*
" " coincidences between *sacred* and *profane history,*

---

* No work gives a better view of man's need of the GOSPEL than LELAND ON THE ADVANTAGES AND NECESSITY OF A REVELATION, as shown from the condition of the heathen, social, civil and religious. ANGUS.

On the coincidences of a minute and statistical character, with the *geography* and *natural history* of Palestine, on each of these subjects different authors have written.

The LITERARY evidence indeed, pervades the whole texture of SCRIPTURE. Some of the coincidences are apparently trifling, as where our LORD went down from Nazareth to Capernaum, *down* expressing the relation of the two localities. Some are pathetic as JOHN 19: 34, " And there came out blood and water." It has been found that blood and water issue from the heart when pierced.

Again, at no time after the destruction of Jerusalem, could the books of the BIBLE have been written in that style, and at no *one* time could the different books have been written.

They are, therefore, by different authors of different ages. Again, after the apostles, all writers called the followers of JESUS Christians, a name not used by Christians in the N. T. of one another. It is also noticeable that the religion of the N. T. is the only one not requiring animal sacrifices, an ordinance which would have pleased both Jews and gentiles.

LITERARY ATTRACTIONS *of the* BIB, LEC by REV J B HAMILTON, AM TR SOCY 1849, is beautiful.

SEC 3 SPIRITUAL EVIDENCE.

MORAL evidence treats of the morality, spiritual evidence, of the spirituality of GOD'S LAW. This kind, though perceived by the intellect, appeals strongly to the heart or conscience.

So far as it comes to man as it finds him, it comes to all; so far as it forms him, only to them who believe 1 COR 14: 22-5, ROM 8: 16.

The first stage consists in the agreement between what an awakened sinner sees himself to be, and what the BIBLE says he is. The BIBLE says, man is wholly depraved, that the " heart is deceitful above all things, and it is desperately sick " Jer 17: 9, and that he "must be born anew." If the reading were found to disagree with the experience, he would reject the BIBLE. But he finds the drawing agrees with the original, the mirror reflecting his own image.

The second stage in evidence is when he finds the provisions suited to his needs. Sinful, guilty, tempted, in a wicked world, and dying, the GOSPEL supplies his every want. Not only so, but the effects on others as portrayed in the GOSPEL narrative, agree with his own experience. Repentance and its fruits, obedience of faith, the increasing light and peace, power of prayer, the change thro conviction, pardon, sanctification; struggles even of the new man, defeats, victories, are sketched to the life through every stage, from birth to death, giving evidence *experimental.*

This evidence is of value to the Christian chiefly, as others cannot understand or appreciate it. It is of such a nature as often to supersede every other. He *feels* the truth which evidences prove. To such, the old controversy between Christianity and infidelity may be of little interest. He has the witness in himself. And

"What we have felt and seen,
With confidence we tell."

OBS. If the saying, The Christian is the world's BIBLE be true, (it being as a sealed book to the sinner), how responsible we are for letting our light *so* shine that men may see our good works, that there be no *cause* of stumbling, walking "even as he walked" I JOHN 2: 6.

"O wad some power the giftie gie us,
To see ourselves as others see us!"

The adaptation of CHRIST's words to every want, is even more than *penetration*, the secret of their power and proof of their inspiration * * * The blade that pierces so deep, bears on its point the balm of Gilead * * * It is half the cure to know the disease. The TEACHER helps to the knowledge of ourselves. He does not apply the remedy till he has cut out the fatal cancer. He shows his skill in the use of the blade as in the balm. INF PRFS.

It is to be observed, the GOSPEL is adapted not to our wants but to our necessities—inward and outward holiness, especially. The Jews wanted a MESSIAH like themselves. The Koran is adapted to nourish sensuality, ambition etc. Hindooism is a baseless fabric, suited to the taste—human nature in that climate. Other faiths adjust themselves to man as he is, this to man as he must be. Those save the convert in his sins, this from his sins.

To the physician entrusted with the cure of a mortal disease, two courses are open:—to treat the symptoms or the disease. If as in a fever, he is anxious only to quench thirst, his treatment is adapted only to the wants of the sufferer. The sounder system treats the disease, and that is the true specific which will remove it. The proof of its virtue is not its palatableness or power of exhilaration, but improvement and health of the sick one, as founded on experience, and confirming the proofs which led to make the trial. And so of the GOSPEL. It may exhilarate, it may please the taste, but the evidence of its truth and being received, is its tendency to *holiness*.

IN CON. We have tried by a short cut, to give our readers a reason for the hope within us. The evidences are so many and various, that it would take a lifetime to examine them

"And still new beauties
And still increasing light" be seen.

For the candid inquirer, any one of these departments often, will be enough; no other system being founded on miracles and prophecy, nor exhibiting such holiness and love.

Yet there is in relation to these evidences, unbelief both among inquirers and Christians. Unbelief, for want of candor or a teachable spirit, which is of itself an evidence of the truth of revelation, being in harmony with the dealings of GOD in the whole realm of nature, providence, and our natural life. Indifference, levity, carelessness, prejudice, lead astray, or hinder from seeing aright. As the SCRIPTURES forewarn, those who love not the truth, shall not understand. So deeply did Grotius feel this, that he regarded the evidences in proof of the BIBLE, divinely

76   INTERNAL EVIDENCES—SPIRITUAL.

adapted to test men's character. "If ye will not believe, surely ye shall not be established" Is 7: 9.

Dan 12: 10, Is 29: 13, 14; Matt 6: 23, 11: 25, 13: 11, 12; Jno 3: 19 etc.

Among Christians, there is weakness of faith through neglect of searching. Baxter says that in early life he was exercised about his sincerity; later, about the truth of Scripture. On examining the evidences, his fears were removed. Internal evidence to Baxter was most convincing, such as came with the witness of the Spirit. The spirit of prophecy says he, was the first witness; the spirit of miraculous power, the second. And now he adds, the spirit of renovation and holiness.

Obs. The reason some are inwardly and outwardly barren in the fruits of the Spirit and good works is, they neglect to have the word of Christ dwell in them richly in all wisdom. I have observed as Bp Foss says, those are most happy and useful, who are most "saturated with the Word." Others there are, the foundations of whose faith in revelation, simply rests on what they have heard parents and teachers say, a kind of traditional evidence.

" A little learning is a dangerous thing ;
    Drink deep, or taste not the Pierian Spring ;
    There shallow draughts intoxicate the brain,
    While drinking largely, sobers us again,"

is more true in application to the knowledge of the things of God than of this life—to the wisdom from above, than of this world. The " lack of knowledge" Hos 4: 6—the Spirit's charge and lament throughout the O T, as the reason for the destruction of the Jews, will account for the inanimate state of many Christians.

Most of the doubts the good have, may be dispelled by Scriptural means. Others, chiefly speculative, may remain in the light of evidence. Even for these however, there is a cure or comfort. Philosophy can not solve them, but faith in God, prayer and work in the Master's vineyard can. If not, the means of grace will bring such to think less of them, and to wait for the perfect day. "If thou wilt go forward in my way, thou shalt know the truth, and the truth shall make you free" Kempis. The proofs, if candidly examined, will cure all honest doubt. Inf Prfs.

Light is sown for the righteous and gladness for the upright in heart Ps 97 : 11.

Ours is a complex nature, and the morbid excitability of one part of our frame may be healed by the increased activity of another. An irritable faith is a symptom of deficient action somewhere, and may be helped by attention to practical duties. Mysteries no man can solve, will melt away in the light and heat of active love.

Who is among you that feareth the LORD, that obeyeth the voice of his servant? He that walketh in darkness and hath no light, let him trust in the name of the LORD, and stay upon his GOD Is 50 : 10.

> "O child of sorrow, be it thine to know
> That SCRIPTURE only is the cure of wo;
> The field of promise, how it flings abroad
> Its perfume oer the Christian's thorny road!
> The soul reposing on assured relief,
> Feels herself happy amidst all her grief;
> Forgets her labors as she toils along,
> Weeps tears of joy and bursts into a song."

"PHILOSOPHY of the PLAN of SALVATION," by a converted skeptic, has cured the doubts and strengthened the faith of both skeptics and Christians.

CHAPTER VI.

THE BIBLE—PECULIARITIES OF.

THE LAW of the LORD is perfect, restoring the soul; the testimony of the LORD is sure, making wise the simple; * * * the judgments of the LORD are true and righteous altogether. More to be desired are they than * * much fine gold Ps 19.

To seek divinity in philosophy, is to seek the living among the dead, to seek philosophy in divinity, is to seek the dead among the living. BACON.

The OLD and N TESTS are like the rolls on which anciently written —one subject from first to last; but the view becomes clearer as we unwind the roll. CECIL.

SEC 1 THE BIBLE A REVELATION OF GOD AND MAN.

THE Bible is a revelation from GOD to man, and a revelation of both, in relation to the office and work of our LORD.

Although traced upon his works and the mind of man, the will of GOD is only complete in his WORD, and preserved from decay.

It begins with Eden, and speaking of man's sin, after a wondrous history, tells of restored union and happiness in heaven through JESUS CHRIST.

More generally, the BIBLE is the store-house of facts, duties and divine truth. It gives light on the history of our world from the beginning, (on which other writings are silent or filled with fable), occasion and consequences of sin, origin of nations and diversity of language. We thus trace the progress and mark the uniformity of the laws on which men have been dealt with, the holiness and mercy of the divine administration, progress of the world and plan of redemption, as shown in every stage, and as influencing GOD's procedure, to be perfected in CHRIST.

All the great questions troubling the minds of mortals, are herein settled forever by authority of GOD, which no one need question, and from which is no appeal.

Sec 2 A Revelation of Spiritual Truth.

The BIBLE record speaks of **our world as** "GOD's world," and destined to become the kingdom of his SON; and the idols of the heathen as imaginary beings, or only parts of his **creation**. The principle of selection, both in its scope and design, is moral and spiritual in both economies, and all looking forward to the coming of JESUS CHRIST and "restoration of all things" ACTS 3: 21.

That these disclosures supply ample materials for inquiry, and (if false) for refutation; and as **never** found false, their antiquity and extent, as Bp Butler shows PT II, is one proof of their inspiration. To teach religious truth is the aim, even of those parts which do not *seem* to be moral.

Being spiritual in nature and design, we **only** study SCRIPTURE aright, as the means of our instruction, conviction, rectification (correction), and holiness. Other knowledge is useful, this necessary. "Take fast hold of instruction * * for she **is thy life**" PROV 4: 13.

We must not study it for other object—"seek the dead among the **living**." And those are rebuked who examine it for the "secret things" which belong "only to GOD."

Again, to disjoin the truth from its spirituality, is next to denying both. Virtue is strong and healthy, only in proportion as **it is molded** after the pattern shown **us in the** BIBLE.

OBS. Many Christians **get** the truth piecemeal. For example, some believe immersion (**one** only of the three modes of baptism), to be Scriptural, thereby confounding a *form* with the ordinance. While others have perverted the holy supper, in mistaking the *sound* or *form* of CHRIST's **words** for the sense. And **this** also is one reason why the body of CHRIST is divided into sects.

Exs. In the first sin, the lesson is clearly moral. **The facts are** given simply. The occasion, result, punishment of the man, woman and serpent are specified, while the hope of a RESTORER is added. In the story, we mark **the** beginning, progress **and** effects of the transgression of GOD's LAW. There **is** the conviction of duty or scruples of conscience, contemplation of the pleasures of sin, hardening of **the heart or** blinding of conscience, **hopes of escaping** punishment, growing of desire and passion, till "she took of the fruit thereof and did eat."

In the history of Cain, and progress and depth of sin and misery on to the deluge, we learn how deeply man had fallen. In Abel, Seth, Enoch and Noah, we find faith in the promise, and consequent holiness. In Abel's offering, Enoch's walking with GOD, Noah only righteous one etc, the doctrine is spiritual.

As the world is repeopled, the divine procedure is changed. Abraham is chosen the depositary of the truth, the youngest instead of the eldest son, and history of his descendants given, with double reference to Israel and seed of the woman. While the institutes of this family illustrate the doctrines of the cross, their sins, repentance and virtues are for our instruction.

Nothing is added not in keeping with the trend of its authorship. History, moral and physical (Gr *phusis* nature) questions might have been answered, but are left to be learned *elsewhere*.

Ex. Assyria is first spoken of GEN 10: 11, but not again till Menahem 1500 yrs after, II KGS 15: 19. And of Egypt there is no notice from Moses till Solomon.

In the prophetic SCRIPTURES, this divine selection is obvious. Prophecy and its *moral* object might have been disjoined without destroying its prescience, but is not. The prophet and history of the future like the past, thus become the handmaid of evangelical truth. In relation to CHRIST, they speak of the dignity of his person, character, office, work; but with reference to us and salvation. And the SON of GOD often calls himself, as not even his apostles called him—the "SON of man."

Though not a revelation of science, the BIBLE is free from error, and contains under reserved and simple language, much concealed wisdom, and turns of expression which harmonize with nature, known to GOD, but not to them for whom first written. All ancient philosophies were as absurd in their notions of science as in their theology.

Exs. The Greeks and Latins believed the sky was a solid vault (Lat *firmamentum*.) The sages of Egypt, that the world was formed by the motion of air and upward course of flame. Plato, that the world is an intelligent being. Empedocles, that there are 2 suns, and Zucippus, that "the stars were kindled by their motions and nourished the sun with their fires."

Eastern nations believed that the stars exerted great influence over human affairs, often evil. Hence the saying "Ill starred."

Hindoo philosophy taught that the globe is flat, triangular, of seven stories; resting on elephant's heads, with tails turned out, feet on a tortoise, which rested on a serpent's head, and their shaking caused earthquakes. Mohammed, that the mountains were created to prevent the earth from moving. And one of the Fathers—Lactantius, said, "The rotundity of the earth is a theory no one is so ignorant as to believe!"

Every ancient system is overthrown by its own physics, while not one of the forty writers of the BIBLE, though living in the midst of these errors, writes a line favoring them. "Of the eighty theories which the FRENCH INSTITUTE counted in 1806 as hostile to the BIBLE, not one now stands."

The agreement of Revelation with modern science is remarkable.

Exs. It speaks of the earth as a globe, suspended on nothing Is 40: 22; Job 26: 7. Of the heavens as boundless space; gives the air weight, as Galileo proved.

Instead of 1022 stars as Hipparchus, or 1026 as Ptolemy taught, they are innumerable, as modern astronomers have discovered. " Lord Ross' telescope has brought to light 400,000,000," * and Herschel speaks of them as " glittering dust scattered on the background of the heavens." When it arrests the sun JOSH 10 12 (i e the earth's rotation), it stays the moon too, necessary on account of the earth's diurnal motion.

As one has truly said, The mechanism of LA PLACE, KOSMOS of HUMBOLDT and latest findings of geology, confirm the account of creation by Moses.

" The astronomer can never find a spot on the SUN of righteousness, nor the geologist upheave the ROCK of ages." DEMPSTER, LECTS.

*The Lick tel Mt Hamilton Cal, says Director Holden, shows abt 100,000,000.

It speaks of physical facts in the language of common life, not to mar the unity of its design and impression, and thus be as a hand-book of science. Also, science would thus have been by revelation, not conducive to scientific research, puzzling the ignorant, and prejudicial it is thought, to religion

No less remarkable is the way in which the BIBLE speaks of abstract questions and ethical science. While the laws of our nature, mental and moral science are known and spoken of, they are not formally taught.

It is in harmony with the laws of our mind, (the Scriptures teach), that habitual attention to its teaching, is the way to get into a holy state. I JOHN 4: 10, 16, 19.

Men believe by "giving heed" to truth ACTS 8: 6, 8, HEB 2: 1. Their impenitence is a consequence of neglect, and neglect, of a bad heart II THESS 2: 11, 12, MARK 8: 18. Holy affection is influenced by attention and faith GAL 5: 6, II COR 5: 11, HEB 11. 7.

SCRIPTURE embodies and acts upon these laws, adding the significant truth that their saving efficacy is through the HOLY SPIRIT, working in and with us.

Attention is the gift of GOD ACTS 16: 14, ZECH 12: 10. Faith from *attention*, is his gift ACTS 10: 44, (See 11: 17, 18.)

The fruit of the SPIRIT is his gift II PET 1: 2, 3; GAL 5: 23. For additional facts and illustration, see CHS V and VI, INF PROOFS —SCIENTIFIC ACCY and TRUTH of the BIBLE.

SEC 3 GRADUAL AND PROGRESSIVE.

THE rising sun scatters the morning mists, and brings to view first one prominence and then another, till hill and valley afar are seen. The landscape was there, but not seen. So in revelation, the progress is not in the truth itself, but in the order and impressiveness with which GOD reveals it to us.

Thus in the beginning, we are taught the unity of the divine nature, while the plurality in the GODHEAD is suggested along in the earlier books.

Exs. As in "Let *us* make man in our image" GEN 1: 26. Also in the use of the plural ELOHIM—GODS, with a singular verb, (as GEN 1: 1), several hundred times. The expressions NUMB 6: 22–7, Is 6· 3, 8· 48, JER 23· 5, 6, compared with the N T benediction, are remarkable.

THE BIBLE—GRADUAL AND PROGRESSIVE. 83

In the later prophets Is 9 : 6, Mic 5 : 2, this doctrine comes forth more clearly, and in the N T is fully revealed. So also the HOLY SPIRIT is spoken of more and more distinctly along in the O T on to the N T, where his personality and work are made manifest. GEN 1 : 2, 6 : 3, Ps 51 : 11.

So also of CHRIST. The first notice GEN 3 : 15, is come to us in mysterious terms. And the first act of worship GEN 4 : 4, HEB 11 : 4, was typical of Abel's faith in that promise.

In the person and worship of Enoch JUDE 14, Noah I PET 3 : 20, Melchisedec HEB 5 : 6, and JOB 19 : 25, there was much both typical and predictive. Still more in Abraham and his descendants GEN 12 : 3, 26 : 4, 49 : 10.

Under the following dispensation, other typical acts, persons, places and things were instituted, and the design of all made known through Moses.

Between Samuel and Malachi, a succession of seers, arose, gradually setting forth the MESSIAH, also the outpouring of the SPIRIT. JOEL 2 : 28, Is 53, 61, alluded to I PET 1 : 11.

While the prophets do not go beyond what was in the first promise, in detail and clearness the progress is marked; and the GOSPEL also in this respect, is as far beyond the prophets as they are beyond the LAW.

It is noticeable also, how revelation spreads equally in the prophetic as in the doctrinal portions. The light that illumes the living spring or harvest field of truth, shows with equal clearness the path to it. The LAW gives precept clearer than previous times, and the prophets are between it and the GOSPEL. They preach personal holiness rather than ceremonial purity, and less about temporal promises. The LAW speaks in tones of authority, and in places, with seeming severity. In the prophets, there is a softened and more attractive feature. Hues from a distant, coming glory, have fallen on its features, illuminating them into its own image. While the LAW says "Thou shalt love the LORD * * with all thy heart," (which nothing could exceed), in the prophets, this first commandment is so expounded and enforced, as to become more luminous and practical.

The PSALMS again, are a great aid to piety, and addition to legal worship, which contains no specific provision for devotion. Herein the SHEPHERD KING and SWEET PSALMIST of Israel (especially), magnifies GOD'S LAW and makes JEHOVAH'S praise GLORIOUS.

If the reader will compare the PENT with the prophets on repentance DEUT 30: 1-6, Is 57: 15, 16; or words of both on the relation between the Jews, or world generally and him who was to enlighten both; or notice the increasing clearness JER 31: 31-4, of the horizon of truth as the dawn approached, he will see the progressive development of revelation. In this consistency and progress, we see proofs of the ONE as Butler says, who is deliberate in all his operations, whether in the seasons, providence, or disclosing of his will.

This suggests the importance of studying the SCRIPTURES in the order the SPIRIT has given them. The chronological order is essential, not only to the explanation of the parts, but to consistent views of the divine character and plans.

This order of development is sometimes spoken of as the ADAMIC, PATRIARCHAL, MOSAIC and GOSPEL dispensations; (dispensation meaning way in which God deals with men.)

The first lasted during man's innocency. The second, 2500 yrs, from GEN 3—Ex 20—the giving of the law, called patriarchal (from *pater* father and *archa* chief), because the head of a family was governor and teacher, as Adam and Abraham. They were the custodians of the divine will, guardians of prophecy, and some more particularly, as Melchizedek HEB 7, types of the SON of GOD.

The covenant with Israel through Moses lasted 1500 yrs, and abounds in typical persons, places and things. GOD'S people were, in their institutions and history, a type of MESSIAH and his church LEV 16: 21, HEBS and I COR 10.

The GOSPEL dispensation (the principles of which are in

the previous economies), is founded on the teachings, works and passion of our LORD. The GOSPELS are of primary importance, as being the seed plot and first stamina of the new dispensation. And they have a like relation as Wesley says, to the ACTS, as *it* bears to the LETTERS. In the ACTS, we have the "good seed" springing forth after Pentecost; in the LETTERS, the further progress and enforcing of the doctrines; REVELATION outlines in obscure, symbolic words, the truth in its struggles with error—Satan and the world, to the end of time.

While we look for no further written revelation, there seem to be as Boyle says, passages whose full meaning is not yet known, reserved to quell some future heresy, or resolve some unformed doubt, or confound some error, or prove by fresh evidence that the BIBLE is from GOD. It is like the ocean, beautifully clear, but immeasurably profound. There is therefore no definable limit to our researches therein *

Popery is the standing illustration of the abuse of this, pleading for the development of truth out of SCRIPTURE, and also in the church. The blessedness of those who die in the LORD, is the germ of their saint worship. CHRIST'S presence in the supper, leads to adoration of the host, the angel's salutation, to the worship of the Virgin—"Mariolatry." The gradual unfolding of revelation is one thing, an accretion which overlays the truth is another. That is the use, this the *ab*-use.

SEC 4 UNITY OF THE BIBLE

THE BIBLE has this requisite of a great book—unity of design from first to last.

In its forty writers and 4100 yrs of maturing, its endless variety of style and matter—now history, then song, argument or dialogue; biography, prophecy, letters, there is no contradiction. Deeper down than these causes of variety,

---

* The ocean like this BOOK, may never be sounded by man. Scientists *think* it may be 8 or 9 m deep. The deepest soundings (near New Guinea), are 26,400 ft.

is found the secret of this agreement—the superhuman care of ONE who is infinite in power and wisdom. "As in the building of Solomon's temple no sound was heard, but every part was prepared and fitted in forest and quarry for its place, suggesting one presiding genius * * the workmen building wiser than they knew ; * * so this BOOK was built in the thought of GOD, before one of its parts was put in the CANON." INF PRFS.

Look at it in its *moral* purpose. It is the story of beings in relation to GOD, first as man, then a family, then a nation, then as a church. Other revelations as the *Shastras* (rel books of the Hindoos), dwell on the origin of the universe; or the Koran, on the physical theory of the future life, or topics which Christians cannot imagine to be of practical importance; as also the Talmuds, legends of the Romish church, visions of Swedenborg and Book of Mormon.* The SCRIPTURES contain no cosmogony, mythology, metaphysics, no marvels, which are not moral. They have no ideal which is not a reality. In all their diversity, their one aim is to knit together the broken relations between GOD and man, man and man, to reclaim and sanctify us.

* MORMON, the last of a pretended line of Heb prophets among a race of Israelites, descendants of Joseph, said to have come from Jerusalem to America about 600 B C, * * * is said to have written the BOOK of MORMON. But the author was Solomon Spalding (from 1761-1816), who had been a clergyman. Joseph Smith obtained this book and claimed it as a revelation from GOD to himself, and used it as text and authority for this new sect. WEBS UN DICTIONARY.

In 1827, Smith professed to have a revelation, and be guided to where the truth was to be discovered—near Palmyra, N. Y, written on plates of gold. In 1830 he published this book—Spalding's, written as a romance, in SCRIPTURE style, which Smith altered. Smith, with one Sydney Rigdon, agreed to palm off this fraud on mankind. * * * June 27, 1844, Smith was lynched at Nauvoo Ills by 200 men, while trying to escape out of prison, pierced by 14 balls. REV SELAH BROWN, GOS in ALL LDS.

The ab is added as a sample of the evidences etc, on which all faiths not Christian, rest.

No Mormon can sing in spirit and truth

"How firm a foundation!"

Again, unity is noticeable in the doctrines taught and believed by the good, in every dispensation. Religion subjective, has ever been faith and obedience—" obedience of faith," toward GOD. And as a system objective, it has never changed.

From the beginning, man has believed in the unity of GOD, the creation, providence, a divine law, the fall, atonement, duty and efficacy of prayer, help of the SPIRIT, need of holiness.

Once more, the LAW and GOSPEL so dissimilar at first sight, prove to be but one complete system (as will appear in following chs.) As both moral and experimental evidences are involved in this connexion, so also, it is the one who has had the vail taken from the heart, who will be most impressed with this truth.

This unity includes teachings beyond our ken. It alludes to GOD's designs in providence, predicts the issue of the conflict between truth and error, analyses man's motives and acts, points out the cause of his misery, and the cure; subjects which the wisest in every age have tried in vain to solve. Though a series of different revelations, the series is one and indivisible.

1 Doctrines brought to light in the NEW, depend for proofs and illustrations, on the O T. The truth under the first dispensations was more elementary and figurative (as in the education of childhood), in order to prepare for the revelation of JESUS CHRIST. So the heathen generally, get a clearer idea of the attributes of GOD and personal holiness from the Old than the N T, as is suggested PT II. c I. SEC 1.

2 " Hence an important test of truth, and relative value of truth. If it be said for example, the sacrifice and priesthood of CHRIST are not revealed in the GOSPEL, or are subordinate truths, we look to the law; and if it be said, in the GOSPEL there is no priesthood or sacrifice, then we have in the LAW observances without reference or meaning—the altar, blood, holy place, propitiatory—types of nothing! * * * " The GOSPEL *is* the end of the LAW. " REVELATION *is* a consistent whole."

Sec 5 Not Systematic

It is both noticeable and instructive, that divine truth has not come to us in systematic form. REVELATION is not a compend of doctrine and duty, of morals and religion made ready to hand; the more noticeable, as in false religions the description of the "faith" is precise, and with directions about observances of little or no value.

And this is natural. In the O T the earlier, and much of the later portions, is historical. Moral truth transpires through narrative, and that fragmentary and concise. GOD had been dealing with man 2500 yrs before he gave the LAW. What he had revealed or how, cannot be known fully from the record. This suggests that there may have been more of revelation than we have an idea of. Indeed, a large part of the BIBLE seems to be not the disclosure, so much as embodiment of truth *already* known.

So of the N T. It does not contain *regular* elementary instruction or articles of faith. The GOSPELS are historical, and imply and suggest the truth, not systematize it.

Religion is subjective or objective—a system of holy doctrine or active principles. The first is truth, the second piety. In SCRIPTURE, both are taught us through example and incidental illustrations.

Exs. The divine perfections are revealed, not defined or mentioned even, but through works, or in connection with a practical end.

The principles of GOD's government are illustrated in his dealings with man. He judges according to every man's work DEUT 10: 17. He hates the wicked and loves the righteous. Ps 11: 5, 146: 8.

Thus, we see scoffing and infidelity in the antediluvians JUDE 14, 15, envy in Joseph's brethren and Cain GEN 4, 37.

Inconsistency in Ahithophel, the friend and traitor II SAM 16:15, faith in CHRIST, but fear of confessing JNO 12: 42, in "the rulers."

Self deceit in David and Balaam II SAM 12, NUMB 22.

In the virtues, we have faith illustrated in Abraham, Patience in Job, Meekness in Moses, decision in Joshua, patriotism in Nehemiah, friendship in Jonathan; pattern for mothers in Hannah; in Samuel, Josiah and Timothy, to children; in Joseph and Daniel, to young men.

To make the lesson complete, we must trace the evidence

of the weakness of the best, as Abraham, Job, Moses, at their strongest points; the first failed through fear GEN 20, the second through impatience JOB 3: 1, the last through irritability DEUT 32: 51. And it will impress us the more deeply, to know that man's power to overcome the world, may not be above his weakest point.

It is only in the life of him who knew no sin—JESUS, that we find an all perfect example for us in duty and suffering. It is this presence in the BIBLE, of men of like passions, that brings it home to our bosoms and business. There is a sense of the human as well as divine, which meets us at every turn. "We feel as we look, that it has a power or charm which, like the eye of a good portrait, is fixed on us turn where we will."

What a requisite in a revelation for all nations and ages! If articles of faith or minute rules of practice (as in the Koran, which insists on prayer at sunrise and sunset), had been given, they must have been retained forever, and with them the heresies and errors they were meant to condemn.

And if such a summary had been given, Christians would have stored their memory with the *words* of the Creed, without *searching* the SCRIPTURES. There would be no tax on reason, demand for investigation, excitement of feeling, or improvement of heart. The Creed being the faith itself, would be regarded with a sort of indolent veneration, as in China and India for example. It is only when the mind is waked up, quickened in the pursuit of knowledge, that it impresses rightly. One has likened the BIBLE to a field wherein is the soil and seeds of precious things, but where nothing is perfected without knowledge and industry.

"I find in this BOOK says Cecil, something which says, I stand alone, am not of your mind. The wise can never exhaust my treasures. I condescend to the ignorant. Leave me as I am, but study me well." * * * As it is—truth being scattered throughout the WORD, we learn to think of doctrine in connection with duty, and duty in connection with the principles by which enforced.

These facts rebuke the Romish church, **which** fosters aversion to the searching of the SCRIPTURES, and encourages indolent submission to what is prepared to hand by a superior, as though " ignorance is the mother of devotion," **as** is charged to her.

OBS. What the U. S. and England are socially and morally, **is** due mostly to an *open* BIBLE. In Rome for ex, where the light **of** CHRIST'S vicar is supposed to shine in his strength—at his *best*, the people, especially females, are ignorant and superstitious. She may be said to take away the **key** of knowledge, and "shut the kingdom of heaven against men."

While the cardinal virtues—faith, hope, love, are **of first** importance, and one may become holy and useful, even without a systematic knowledge of the ORACLES of GOD, he would be more **so with such** advantages. Ignorance and sin are inexcusable, **two** things GOD has no use for. Systematic divinity is, perhaps, the last perfection of knowledge, though not necessarily of character. While religion is founded in knowledge, it is not of the head only. We are admonished **to search** the SCRIPTURES *devotionally*, **with** desire to learn the whole **will of our** FATHER. They **are** so handed down, that every **one may find what** he seeks, whether the eye be single **or evil.** Hence **they are** used by the devil even, **to** deceive some and tempt **others** I KGS 22: 22, MATT 4. It is **necessary to a** symmetrical character that not only the sense of *some* portions (as **most** content themselves with), be studied, but the mind **of the** SPIRIT through his different dispensations, or REVELATION **as a whole.** And more is *suggested* than expressed.

While systematic treatises are **useful in defining and preserving** the unity of the faith, **they are, unlike the** books **of the** BIBLE, wanting in example, **feeling**, power; **in** patterns of holiness, touches of nature, **etc.** Remember therefore, **that** the divine means for perfecting our spiritual manhood is that BOOK which abounds in examples of faith and works, giving forth tones, looks and words, at once human and divine, and ever new—the BIBLE.

> Here the fair tree of knowledge grows,
> And yields a free repast.   ANNE STEELE.

PART II.

INDUCTIVE STUDY.

CHAPTER I.

INTERPRETATION.

Sec 1 Necessity of Care in Studying the Scriptures

Man can weary himself in worldly affairs, but to search the Scriptures is a wearisome task. Locke.

"But little profit can come of reading the Word cursorily."

The meaning and relation of tropical and literal, is the same as the figurative and grammatical sense of the sacred writings. Marsh, Lects.

A KNOWLEDGE of the writers, their employment, character, aim; the time, place, circumstances, persons addressed etc, is necessary in order to read the Bible aright, as such things had much to do with the ideas and language.

They were written by scholars as Moses and Paul; warriors, kings and poets, as David and Solomon; priests as Ezra, prophets as Isaiah, herdsmen as Amos; statesmen as Daniel, fishermen, and "unlearned," as Peter and John.

They were written in dead languages, for all nations and both worlds.

Moses lived 400 years before the siege of Troy, 900 before the ancient sages—Thales, Pythagoras and Confucius. John, 1500 after Moses.

They were composed in Asia, sands of Arabia, deserts of Judea; porches of the temple, schools of the prophets at Jericho and Bethel, palaces of Babylon, banks of the Chebar; in Europe, Asia Minor, the sea.

Moses frames laws, others write history, David psalms, Solomon proverbs, Isaiah prophecies, the evangelists biography, the apostles letters.

Books and portions of books, as Isaiah and Nahum, are about the gentiles, others to the Jews. MATT is to Jews, LUKE to Greeks and Romans; while ROMS is in part to the self-righteous, JAMES to the formal Christian.

The state of man since the fall, is such that he cannot understand spiritual things abstractly in words, but through natural objects. GOD having stamped his image on material things, uses them as symbols, to lead the idea, in a childhood state, to spiritual things—"the visible world being a dial plate of the invisible." To the spiritual mind, the seen and unseen are so related as to be as one—nature leading thus to nature's GOD.

Hence it is, that the figures of HOLY WRIT have come to us as the offspring of good taste and sound piety.

Most words in the beginning of the race, were chosen from analogy of material to spiritual things.

Exs. Spirit meant in its derivation, breath. The mind is said to *see* truth. To reflect was literally, to bend back; now, look around our thoughts. Attention is a mental state, analogous to stretching the eye to see a distant object.

And such language makes the idea more vivid. "It charms the imagination, instructs the judgment, while it impresses memory and interests the heart."

1 *Human affections* and *actions* are ascribed to GOD.

Exs. He is spoken of as having hands, eyes and feet; as our FATHER—the CREATOR and supporter of life. GEN 6, "It repented the Lord that he made man"—as having no longer pleasure in him. JER 7 : 13, "I spake * * rising up early" i e, to express his interest in them.

As in the above e g, "hand" is suggestive of GOD's infinite power, so the figure is not beyond, but far short of the reality in SCRIPTURE. When the church is called the bride of CHRIST, and earthly kingdoms figures of CHRIST's kingdom, they are but *faint* images of the things prefigured.

CARE IN STUDYING THE SCRIPTURES. 93

2 *The figures* are often used in different senses.

Exs. God is **said to repent** and turn from the evil threatened. Again, he is not a man **that he** should repent. The first, meaning that he changes when sinners turn, and the second, that there is no fickleness in him. Again, the same word in Hebrew—*barak*, means bless and curse. This word originally meant "bend the knee," and the act was equally appropriate in asking favor for others, or denouncing them.

3 *The Jews,* their **customs, religion etc, are** suggestive of spiritual **truths.**

Ex. Holiness (for which the heathen had **no word, in the** Christian sense), was taught by the division of animals into clean and unclean. From the first, one was chosen without spot or blemish. One tribe chosen from the rest was to offer it. Both the victim and priest were washed in pure water. But neither priest, people nor sacrifice, were worthy to come before God, so the offering must be made without the holy place. The idea of his holiness was thus suggested; and moral purity under the law, to mean purification for sacred uses. But under the GOSPEL, inward holiness.

The demerit of sin and atonement, were from equally significant rites. The **blood**—"the life" of the sacrifice, was sprinkled on the mercy seat and toward the holy place. While the people prayed without, they saw the volume of smoke ascending from **the** victim burning in their stead. How must this have suggested that God's justice is a consuming fire, and that their souls escaped only through vicarious atonement! The *ideas* were intended to be continued through all time.

The priests again, **were** clothed **in white and royal apparel,** prefiguring the purity and **dignity** of Christians **and** the redeemed.

4 *The whole Jewish history* was typical, suggestive of **spiritual** things.

Exs. Men are the "slaves" of sin, their road through a "desert." They cross the "Jordan" of death, enter the "rest" that remains, have their "forerunner," "prophet," "priest," who is also, after Saul's day, called "king."

Many words in the N T are **used in a** new sense, unknown to the Greeks.

94 TROPICAL WORDS, ALLEGORY, TYPE, SYMBOL.

Exs. Humility meant in classic Greek, mean spiritedness. The Greeks had no virtue under this name, and Cicero calls it a blemish. *Grace* (as unmerited favor), *justification* by faith, GOD as holy and merciful, *faith* in justifying and sanctifying, are all used in the GOSPEL with a peculiar meaning. Virtue (Gr *arctas* II PET 1 : 5), meant courage in war. With the new religion, came to us a new or *purified* language—The advent of JESUS gave man a new lexicography, like as the HOLY SPIRIT gives (with a new, clean heart), a **new BIBLE.**

All languages exhibit changes. Calamity meant loss of standing corn (Gr *calamos* stalk, corn,) Sycophant (Gr *sukophantos*), meant fig informer, now, flatterer. As man rises in intelligence and piety, the meaning of words intensifies, becoming more spiritual and abstract.

SEC 2 TROPICAL WORDS, ALLEGORY, TYPE, SYMBOL.

As SCRIPTURE abounds in analogical words and teachings, it may help the reader to classify and define them according to the rules of grammar, adding exs.

When a word, usage has applied to one thing is transferred to another, there is a trope (Gr *trepo*, turn), and the expression is figurative. If the first signification should be disused, the tropical becomes the right one. The Heb "to bless" e g, being no longer used in its original sense, the tropical becomes the right one.

METAPHOR is founded on resemblance between two objects; as "Judah is a lion's whelp" GEN 49. "I am the true vine" JOHN 15.

SYNEC'DOCHE is putting a part for the whole, or whole for a part; or where there is no resemblance, but a connection simply; as "There shall not a hoof be left" Ex 10: 26. I Cor 11 : 27, *cup* is put for thing contained.

METON'YMY is where cause is put for effect, or sign for thing signified—one thing for another; and where also the connection is only in the mind; as "They have Moses and the prophets"—their writings. "The blood * * cleanseth us from all sin"—merit of CHRIST's sufferings.

The above refer to words or single expressions. The

following refer to several words—a subject, story or discourse—

ALLEGORY is story or narrative, teaching a moral lesson. It is to narrative what *trope* is to single words, adding to the literal, a spiritual sense.

Exs. Jotham's JUD 9, II KGS 14, thistle and cedar, the vine Ps 80, the vineyard Is 5, prodigal son LUKE 15.

When the allegory is in the style of history, of things that have or may have been, it is called *parable*.

The above are parables. The parables of JESUS are purer than those of the O T. JESUS' teachings abound in parable. There are eight in MATT 13. Some, as that of the "GOOD SHEPHERD" JOHN 10, are allegory.

When of things that could *not* have happened, it is *fable*. Jotham's, and Jehoash's to Amaziah, are both parable and fable. Thus we see the better sort of fable is parable, both pointing a moral.*

When the allegory is abstruse, it is called riddle, as Samson's.

TYPE. Gr *tupos* mark, print, caused by blows. Hence pattern, example, model after which a person or thing is to be made. A type is agreement between two persons or things, and future. Type becomes antitype when fulfilled. Adam, Abraham, Moses, David, ark, tabernacle; holy place, passover, scape goat, pillar of cloud, were types of CHRIST and "copies of things in the heavens." Type has its representation in a person or thing, action or object, as allegory has in words.

SYMBOL (Gr *sum-ballo* to cast, throw together), is a sign of something moral or spiritual, from natural objects, an emblem.

Exs. Baptism and the LORD's supper are symbols of regeneration, and of the body and blood of CHRIST. The symbol relates to something past or at hand. Some things are both symbol and type, as the passover and supper. They prefigure and commemorate also.

As the SCRIPTURES come to us in dead languages, are in

---

* Æsop's Fables is a precious vol of uninspired pars.

a degree analogical and figurative, their **truths and precepts** such as **reason** and experience are little **conversant** with; so, much research external and internal must be brought to bear upon them.—A *little* learning herein, may prove a dangerous thing to the Christian, as well as to the "ignorant and unsteadfast" II PET 3: 16.

The subjoined **extract from a spiritual** writer is suggestive.—The differences **in the seeing** capacity and views **of the BIBLE** among its readers, may be illustrated by the different views one sees **in climbing a high** mountain. At the foot, he has a **limited view, true so far** as it reaches. As he climbs higher, the range is more widespread. On the top, the landscape **in variety and grandeur,** spreads away **before his** face, making an impression never to be forgotten,—a perfect view, bounded and limited only by his powers of seeing **and comprehension.**

Thus we must **come by the** knowledge **of the** WORD. And while different **views may** be explained **by** different stand points, the inference is, that *our* view may not be the *only* right or complete view of the truth. H. W. S.

SEC 3 ON SEARCHING THE SCRIPTURES

"OPEN thou mine eyes, **that I may** behold **wondrous things out of** thy LAW" Ps 119: 18.

"If thou seek her as silver and search for her as for hid treasures, then shalt thou * * * find the knowledge of GOD" PROV 2: 4.

"The meek will he guide in judgment * * * and teach his way" Ps 25: 9.

"When he the SPIRIT of truth is come, he shall guide you into all the truth." JESUS, JOHN 16: 13.

> Come Holy Ghost, for moved by thee,
> The prophets wrote and spoke,
> Unlock the truth, thyself the key;
> Unseal the sacred BOOK. C WESLEY.

* * * In divine **things therefore, it is necessary to love** them in order to know them, and we enter into truth only through charity. PASCAL.

He who has not believed will not experience, and he who has not experienced, cannot know. ANSELM.

ON SEARCHING THE SCRIPTURES.

The theologian must believe the doctrine which he studies. Without faith, he cannot know the truth. THOLUCK.

An inward interest in theology is needful for a Biblical interpreter. * * * * The truth will not be rightly comprehended unless the SPIRIT himself be the interpreter—the *angelus interpres*. HAGENBACH.

Pectus est quod facit theologum. NEANDER'S motto.

THE above from best authors, inspired and uninspired, suggest both the spirit and means whereby we are to search the SCRIPTURES.

It is believed as Stalker says, that JESUS was a diligent student of the SCRIPTURES—the HEB (then only a written language), and SEPT. These he mastered in the letter and spirit, if not memorized also, himself being the end and expounder of the LAW. Deuteronomy, Psalms and Isaiah it seems, were favorites, as he oftenest quotes them. The WORD he committed, for weapons offensive and defensive; also for his own inspiration and guidance.

In the walks and groves of the O T, our LORD met and communed with kindred spirits—Enoch, Abraham, Joshua, David, Jeremiah, Daniel, in some sense as with Moses and Elijah, in his transfiguration on the mount. IMAGO CHRISTI.

If our SAVIOR must come by his infinite understanding of the LAW of GOD through study (even of a dead language), it suggests an impressive lesson for our imitation. And one of the secrets of our TEACHER's wonderful wisdom and power was, the LAW of his GOD was in his heart—he had *searched* the SCRIPTURES.

While it is the SPIRIT of truth we are dependent on to enlighten us therein, a reverential attention and desire after it, is necessary. Although this may not be a law of interpretation, it is essential to the application of all rules. To appreciate poetry, there must be a poetic taste. Proficiency in philosophy requires a love of that science. This principle need not be questioned in application to the BIBLE.

Men need *divine* teaching * * * because without it, they will not and cannot know divine truth.

When **Christ** came, the light shone "in the darkness and the darkness apprehended it not."

> "A dark pall enveloped the nations in its benighted shadows.
> Reason shed a faint glimmering on the minds of men,
> Like the cold, inefficient shining of a distant star."

Unholy affection had surrounded the mental eye with the opposite of clear "dry light," impairing the organ itself. Blindness of mind produced ignorance, and alienation from God was the effect of an understanding darkened Eph 4: 18. Christians are all taught of the Lord. "If any of you lacketh wisdom, let him ask of God * * * and it shall be given him." Jas 1: 5. Childlike docility and a prayerful spirit, are keys to unlock the truth. *Bene orasse est bene studuisse*—to pray well is to have studied well, though an aphorism of Luther, is really of God.

The church holds that God does not reveal doctrines not in the Scriptures. He makes us wise up to what is written, not beyond Luke 24: 45. What then is found contrary, or in addition to the Word, or without it, may be ascribed to the spirit of error, or ourselves. But the

> "New beauties
> And still increasing light"

therein, which the growing Christian finds, may *it* be the experience of both writer and reader! Amen.

> O may the gracious words divine,
> Subject of all my converse be!
> So will the Lord his follower join,
> And walk and talk himself with me.
>   C Wesley.

Obs. 1 Even where revelations were received through those set above, over the conscience, who might not *intentionally* deceive, the inquirer at oracles and divination was left in as much doubt, as the other was ignorant of the "secrets of fate." The privileged ones as kings and nobility, favored with responses, brought gifts and sacrifices, and could have access only at intervals, as once a month or year.

2 How favored is the humblest Christian (in the light of the R

V), above the most enlightened heathen! Having not those "cunningly devised fables," but the "living ORACLES" of GOD, as clearly shown, he may know what is the mind of the SPIRIT, every one for himself. For it is JESUS our oracle, priest and prophet, who speaks to us through the WORD. That WORD as Phœbe Palmer says, " is the voice of GOD to us."

As in SCRIPTURE there is no ideal that is not also a reality, so every one may find to satisfaction, his idea of perfection of character (including examples of greatest wickedness),—of goodness, greatness etc, divine and human, in the active and passive virtues. But all merely human ideals pass away as stars at sunrise, when the opening eye of faith, learns to read the life and character of JESUS, as sketched in the GOSPEL.

CHAPTER II.

RULES OF INTERPRETATION.

SEC 1 SENSE OF THE WORDS.

Grammatical analysis and rules of exegesis, lead to the same views, as the theologians who bring to the study of the SCRIPTURES, strong sense and piety THOLUCK.

The controversies have led to the conclusion that the protestant views of the sacred text, are the correct ones WINER.

The most illiterate, if he can read his BIBLE, may not only become wise unto salvation, but be able to refute every argument against his religion BP HORSLEY.

WHETHER the words be literal or figurative, the first rule is to find the sense. As the authors wrote to be understood, we are to explain by the *usus loquendi*—language of common life.

Exs. "None doeth good" i e by nature. "All flesh had corrupted his way," is the same thought in other words.

The teachings of the BIBLE—being and perfections of GOD, our sin and misery, CHRIST's redemption—all the doctrines, are stated in words equally plain. If language have meaning, these truths need not be misunderstood.

And yet this rule is violated by some—

Ex. Origen in Abraham's second marriage, finding Keturah means "sweet odor," and this applicable to such as have the fragrance of piety in their lives, concluded that Abraham became very holy in old age.

A kindred error changes BIBLE history into fable, and the works of CHRIST, to common occurrences mystically related. On this principle, the WORD may mean nothing definite, or anything fancy or imagination may give it.

Yet *there are* peculiarities in the originals. Our translation being quite literal, often gives the idioms of the Heb—

Exs. The Jews often used a qualifying thought, not by an adjective but noun, noticeable in the Heb Greek of the N T also. "Your work of faith, labor of love and patience of hope," means your believing work, loving labor and hopeful patience. "SPIRIT of promise"—promised SPIRIT.

The Hebrews called a person having a quality good or bad, the son or child of it.

Exs. Eli's sons I SAM 2: 12, are "sons of Belial." "Son of peace" LUKE 10: 6, means one friendly to CHRIST or his GOSPEL See EPH 6: 5-8.

Their mode of comparison may be illustrated LUKE 14: 26, where "hate" means MATT 10: 37, to love less. So ROM 9: 13, Jacob and Esau.

Names of *parents* are given to their posterity.

Exs. GEN 9: 25, Cursed be Canaan—his posterity. Melchizedec, Abimelech and the Syrophœnician woman were Canaanites, and not cursed.

Son is used for descendant.

Exs. The priests are called sons of Levi. Mephibosheth is the son of Saul, though of Jonathan. Son is used for any descendant, as father is for any ancestor I CHRON 1.

Brother is similarly used. GEN 14: 16, Abraham is Lot's brother, though uncle. Jair is the son of Manasseh, because his grandfather had married a daughter of one of the heads of that tribe.* "Mary

---

* NUMB 32: 41, I CHRON 2: 21, 22.

is thought to have descended from David in this way; so that our LORD was David's son on the maternal side also."

There are other peculiarities.

EXS. In numbers, ten often means several GEN 31: 7, DAN 1: 20. Forty means many. Persepolis is called "city of forty towers" in Eastern parlance, though it had more. 7 and 70 mean a large, complete No. PROV 26: 16, 25. Ps 119, "Seven times a day do I praise thee." "Seven other spirits" MATT 12: 45—an indefinite or perfect number.

Sometimes a round for a definite number is used.

EXS. 24000 NUMB 25: 9, is 23000 I COR 10: 8. JUD 11: 26, 3.0 yrs is for 293. Compare JUD 20: 35, 46.

Different persons have often the same name. Pharaoh (ruler, from *Phre* sun) was the name of the Egyptian kings till the invasion by Persia 525, as Ptolemy was after Alexander. Abimelech (my father king), of the Philistines. Agag of the Amalekites, Benhadad (son of the sun), name of the kings of Damascus. Augustus was the title of the Roman emperors. The one LUKE 2: 1, was the second (reckoning Julius Cæsar as the first.) Tiberius was emperor when CHRIST was crucified. The one Paul appealed to ACTS 25: 21 ("the Augustus" marg), was Nero. Domitian 81 A D, was the last, and last of the "12 Cæsars" also.

Herod the Gt was king when CHRIST was born. He was notorious for his jealousy and cruelty. The half of his kingdom (including Judea and Samaria), was given to his son Archelaus. Most of Galilee was given to his son Herod the Tetrarch LUKE 3: 1; other parts of Syria and Galilee to his third son Philip Herod. It was Herod the Tet who beheaded John, and mocked our LORD in his trial.

He married the daughter of Aretas, but dismissed her on becoming enamored with Herodias, his niece and brother Philip's wife, whom he married. After the murder of John at the instigation of Herodias, he went to Rome to be made king. He was there accused before Caligula by Herod Agrippa her own brother, and banished with her, to Lyons in Gaul abt 39. Afterwards, attempting to regain his place, was banished to Spain and died.

The dominions of Herod and Philip were given to the

brother of Herodias—Herod Agrippa, called Herod in SCRIPTURE. Herod came by all Palestine, which had belonged to his grandfather Herod the Gt. He killed James the brother of John, was struck by the angel and eaten of worms at Cæsarea. His son Herod Agrippa (Agrippa of ACTS 25, 26), is the one before whom Paul was brought by Festus.

Pilate, who was induced to sentence JESUS, was hated by Jews and Samaritans, was accused to Vitellius and sent to Rome, and is said to have been banished to Vienna in Gaul, and to have committed suicide about 41 ROBINSON.

Different persons and places have different names.

Exs. Jethro is called Hobab. Reuel is thought to be Moses wife's grandfather, called father Ex 2: 18. Levi is called Matthew. Thomas and Didymus are synonyms, and mean twin. Thaddeus, Lebbæus and Judas are for Jude. Sylvanus, Lucas, Timotheus are Latin for Silas, Luke, Timothy.

Abyssinia is Ethiopia, sometimes Cush; the latter being applied generally to Arabia or India; hence probably, Chusistan. Greece is Javan and Greece Is 66: 19, ZECH 9: 13. Egypt is Ham and Rahab Ps 78: 51, Is 51: 9.

The Dead Sea is Sea of the Plain, R V *Arabah*, on which Sodom and Gomorrah stood, the East Sea (as E of Jerusalem), and Salt Sea II KGS 14: 25, GEN 14: 3.

The Mediterranean is Sea of the Philistines, the hinder Sea and Great Sea Ex 23: 31, DEUT 11, NUMB 34.

Gennesaret is Sea of Galilee and Tiberias MATT 4: 18, JOHN 21: 1.

The Holy Land is Canaan, Land of Israel, of Judea, Palestine, Land of Shepherds and Land of Promise.

The rule applying to proper names is important.

Exs. Ahaziah son of Jehoram II KGS 8: 29, II CHRON 22: 6, 21: 17, is Azariah and Jehoahaz. Jehoahaz son of Josiah is Johanan and Shallum II KGS 23: 30, I CHRON 3: 15, JER 22: 11.

Jehoiada is Johanan and probably Barachias II CHRON 24: 20, I CHRON 6: 9, MATT 23: 35. Uzziah is Azariah; Nathaniel, Bartholomew. In the above, the meaning is the same or similar.

SEC 2 CONNECTION.

As a word often has various meanings sanctioned by usage, we must ascertain the sense it has in the *connection*.

Exs. Thus *faith* is GAL 1: 23, found to mean the gospel; truth or faithfulness ROM 3: 3; proof or evidence ACTS 17: 31; conscientious conviction of duty ROM 14: 23. And comprehensively, faith means the state which receives the truth HEB 11; or specifically, repose in JESUS' perfect righteousness as in ROM 3: 28, 8: 1.

Flesh means tender, teachable EZEK 11: 19—"a heart of flesh;" human nature simply, JNO 1: 14; usually as sinful ROM 8: 5, or the ceremonial in religion—the "fair show in the flesh" GAL 6: 12.

Blood means one common nature, "made of one blood" ACTS 17: 26. To give the wicked blood to drink, is to put in hand the cup of death. "His blood be on us" MATT 27: 25, means the guilt of it. In "justified by his blood" ROM 5: 9, " cleanse your conscience from dead works" HEB 9: 14, "the blood * * * cleanseth us from all sin" I JNO 1, blood (by *metonymy*), is for CHRIST's obedience unto death, *merit* of his blood.

This rule helps us also, as to whether the words are used literally or figuratively.

Exs. Christians I PET 2: 5, are called "living stones;" ROM 13: 12, we are to "put on the armor of light." The "washing" I COR 6: 11, is "by the SPIRIT of our GOD." "Leave the dead to bury their own dead" MATT 8: 22, means let worldly minds tend to their own concerns.

The connection under rule 2nd, fixes the sense.

In the use of tropical terms, the writers choose on the principle of resemblance.

Exs. The heavenly bodies, mountains etc, are used to designate kingdoms and rulers. Earthquakes, tempests, eclipses—political changes.

Dew, showers, streams &c, spiritual blessings. Light, darkness express joy, sorrow, knowledge, ignorance &c. Marriage and adultery, a covenant with God and its violation.

SEC 3 CONTEXT.

1 When the words or connection do not satisfy, we examine the *context*, and there find the meaning explained or suggested.

Exs. In HEB 11, *faith* is defined and then illustrated. "Now faith is the assurance of things hoped for, the proving of things not seen." The first part refers to future good. Things not seen are past, present or future, more and greater than things seen. Examples are given of **each**. In Noah, it was persuasion concerning the deluge. In Abraham, of the promise to him, his posterity, and of CHRIST. Is there a passage suggesting the difficulty of a good translation, or the divine wisdom in giving us a BIBLE teaching by example and illustrations, like this?

Substance (Gr) is a literal rendering and means what stands under, sustains. In 1 : 3 (A V), it is *person*, and II COR 11 : 17, *confidence* of boasting. Faith is therefore, as to things hoped for, that on which real, substantial confidence may rest. And as to things not seen, it is evidence which silences doubt and fear—proof. These are the sense, and all this extent is in the original, which no one word can express.

What depth and illumination in the writer does this SCRIPTURE suggest!

PERFECTION Ps 37 : 37, is synonymous with uprightness, sincerity, goodness—its general meaning in the O T In the N T, "It means 1, a clear, accurate knowledge of divine truth; or 2, possession of ALL the graces of Christian character in a higher or lower degree" ANGUS. The first is its meaning HEB 5 : 14, I COR 2 : 6, where " full grown " is in marg *perfect*. The 2nd in JAS 1 : 4, where perfect is defined as " entire, lacking nothing." In II PET 1 : 5-7, the graces which make the perfect man are enumerated— " adding all diligence etc."

From GEN 48 : 8, 10, we infer that Jacob's blindness was partial.

2 *The sense* is sometimes fixed by analogous expressions.

Exs. Covenant GAL 3 : 17, means promise (to Abraham). In ROM 4 : 5, worketh is explained. So in several places in the chapter. v. 2, it is " justified by works." v 5, it is the opposite of " believing on him who justifieth." So in JAS 2 : 14, the faith that cannot save is the faith that is in words not deeds, and not Abraham's v 23.—" Justified by works " therefore in Paul, means to reject CHRIST, while the " works " in James imply faith in CHRIST.*
This truth is taught JOHN 3 : 36—" He that believeth on the SON hath eternal life; but he that obeyeth not the SON, shall not see life." So that as Doddridge observes, saving faith implies unreserved obedience.

For inattention to the connection, some have miscon-

* Faith " working through love," purifying the heart.

strued the teaching on faith and works in Paul and James.

Under this head SCRIPTURE parallelisms may be classed. Some as the 1st Psalm, are synonymous and gradational.

Exs. "Blessed is the man
That walketh not in the counsel of the wicked,
Nor standeth in the way of sinners,
Nor sitteth in the seat of the scornful."

Walketh means to have casual intercourse.
Standeth   "   "   intimacy.
Sitteth   "   "   permanent connection.

So counsel, way, seat, ungodly, sinners, scornful, mean downward steps in sin—a "toboggan slide." See also Ps 24 : 3, 4, Is 55 : 6, 7. Also Ps 132, 135.

3 SOMETIMES the sense is suggested by allusions, or reasoning of the context.

Exs. The counsel of Ahithophel is *good*, and the unjust steward *wise*, only in regard to the end they had in view.

In JAS 5 : 14, in "The prayer of faith shall save the sick," *save* refers to *health* v 15, 16. Rome founds extreme unction on this, to save the *soul* of the dying. James speaks of one already saved.

I KGS 22 : 15, Go up and prosper, Micaiah's answer to Ahab, and "Cry aloud for he is a god," Elijah to Baal's prophets, are exs of the ironical, sarcastic in our BIBLE.

The SCRIPTURES abound in abrupt transition, and distant events as in prophecy, are often in close proximity. The conclusion is omitted, premise suppressed, or objection answered which is not stated.

Exs. of all these difficulties may be found in ROMS 3 : 22-4, 8 : 17, 18, 9 : 6, c 3, 4.

The context aids in ascertaining whether the language is tropical or literal; also the sense.

Exs. "He that eateth me, he also shall live because of me" JOHN 6 : 57, the Jews misunderstood. CHRIST had already explained as believing—receiving him in his word and SPIRIT. Catholics take the words literally, in the Eucharist.

"Himself shall be saved, * * as through fire" I COR 3 : 15, is quoted in favor of purgatory. But the context shows that the words,—foundation, gold, silver, wood, hay, are all figurative. "Fire," the symbol of the SPIRIT'S purifying, is to prove every man's work—teacher and the taught, in the day of judgment. Therefore the fire of purgatory must be coeval with the day of judgment. WESLEY.

OBS. Saved as through the fire, suggests that some, though built on the teachings of CHRIST, will be saved with little or no reward.

SEC 4 SCOPE.

WHEN the words, connection and context fail to clear up the sense, we look to the *scope*—the design of the book, or a section of it. The last rule touches this, and indeed all the rules glide into one another.

Sometimes the scope is mentioned—

EXS. That man is justified by faith alone, is Paul's conclusion ROM 3: 28. The design of PROVERBS is told 1: 1–4, 6. Of the GOSPELS JOHN 20: 31, and of the BIBLE ROM 15: 4, II TIM 3: 16, 17.

The purport is sometimes gathered from the occasion on which written.

Ps 90 is thought to have been by Moses when Israel was sent back to wander in the wilderness.

COLOSSIANS, EPHESIANS and GALATIANS, were written to illustrate the doctrines of the GOSPEL, and refute Judaizing teachers. Reference to ACTS will explain some parts as c 15, where is found the history of what these LETTERS discuss.

A knowledge of the scope sometimes requires repeated study of the book itself. When once this is mastered, it will enlighten particular expressions, and illustrate other parts of the BIBLE in a way both instructive and surprising—

"To understand the precept of our LORD Matt 19. 17— 'If thou wilt enter into life, keep the commandments,' we look to the scope. An inquirer proud of his own righteousness, asks what he must *do* to obtain eternal life, and our LORD refers him to the LAW, to rebuke and humble him." ANGUS.

OBS The case of this "ruler" (probably a Pharisee, given also

Mark 10, Luke 18), in connection with the MASTER'S treatment, is most instructive and suggestive.—It was at his weak point he failed, when CHRIST applied the test—give up all—self righteousness, deadly doings etc, and follow me. For the best elucidation of this story see WHEDON.

Thus the subjects of Is 1–39, are usually plain. CHS 51–55, are a continuous prophecy. 53–4 speak of the sufferings and work of MESSIAH.

Sometimes we do not know whether to interpret by the connection or scope of the book—

EXS. In LUKE 15—the prodigal son, we do not know whether the elder and younger son mean the Pharisee and sinner or Jew and gentile. The scope of the context favors the first, while that of the book (Luke being to the gentiles), the second. In such case, both interpretations are consistent.

OBS. What wisdom and insight of the heart does our LORD show in this parable! Truly, the SPIRIT of the LORD, of understanding, of counsel and might rested on JESUS, to make him of quick understanding in the fear of the LORD. Is 11: 2.

As the bread multiplied in the LORD's hands, so the WORD grows exceedingly as we proceed in its study

"A vast, unfathomable sea,
Where all our thoughts are drowned."

By the same rule, we compare Paul and James on *justification*. In Roms, Paul is proving that by the works of the LAW, we cannot have pardon and peace. James is teaching the difference between a dead and living faith.

SEC 5 COMPARING SCRIPTURE WITH SCRIPTURE.

Things spiritual with spiritual I COR 2: 13. This is the most comprehensive rule, and by this alone we ascertain the divine teaching on faith and practice. A SCRIPTURE truth and duty, is the consistent explanation of all teaching there is on it. It is in revelation as in nature—we examine facts and phenomena, then refer to, and classify with similar facts, then explain the whole. This is called a general law.*

* This suggests the importance and use of a HARMONY of the GOSPELS.

The mistakes of the Jews are chargeable in part to neglect of this rule.

Exs. "We have heard Is 9: 7, (said they), that CHRIST abideth forever, and how sayest thou that the SON * * must be lifted up?" Is 9, DAN 7: 14, speak of his death (not for himself), and everlasting reign.

In I SAM and ACTS, David is called a man after GOD'S own heart. Compared with other places, we gather that it is his kingly, and not personal character that is meant.

GAL 6: 17, "I bear * * the marks of JESUS." In II COR 4, 11, we find Paul speaks of his sufferings, not the *stigmata* of the cross.

NUMB 22-24, leave us in doubt as to the character of Balaam. Comparison with Peter, tells us covetousness was his snare, and Jude classes him with Cain and Korah.

It is by comparing SCRIPTURE with SCRIPTURE, different expressions are harmonized.

Ex. GOD'S offer of 7 yrs famine II SAM 24: 13, includes the 3 preceding yrs the famine had been, 21: 1. In I CHRON 21: 11, 12, is no reference to the past, so 3 yrs is named.

1 *In verbal* parallelisms, 1st find the sense the words bear in other parts of the author, in other writings of the same date, then throughout the BIBLE. The sense may change, and all do not use the same word in the same sense. Admit no meaning inconsistent with the context, or reasoning of the author. In ROMS and GAL e g, "works" means performance of legal duties; In JAMES, *obedience* and *holiness* through faith. So in JNO 1: 1, "WORD" cannot be explained by II TIM 4: 2. WORD in the first means the divine nature, in the second, GOSPEL.

2 *Comparison* of the facts or doctrines, to get a complete view of a truth, is called parellelism of ideas—

Exs. If we wish to know whether the wine in the holy supper is for all, or the priest only, we compare MATT 26: 27 with I COR 11, and find that the bread and wine (mentioned six times) are enjoined on all Christians alike.

Again MATT 16: 18, CHRIST says "Thou art Peter, and on this rock I will build my church." I COR 3: 11, tells us "other foundation can no man lay" but CHRIST. ACTS 2: 41, c 10, 15: 7, we learn that Peter's preaching was a means of the first conversions. Augustine and Luther say "rock" means Peter's confession. Wesley, that CHRIST probably pointed to himself (the only foundation) when he spoke.

In parallelisms, the most important rule is to interpret what is obscure by what is more clearly stated—

Exs. Justification by faith alluded to PHIL 3: 9, is explained in ROMS and GAL.

The charity I PET 4: 8, is "brotherly love," and covers a multitude of sins. Not because it extinguishes them and so justifies, but (see PROV 10: 12), because it quenches contention and strife.

When a passage is explained by the general tenor of the WORD, it is called the *analogy* or *rule* of *faith*.

Ex. In GAL 6: 14, I COR 15: 3–11, Paul speaks of the death and resurrection of CHRIST, then deduces other doctrines from them.

The analogy of faith is called I COR 15: 3, 4, the "SCRIPTURES," "the whole LAW" GAL 5: 14, "mouth of all the prophets" ACTS 3: 18. Paul ROM 12: 6, exhorts to expound (prophecy), according to the proportion (analogy) of faith. It is the whole tenor of SCRIPTURE—the result of all the texts on any one doctrine.

It is thus that philosophy interprets nature. When a principle is established, phenomena seeming to disagree are examined, and the one agreeing best with the general law, chosen. Such is the connection of nature and revelation. And how beautiful is the order, as alluded to by Paul!— "That is not first which is spiritual, but that which is natural; then, that which is spiritual" I COR 15: 46.

In ACTS 2: 21, we read "Whosoever shall call on the name of the LORD shall be saved." In MATT 7: 21, "Not every one that saith unto me LORD, LORD, shall enter * * heaven." Comparing with ROM 10: 11–14 and I COR 1: 2, we find that the words (from Joel), imply saving faith in CHRIST.

In figurative language, similitude in some respects only, is sufficient to justify the metaphor.

Ex. CHRIST calls his disciples sheep, and the points of comparison are evidently his affection and care for them, and their confidence and love for the SHEPHERD. And CHRIST is called with smaller limits, the LAMB, with reference to his character and sacrifice. The analogical portions have, by pushing the analogies too far, proved a fruitful source of error. Sanctified common sense will limit their application.

To ascertain then the meaning of a SCRIPTURE, whether the words be used literally or tropically, we ask What is the sense? **If they have but one, that is** the meaning. If several, we ask what is required by the **rest** of the sentence? **If 2 or more remain**, then, What is required by the context? **If still more** than 1 remain, then What is required by the general scope? If this fail, then What is required by other **passages?** If more than **one may be the sense,** both are true, and we take the **one meeting best** the conditions.

Whether the words be literal or figurative, in history or prophecy, simple narrative or allegory, the above rules **are** applicable—as applicable **as in** the common intercourse **of** life. SEE first of this CHAP.

1 Rules are for the difficult, rather than **plain portions of** SCRIPTURE.

2 And we have **need to study the** WORD (in order to *prove* its meaning, which is also one branch of our education and discipline in the school of CHRIST).

Revelation is proposed as *the* text BOOK in **our course,** and it is the TEACHER's will that its lessons be mastered.

Solomon, **who next to the** SON **of David,** had perhaps the clearest light in divine things—"wiser than all men" I KGS 4: 31, whose fame attracted the queen of Sheba, and "all kings of the earth" 4: 34, to his court, has spoken of the means of getting wisdom. PROV 3: 13–18, he breaks out in impassioned tones—

> "Happy is the man who findeth WISDOM! * * *
> None of the things thou canst desire
> Are to be compared to her."

Impressed with its importance, he continues to dwell upon it c 4, exclaiming

> " WISDOM is the principal thing!"

And JESUS, "greater than Solomon," whom the wisdom of Solomon personified, on the same subject—his doctrine and the experience, compares it to hid TREASURES, and the "PEARL OF GREAT PRICE," of more value than the riches of all this world.

So dependent are we in divine things on the motive and temper brought to the ORACLES of GOD, and that SPIRIT which

"Brightened Isaiah's vivid page,
And breathed in David's hallowed lays,"

that one with few advantages, may find a more Scriptural knowledge and experience, than one of much learning but feeble piety.

Apollos was "mighty in the SCRIPTURES," but Priscilla and Aquila who had learned of Paul, "took him unto them, and expounded unto him the way of GOD more carefully" ACTS 18: 26.

The interpretation of SCRIPTURE is not every sense it will bear. It is getting at the mind of the Spirit though the writer himself was sometimes ignorant of its full import.

No doctrine founded on a single text belongs to the analogy of faith.—Theology is the whole meaning of the WORD, as explained and limited thereby.

CHAPTER III.

INTERPRETATION CONTINUED. EXTERNAL HELPS.

SEC 1 OPINIONS AND IDEAS.

"Every scribe who hath been made a disciple (instructed) to the kingdom of heaven, is like a householder who bringeth out of his treasures things new and old" MATT 13: 52.

The BIBLE resembles a garden, with variety and profusion of fruits and flowers * * * But it is only to the pure in heart, that GOD is manifested therein as not to the world. CECIL.

AS a knowledge of the OPINIONS and IDEAS prevalent, HISTORY, CHRONOLOGY, NATURAL HISTORY, GEOGRAPHY, MANNERS and CUSTOMS of BIBLE times, is needful to the intelligent reading of the BOOK, a lesson under each of these topics will be interesting and profitable here.

Before his coming, there was expectation of the MESSIAH among both Jews and gentiles, and his times were spoken of as "The world to come," "kingdom of heaven" or of GOD, Heavenly Jerusalem etc. While some, like John, Zacharias and Elizabeth, Simeon and Anna, knew about the nature of CHRIST's kingdom, most had erroneous views of his person and work, which he and his apostles had to meet and correct. Knowledge of the ignorance and prejudices of the people, will therefore, enlighten many things in the N T.

Exs. A proselyte by circumcision or baptism, was said to be "born again." CHRIST JOHN 3, alludes to this error and corrects it.
"Bind" and "loose" meant to forbid as unlawful, or allow as lawful.

The Sermon on the mount is more impressive, for knowing that the Pharisees taught that the thoughts are not sinful MATT 5:28. The Scribes, that the gifts on the altar expiated offences v 24. Maimonides, that oaths by heaven and earth might be taken collusively—secretly, to defraud v 34.

The chief sources of the opinions of the Jews are the *Targums, Talmuds* * and R Simeon of the 2d cy. Simeon has written well on MESSIAH, and illustrates both the faith and unbelief of his nation.—The passages in PSALMS and Isaiah on MESSIAH, and quoted in the N T, are applied to CHRIST. Yet in him who fulfills them all, they do not believe!

The plagues of Egypt are the more instructive for knowing that they were inflicted on the objects they worshipped.

Some converts from the oriental philosophy, like the Gnostics, (who held there were emanations from the GODHEAD—WORD, LIFE, LIGHT etc), tried to mix the two systems together. John is believed to have reference to

* The *Mishna* and *Gemara* compose the *Talmud*, which means *to teach*.

these errors 1 : 1–18, using the words as applicable to CHRIST and to prove his divinity.

Of the Greeks, the Epicureans taught that GOD took no interest in the affairs of the world ; the Stoics, that he was the soul of the world. Paul ACTS 17 : 18–31, rebukes both, and reveals to them the resurrection and atonement of CHRIST.

SEC 2 HISTORY

GEN 46, " Every shepherd is an abomination unto the Egyptians," is the reason given for settling Jacob in Goshen, on the borders of Egypt. Hales and Faber tell us (from Manetho), that abt 2259 B C, Egypt was invaded by Cushite shepherds from Arabia, who after 2 or 3 hundred years of domination, were expelled by the princes of Upper Egypt and returned to Palestine (Land of Shepherds, in SCRIPTURE Philistia), before Joseph's administration.

This seems to be the reason for the prejudice against Israel, who was from those quarters. So WHEDON in loco.

Recent discoveries in Palestine, Egypt and Assyria, confirm portions of O T history.

The best comment out of the BIBLE, on DEUT 28, and predictions about Jerusalem, is found in Josephus, who in turn, is confirmed by cotemporary historians and Titus.

MATT 2 : 2, 3, is enlightened by knowing that in the East, there was expectation of a great prince to appear and have universal dominion.

JESUS MATT 24 : 15, 16, forewarns his followers to escape out of Jerusalem. Josephus says that Cestius Gallus, after beginning the siege, suddenly withdrew without any assignable cause, and that many taking advantage of this, fled to the mountains, some to Pella over Jordan, others to Libanus.

OBS. JESUS cares for his own.

The " rest," R V peace, ACTS 9 : 31, may have been due

not to Saul's conversion, for the persecution lasted 3 yrs longer; but to Caligula setting up his statue in the Holy of Holies, which diverted the Jews *pro tem*, from persecuting.

ACTS 24: 25, As Paul "reasoned of righteousness, and temperance, and the judgment," Felix trembled. Josephus tells us Felix was oppressive, and living in adultery with Drusilla, wife of the king of Edessa. This may illustrate Paul's courage, and suggest his reasons for speaking so, and Felix trembling under his masterly words.

SEC 3 CHURCH HISTORY

ECCLESIASTICAL history tells us, that before the destruction of Jerusalem, the GOSPEL had been preached and churches formed in Macedonia and Syria by Jude; Egypt and parts of Africa by Mark, Simon and Jude. Ethiopia by the Eunuch of Candace and Matthias; Pontus by Peter. "The seven churches" by John; Parthia by Matthew. Scythia by Philip and Andrew; Persia by Simon and Jude. Media by Thomas; in Italy and Greece by Paul.

The duty of all to study the BIBLE is taught and implied II TIM 3, JNO 5, ACTS 17; LUKE 16, MATT 22, II PET 1, I THESS 5, etc, in addition to the many commands and exhortations in the O T. So it is found that the early Fathers enforced this on Christians in the strongest terms. Chrysostom, Jerome, Origen and Augustine do this. They even affirm that the cause of the evils of their times, was due to the fact that the "SCRIPTURES are not known."

Corruptions and errors foretold therein, are recorded in history—

Exs. The Bishop of Rome is called universal Bp 606, then pope. Council of Trent 1545, canonizes the Apocrypha, VULGATE and traditions. 666 Latin for the vernacular in worship enforced. Transubstantiation first taught in 8th cy. Cup taken from the laity in 11th cy. Seven sacraments adopted 12th cy. Purgatory, merit of penance and prayers for the dead, begun in 7th cy, confirmed 1140. Indulgences by the Pope in 12th cy. Auricular confession by the 4th Lateran Council 13th cy. Celibacy of the clergy compulsory, enjoined in 4th, confirmed by Gregory the Gt 11th cy—

Col 2 : 23, " Which things have indeed a show of wisdom." Compare with II Thess 2 : 7–12—" For the mystery of lawlessness " etc.

The comparatively recent origin of these dogmas proves that Popery is a novelty, being unknown to those nearest the times of Christ and his apostles.

Sec 4 Chronology

The order of events and intervals between, are essential to understand some parts of Scripture; and chronology, the science of adjusting epochs to facts, supplies this information—

Exs. Depravity in the course of sin, is made the more remarkable for knowing that in the second generation, all flesh had so corrupted his way, that " it repented the Lord that he had made man " Gen 6 : 6.

That Noah their progenitor had not been dead 100 yrs, ere Sodom and Gomorrah were ripe for their judgment.

The judgment on Eli's house began with Hophni and Phinehas, but was not finished (in Abiathar's removal to Zadok), till 80 yrs after I Kgs 2 : 26.

"The mills of the gods grind slow."

From II Kgs 23 : 13, we learn that the high places built by Solomon to Ashtoreth, Chemosh and Milcom, continued till Josiah—350 yrs.

"The man of sin" II Thess 2 : 3, some refer to Caligula, but it was not written till twelve years after his death.

"Honor the king" I Pet 2 : 17, derives the greater force from the fact that Nero was then the ruling tyrant.

4000 yrs elapsed from the first, and 400 from the last prediction, till Christ came.

" Learn to wait, life's hardest lesson,
   Conned perchance, through blinding tears,
   While the heart throbs sadly echo
   To the tread of passing years."

From Gen 5, it appears that Noah could have received the history of creation from Enos or Lamech, his own father. Lamech was 56 yrs cotemporary with Adam and 100 with Shem. Shem was 150 yrs cotemporary with Abraham and 50 with Isaac Gen 11 : 10. The communication from Adam to Isaac therefore, may have been only 2 links. How easy to transmit truth from earliest times!

Enoch "the seventh from Adam," was translated while but a youth (for his times), only 365.

Methuselah lived 969 yrs to the flood, and may have been drowned in it. It is probable some lived over 1000 yrs.

From GEN 6, 120 years notice of the judgment was given, and Noah warned the people 120 yrs to the flood. The earth was cleansed by this washing of water—baptism, from the filthiness of its inhabitants.

From GEN 7 : 11, 8 : 14, we learn Noah was 1 yr and 10 ds in the ark.

All that the SPIRIT has given us of the first period—the "world of the ungodly," nearly 2000 yrs, is in the first 7 CHS of GENESIS.

Ons There is a chart of the history of our world, the stream of time running thro the centre, with lines across the map dividing it into centuries. On this panorama, is illustrated in colors from left to right, with name, date etc, the important characters, empires, cities, monuments, reforms etc, in the BIBLE and history. The account begins with creation, our first parents in Eden, sin, expulsion, ark, flood etc, (including 2 pillars of stone, on which tradition says was written the history of the antediluvian world), and continues down to our times.

Such a representation (the one described abt 2½x30 ft), through the eye, of GOD in revelation and history, aids in fixing in the mind the order and relation of events, and gives us a more vivid conception of JEHOVAH's sovereignty in the natural and spiritual realm.

Every nation has some memorable epoch or era from which to reckon. Christians reckon from the birth of CHRIST, the Romans from the foundation of their city A. U. C.* 753, the Greeks from the 1st Olympiad 776 B C, the Mohammedans from the Hegira 622 A D.

As the SCRIPTURES have events of historic and religious importance, so there are divisions corresponding The Jews reckon from the creation, from the flood, the Exode NUMB 33 : 38, I KGS 6 : 1, and Solomon's temple II CHRON 8 : 1.

*Ab Urbe Condita—from the building of the city.

CHRONOLOGY.   117

The duration of the **1st era** is found by summing the age of the 10 patriarchs at the birth of their eldest son. This is the one from the Heb by Abp Usher, modified by Bp Lloyd, and received as correct.

	Usher.	Sept.	Jos.
From creation to the flood	1656	2262	2256
To call of Abram	427	1207	1062
" the Exode	430	425	445
" Sols temple	479	601	621
" return from Babylon	476	476	493
" Christ	536	537	534
	4004	5508	5411

The Exode then was 2513 A M, 857 from the flood. Israel was 215 yrs in Egypt. Abraham was 75 Gen 12, and at 100 begat Isaac 21 c. Isaac was 60 and begat Jacob 25 c   Jacob at 130 went to Egypt. $25 + 60 + 130 = 215$. The Sam reckons 1307 to the flood. The modern Jews 3760 from the creation to Christ.

Abp Usher from I Kgs 6 : 1, makes the 4th period 479 yrs 16 ds. But the LXX does not adopt the reading. In II Chron 3 : 2—the parallel passage, is no date. Josephus, Theophilus and Eusebius do not seem to adopt it. Paul Acts 13 : 20, seems to say 450 from the division of Canaan to Samuel. If so, it was 579 ; i e, from the Exode till division of the land 46, from Judges to Samuel 450, from Saul and David to 3rd of Solomon 83–579. Usher thinks the 450 means from after the birth of Isaac to the entrance into Canaan. Jos says 592, Hales 621, Greswell 594.

In Judges the time is not solved. Six servitudes—111 yrs, are noticed and 14 Judgeships, not including Joshua, Eli and Samuel, covering 279=390 yrs. Adding the 46 and 83 as above, we have 519 to Solomon's temple. But are the servitudes and Judgeships cotemporaneous? Usher thinks so. Hales thinking Jud 2 : 18 applies to all, thinks not. Again we are not told how long Joshua and Elders after him ruled, except Othniel his son in law. Neither are we told whether Eli was a ruler, or priest only. If the latter, his time must be left out. Neither can we find the time between Samson and Saul.

In conclusion, if we set aside I KGS 6: 1, and are uncertain of ACTS 13: 20, we have not materials for finding the time between the Exode and Solomon's temple.

The fifth and sixth periods nearly agree, the first from SCRIPTURE, the 2nd from history.

The comparative claims of these systems is unsettled.

The HEB is deemed more likely than the SEPT to have been altered, being more confined to the Jews. For among them was a motive after CHRIST came, for shortening the time their expositors had fixed on, to make it appear that it was not past.

The SEPT, Josephus and SAMARITAN, make the time from the flood to the birth of Abraham abt 1100 yrs, which is thought by some to account better for the apparent increase among the nations than Usher's—350.

While such differences in the chronology may be charged to mistakes in copying, and consequent various readings, GOD has permitted this uncertainty of the past, as he veils the times and seasons future, from us.

Differences also arise from different modes of reckoning. Some nations have two or more modes, or beginnings of the year—civil, consular, ecclesiastical etc. Also, the year does not begin with actual time—

Ex. The Julian year 365 d 6 h, was 11 m 9 s too much. From A D 1 to 1836 therefore, this mode makes the yr $14\frac{1}{2}$ ds in advance. The council of Nice struck out $2\frac{1}{2}$ ds, and in 1582 Gregory the XIII corrected the calendar, making the 5th of Oct the 15th, disposing of 10 ds more. In Eng the 3rd of Sept 1751, was reckoned the 14, and in 1800 the 29 of Feb was omitted. So that from 30 to 1836, we have within a few hours, 1806 yrs, thus correcting the Julian mode.

Peculiarities of reckoning—

EXS. The SCRIPTURES speak of a part of a day or yr as one. As in the reign of a king, though but 1 yr and 2 mos, the one mo falling in the first, the other in the last, it is 3 yrs.

As the son often reigned with his father, the time of each is sometimes included, sometimes excluded. Jotham reigned 16 yrs II Kgs 15 : 33, and in v 30, 20 yrs.

For 4 yrs he seems to have reigned with Uzziah, who was a leper.

GEN 15 : 13, the 400 yrs means from the birth of Isaac. GAL 3 : 17, 430 is from the call of Abraham to the giving of the LAW, 3 mos after the Exode.

GEN 46—All that went with Jacob into Egypt were 66. Jacob, Joseph and 2 sons added—70. In ACTS 7, Steven says 75. This includes the nine wives of Jacob's sons (Judah and Simeon's were d), 66+9=75.

Comparing Ez 2 with NEH 7, "42360" returned from Babylon, of which the number of Judah, Benjamin and the priests are given —Neh 31089 Ez 29818.

Add to NEH 494 named only in EZRA, and to EZRA 1765 only in NEH, they agree—31583. The difference 10777, are not named, because they had no register, or belonged to the 10 tribes.

RULES FOR FRAMING *a system*. 1. Find the important epochs and reckon forward or backward. The birth of our LORD is the centre of modern chronology and much of ancient. The council at Jerusalem, or d of Herod, is the key to that of ACTS, as the date of Paul's conversion is to his LETTERS.* The return from Babylon, destruction of Jerusalem, and the first temple (reckoning upward from A D 1), are epochs of O T chronology.

2 *Test chronology* by astronomy—

Ex. The passover began on the day before the moon fulled, between Mar 18 and Apl 16. As the moon can be eclipsed only at the full, this feast will fall on any day before an eclipse, between the above dates. The passover was on the 14th of Nisan, and reckoning backward, we find the first day of each yr. Fifty days after 14th of Nisan was Pentecost. 177 ds from the full of the moon of Nisan— 6 lunations, was the feast of Tabs. The great day of atonement was 5 ds earlier—10 of Tisri.

So also CHRIST's crucifixion is reckoned to be Apl 5 or 6 30. So S S JOURNAL.

* From 33–35. Herod Agrippa died at Cæsarea on "the fifth day" after the angel smote him, Josephus says, 44. The council at Jerusalem Acts 15, compared with Gal 1 : 18, 2 : 1, was 17 yrs after Saul's conversion—50–52. ANGUS, WESLEY, CLARKE.

Sec 5 Natural History

Ps 92 : 12, "The righteous shall flourish like the palm." This species flourishes best in the desert, bears best dates at 100, sends from its roots a forest of suckers. Its verdure apparently springs from the scorching dust. "It is says Laborde, as a friendly light-house, guiding the **traveller to where water is found.**" It is beautiful, tall, crowned with a leafy canopy—a waving plume, emblem of praise and victory ; **the** redeemed have palms in their hands Rev 7 : 9. It never fades, dust never settles on it. "Plutarch **says, it has the** property of rising under pressure, **and** flourishes in proportion to the weights on it. It preserves its vigor in old age, so that the ancients accounted it immortal. It grows not from external accretions, but inward **additions.**" Happy Islands or Paradise Restored.

The Syrians speak of 360 uses the palm is applied to.

What a symbol of a growing Christian in a guilty, desert world !* It is instructive that the palm, once the symbol of Palestine, is now rarely seen there.

Again, same verse, "He shall grow like a cedar in Lebanon." The cedars of Lebanon are proverbial for fragrance. The cedar grows best near water, its roots are in the rocks, it is evergreen like the palm, is sound to the heart. After living a thousands yrs, it preserves all it touches and beautifies the house of the Lord.

Deut 32: 11, God is said to have taught Israel as the eagle trains her young. When the eaglets are old enough, she tears up her nest, compelling them to fly ; flutters over, catches them on her wings when falling or unwilling to fly, shakes them off, darts between them and an enemy. The

* "There grows in Euphrosyne, a tropical plant of the cereal class, which also symbolizes the higher life. Like other plants, it has its roots in the earth ; but when it has reached up and laid hold of something above, it quits the ground and flourishes better, suspended from the heavens, filling the region round about with its perfume. H. Is or Par Restored p 161.

eagle is the only bird having such an instinct. The story of Israel, and the church in the two dispensations, and life of our LORD above all, are suggestive of GOD's way in dealing with us individually.

It had come to be a sign of poverty or humility in the time of our LORD, for great men to be seen in public on an ass. Comp ZECH 9 : 9 with MATT 21 : 4, 5, where we have prediction—"Thy King cometh unto thee * * riding upon an ass," and its accomplishment.

The SCRIPTURES abound with expressions and figures from natural history; and a knowledge of Eastern botany (much increased since James' VERSION), adds no small interest to our NEW VERSION.

JAS 5 : 14, "* * anointing him with *oil* in the name of the LORD ; and the prayer of faith shall save him that is sick." The oil of the olive soothes pain and promotes health. It was used for counteracting poison, and is used tropically, for the healing effects of the GOSPEL. "This gift, CHRIST committed to his church MARK 16 : 18, remained long after others gifts failed, and was designed to have remained forever. * * * This was the whole process of physic in the church till abused, and so mostly lost through unbelief. Extreme unction for the dying, bears no resemblance." WESLEY.

JER 8 : 22, "Is there no balm in Gilead?" The myrrh and balm (balsam) of the East, are aromatic, exuding from trees, and in demand with the merchant. The balm of Gilead had great medical properties, and was also used by the SPIRIT, as a symbol of the healing virtues of JESUS, our GREAT PHYSICIAN.

CHAPTER IV

INTERPRETATION CONTINUED

Sec 1 Manners and Customs.

HABITATIONS. The progenitors of Israel dwelt in tents. The first notice of tent is in Gen 4: 20. The tabernacle was tent fashion. When Israel came into Canaan, they occupied the houses of that people. Architecture made progress. Solomon's palace, built with the aid of the Phœnicians, was magnificent.

The houses of the poor were daubed with mud, and hence were used as figures of human frailty, being easily destroyed Job 24: 16, Matt 6: 19.

Those of the better class had a porch, leading by a side door into a waiting room, which led into a court open at top, surrounded by the inner walls of the house. The roof was flat, surrounded by a battlement, with a balustrade of lattice work around the court. In summer, the people slept on the roof, which was used also as a place of rest, mourning and devotion.

These facts explain Deut 22: 8, I Sam 9: 25, II Sam 11: 2, Is 22: 1, Acts 10: 9, Mark 13: 15, 2: 4.

The doors were double, and moved on pivots secured by bars. Deut 3: 5, Jud 16: 3. Locks were often, merely wooden slides. The street doors and gates of towns, were adorned with lessons out of the law Deut 6: 9. The windows were of lattice work, covered with a veil etc, in winter. For want of chimneys, holes were sometimes made above for the smoke. In some houses, coal was used for fire Jno 18: 18.

Articles of furniture were few and simple. The seat was a rug, mat, a legged stool or chair I Sam 1: 9, Prov 9: 14, Matt 21: 12. Beds were of mattresses and quilts. Sheets,

MANNERS AND CUSTOMS. 123

blankets and bedsteads were not known, though on the roof a settee or frame work was used, on which to lay the bed.

The towns were small but numerous. Jerusalem, Samaria and Cæsarea were the largest. The streets were narrow, dull and unpaved. They had high walls with bars and gates, to protect against robbers etc. The people lived so much in this way that, as Bp Simpson says, there seemed to be no country in Palestine. Matters of public interest were transacted in the gate as a court. It was here that Abraham bargained for Machpelah GEN 23, and Boaz for his bride RUTH, c 4.

DRESS consisted of a frock or shirt to the ankle, with a loose robe over that. In doors the first was often worn. It was like an undress, not worn on visits or abroad. In the first, one was said to be naked Is 20: 2, JNO 21: 7. The dress was fastened with a girdle. When great effort was required, the sleeve was rolled up Is 52: 10—"The LORD hath made bare his holy arm." The sleeve was long, so as to conceal the hand during visits of ceremony.

The outer garment (mantle or plaid), was sometimes used for a cover or bed at night. Some of the wealth of eastern nations consisted of garments, which were exchanged, or given and worn in respect or affection GEN 45: 22, II Kgs 5: 22. The garment was rent in token of grief or sorrow GEN. 37: 34. The art of embroidery was known to the Hebrews EX 35: 35. White, blue, red and purple are the favorite colors in SCRIPTURE.

The feet were "shod with sandals" of wood or leather, strapped over the foot MATT 3: 11. In transfering property, it was the custom to deliver a sandal RUTH 4, as it was a glove in the middle ages.

To throw a shoe over a land, was a sign of possession Ps 60: 8. To remove or unloose. a sign of reverence EX 3: 5, as to bear, was of servility MARK 1: 7. Stockings were not worn except in winter.

The head was covered generally, with a cloth or kind of turban. The women wore veils.

The hair and beard were allowed to grow. The latter was respected as a sign of manhood, and to shave, to spit on or pull (except in saluting), was a great insult II Sam 10 : 4–6.

Food. The living was simple, little flesh even of clean animals was eaten. Blood, the fat and swine, were forbidden by God.

Obs. As the eater must assimilate and partake of the nature **and** qualities of what is eaten, reason and religion teach us to live **on** what may be healthful to body and soul. "Most people dig their graves with their teeth" as one says, who has written on this subject. As the hog was eaten by the heathen, its restriction in Israel among the creatures as "unclean," is the more instructive to us.

Milk, butter, cheese, bread, fruit and honey, were much used. Our Lord and his disciples often ate bread and fish.

Locusts were eaten. John ate locusts and wild honey.

Bread was baked daily, in the form of cake, roll or biscuit **on** the hearth, metal plates, sides of earthen vessels, or of a pit in the floor.

The grinding of corn and baking was **done** by the wife and daughter at first, but afterwards by the servant. The bread was not cut but broken.

The Jews commonly ate two meals a day, the principal one about 5 P. M. The guests reclined on the left side on couches. The food was eaten with the hand; hence the custom **of** washing before and after meals Mark 7 : 5.

The drink (after eating) was water, or wine diluted with water, called *vinegar* Ruth 2 : 14, Matt 27 : 48.* This is what the soldiers gave Jesus when he cried "I thirst!" The wine and gall or wine and myrrh given him before Matt 27 : 34, Mark 15 : 23, was given to those condemned to die, to stupefy them. Our Lord refused this, to endure "the cross, despising the shame." It was a custom to anoint with oil or perfume at banquets Ps 23 : 5. Christ

---

* God's people do not seem to have learned to drink tea and coffee, two of those stimuli Americans indulge in, and the taste of many is really enslaved to, so *pernicious* to *health* and even *morals*. For what injures the bodily organism, affects our mental and spiritual nature also. On this see Home, Hlth and H. Economics.

was thus honored **Mark 14: 3**, with costliest ointment, worth about $50.

"Supper," the chief meal, was in the evening. The light and joy in the house was used betimes to represent heaven, and without "outer darkness," the misery of the lost **Matt 8: 12**.

Sec 2 Revenue and Tax.

After the land was made a Roman province, Pt III c V Sec 3, a census was taken **Luke 2: 2**, of the name and fortune of the people, as the basis of a capitation tax. This was an occasion of dissatisfaction to the Jews, and of more than one insurrection **Acts 5: 37**, Judas of Gal. Christ **Matt 22: 17**, was tempted by the Pharisees, through the Herodians, about this tribute. The *denarius* or penny, was paid to collectors in Roman or Grecian (*drachma*) coin. When in the latter, it had to be changed to Roman by the "money changers," whose seats our **Lord** overthrew **Matt 21: 12**.

Also, there were customs on imports and exports **Matt 9: 9**. These were levied by the farmers through their servants. Those, as Zaccheus, were called chiefs, and these as Matthew, publicans. They were notorious for their exactions, and hateful to the Jews.

There was also the half shekel—temple tax, required by the law "of every Jew" **Angus, Robinson**. "Of every male" **Clarke**. "Of every head of a family" **Wesley**, even of those living out of Palestine. The brokers exchanged the foreign for current coin in the temple **Matt 21: 12, John 2: 16**.

This is the "tribute" **Matt 17: 24**. R V reads "half shekel," and for "piece of money" v 27, "shekel," with *didrachma* and *stater* in mar. A better rendering than the A V.

The distinction between the above three taxes is expressed in the Greek, and generally in our translation.

Sec 3 Coins and Measures.

Mite λεπτον	Mark 12:42	⅟₈c	Digit "finger," Jer 52:21	⅞ in*
Farthing κοδραντης	" "	⅖	Handbreadth Ex 25:23	4 "
Penny	Matt 22:19	17¼	Span " 28:16	9 *
Pound (mina)	Luke 19 13	$15.60	Cubit Gen 6:15	18 *
Shekel	Matt 17 24	62½*	Fathom Acts 27 28	6 ft
£1 Eng		4.84*	Ezekiel's reed Ezek 40:3	10 ft 11 in
Talent silver		£342 3s 9d	Furlong Luke 24:13	⅛ m
" gold	16 times more		Ephah tenth of a homer,	
"Pieces of silver" Acts 19:19, may be shekels			Ezek 45:11	3 pks, 3 pts
			Bath I Kgs 7:26	7¼ gal
			Firkin John 2:6	8⅝ "

Money being scarcer then, was of greater relative value, and would buy many times as much as now.

A sabbath day's journey Acts 1:12, less than a mile, was so called because the distance between the tabernacle and outside of the camp.

Sec 4 Time, Modes of Reckoning etc.

The sacred year began Ex 12:1, with Abib (Mar or Apl), according to the moon. The civil with Ethanim I Kgs 8:2, the 7th month (Sept or Oct)—beginning of seed time. The year was divided into 12 lunar months, and every third year, a 13th mo added. The first month—Abib —"green ears" Ex 13:4, or Nisan "flight" Est 3:7, is the only one with *name*, till after the exile, when Babylonish names were used.

The natural day was from "sun to sun," the civil from 6 P M to 6 P M the next day, differing from the Roman which like ours, was from midnight to midnight.

The night at first was divided into three watches Jud 7:19. But in the N T under the Roms, into 4 equal parts from 6 P M to 6 A M Mark 13:35. The third watch was "cock crowing" Matt 26:34.

A *knowledge* of the customs and modes of reckoning, will explain many passages.

Exs. Matt 20:6, "The eleventh hour" was 5 P M.
Luke 23:44, the *darkness* was supernatural, as the sun is never

* Webs Unab Dicy, adopted where standard authorities differ.

eclipsed at full moon. JOHN 19: 14, Pilate brought JESUS forth about "the sixth hour." He may either read τριτη third. for ἑκτη, or suppose that John uses the Roman reckoning, adopted after the destruction of Jerusalem.

MATT 27 : 63, "After three days I will rise again." From sunset till Sunday morning was reckoned "three days." So also a week is called " eight days" JOHN 20: 26.

In Rome children were adopted, and the adoption was afterward ratified in public, thus making them heirs of their foster parents. So ROM 8 speaks of *our* " adoption " by GOD the FATHER, and redemption of our bodies v 23, at CHRIST's coming.

The salutation was a kiss, sometimes on the beard or cheek. When on the brow, in token of respect. On meeting, the Jews used much ceremony, and persons charged with urgent business were forbidden to salute by the way II KGS 4: 29, LUKE 10: 4. The usual greeting was, Peace be with thee. JESUS the SON of peace, used this to comfort his sorrowing disciples in a new and holier sense, where he says, " *My* peace I give unto you, not as the world giveth " Other beautiful forms are given for us RUTH 2: 4, 3: 10, Ps 129: 8.

In early times, travellers waited in the street or at the door till provided for. GEN 19, the two angels in Sodom ; JUD 19, the Levite and concubine in Gibeah.

Mourning for the dead—weeping, rending the clothes, sackcloth and ashes, sprinkling dust on the head, was practiced. The body was closely wrapped and placed on a bier, and borne away within 24 hours after death. Embalming was common, though not carried to the perfection it was, in Egypt.

Crucifixion was a Romish punishment, not for a Roman, but slaves, and the vilest criminals. Our LORD was numbered with such LUKE 22 : 37.

At the feast of tabernacles on the "last day, the great day of the feast," JOHN 7: 37, they drew water out of Siloam, some of which was drunk, singing—" With joy shall ye draw water from the wells of salvation " Is 12 : 3. The rest was poured by the priests on the evening sacrifice. The

giving of water from the rock was **commemorated, and
prayers** for **rain** offered.

It was the custom **with** the kings of Syria to visit Rome
—the emperor and senate, for honors. Herod the Gt and
his sons went **to** Augustus. They went, as CHRIST says of
himself, to **receive** " a kingdom and return " LUKE 19 : 12.

For more under this head, HAND BOOK OF MANNERS AND CUS-
TOMS, J. M. FREEMAN, D.D., is best.

CHAPTER V.

INTERPRETATION CONTINUED.

SEC 1 GEOGRAPHY.

IN the neglect of BIBLE history and geography, the SCRIPTURES
as a whole, can never be understood. Even its doctrinal teachings
will not be so clearly apprehended without these. F G HIBBARD
DD, PAL.

THE **BIBLE** tells **us** that Armenia **and** the plains
between the Tigris and Euphrates—Mesopotamia
(between the rivers), were settled first after the flood.

After the dispersion at Babel, Shem settled between the
Indian Ocean and Black Sea. Ham chose Africa, Japhet
Europe and part of **Asia.**

Going S W from **Ararat, we come to** Lebanon, and have
before **us** " **the lands of the BIBLE."** From this position
southward, far over **the** Syrian desert, we have the
Euphrates and Tigris, **which rising in** Armenia, run into
the Persian Gulf. On the first arose Babylon, on the
second Nineveh.

Between the Euphrates and table land E of the Jordan,
is Arabia Deserta. Southward, Arabia Petrea (rocky)
with *Petra* the capital. S of this, E of the Red Sea,
stretches Arabia Felix (the fruitful), whence the gold and
spices of **ancient** story.

Still looking S and **below** us, stretches away Palestine,

having Phœnicia (coast of Tyre and Sidon) on its northern seaboard, and Philistia for its Southern.

Now suppose we stand on Hermon, where Libanus and Anti-libanus join, we see these two ridges running through Syria till lost in Asia Minor, enclosing Cœle (hollow) Syria, called also plain of Lebanon, with Baalbec for its capital. Southward, these ridges run through Palestine, the left one losing itself in the Red Sea, the other in the peninsula of Sinai, where Israel wandered 40 yrs. Where

> By day, along the astonished land,
>   The cloudy pillar glided slow;
> By night, Arabia's crimsoned sand,
>   Returned the fiery column's glow. SIR W SCOTT.

West of this lies Egypt.

Below to the left, is Damascus, famed for fruitfulness and bigotry. On the right, lay the blue, tideless Mediterranean, connecting the traffic of Europe with the Orient; and in succession Cyprus, Crete, Malta and Sicily—" the isles of the sea." On our right also is Asia Minor, spoken of in Acts as the scene of Paul's early trials and triumphs, and REV 1 : 4, where "the seven (principal) churches" had been planted. Beyond the Ægean Sea is *Hellas— Achaia*, with Macedonia on the N.

Looking still Southward, E of the Jordan, lay the high lands of Gilead and Bashan, diversified with mountains, hills and vales, a goodly land DEUT 8: 7–10. Still Southward lay in order, Ammon, Moab and Edom.

Between the ridge running through this district, and ridge of Lebanon running also S, on the W side (called mountains of Naphtali, of Ephraim or Israel, and mountains of Judah), lies the Jordan valley, with Gennesaret on the N, the sacred stream losing itself in the Dead Sea. Although between Tiberias and the Salt Sea, is only about 60 miles, the channel of the Jordan is about 200 m long. It is from 50 to 150 feet wide. Gennesaret is about 6 m wide and 12 long.

The valley opening to the sea at Carmel, has been successively called Esdraelon, Jezreel and Megiddo. The Kishon "that ancient river," flows through it into the "Great Sea." JUD 4 : 13, 5 : 21. Nazareth and Tabor are on the N.*

On this battle field of **nations**, Deborah and Barak fought Sisera, Gideon destroyed the Midianites, Saul met the Philistines, and he and Jonathan fell on Gilboa. Ahab met Ben Hadad, and Josiah Pharaoh Necho. Here the Assyrians and Persians, **Crusaders** and Saracens, Egyptians and **Turks**, the **Arabians and Franks** have fought, and **Bonaparte**.

JUD 4 : 12, I SAM 31. I KGS 20, II KGS 24.

And this seems to be the " Har-Magedon," where the kings of the whole world gather themselves unto the war of the great day of GOD the ALMIGHTY REV 16 : 14–16. Wesley connects and makes this the same with the overthrow of the beast and false prophet c 19 : 20, before the " thousand yrs " 20 : 2.

HEBRON.—One of the oldest cities in the world ("built seven yrs before Zoan" NUMB 13 : 22, the capital of lower Egypt), is 20 m S of, and about midway between Jerusalem and Beersheba. JOSHUA 14 : 15, it is Kirjath-Arba (city of Arba), "which Arba was the greatest man among the Anakim." GEN 23 : 19, it is Mamre. In this picturesque and romantic spot sojourned Abraham, Isaac and Jacob. Here they received the promise and seal of the covenant, and here they and their wives were buried. Joshua took it and gave it to Caleb. It became a Levitical city. Here David was anointed king, reigning seven yrs and six months. It was the capital till he took Mount Zion from the Jebusites. Here Abner was assassinated, and Absalom made himself king II SAM 15 : 10. Over one of its pools David hung the assassins of Ishbosheth. "One of the two ancient pools, on the S side, is 133 feet square, of stone, 21 ft 8 in deep, with 14 feet of water. The pool on the

---

* This valley reaches from Carmel to Jordan, mean width about 12 m. J. M. BUCKLEY, D.D.

N side is 85x55 ft, 18 ft 8 in deep, water 7. MAY 24 1838" HIBBARD. It seems to be the "city of Judah" LUKE 1: 39, where John the Baptist was born. The Arabic name is *el Khulil—the Friend*, in honor of Abraham. Population 6000.

JERICHO about 20 m N E of Jerusalem and 5 from Jordan, on the western edge of the valley, was a royal city JOSH 12: 7. It was the first destroyed by GOD miraculously, for an example and sign to the wicked and the righteous to all generations, and the ruins, and the man who should try to restore them, cursed; fulfilled on Hiel the Bethelite I KGS 16: 34, about 520 yrs after, in the days of Ahab and Jezebel. "By faith Rahab * * * perished not" HEB 11. "A new city had arisen near, few it seems caring to occupy the doomed site, which lay desolate" HIBBARD. It was E of Jordan from Jericho, that Elijah was taken to heaven in the chariot of GOD by a whirlwind. Here was a school of the prophets, Elijah and Elisha seem to have been connected with. Herod died here of grievous, incurable diseases. Riha a village, stands on the supposed site, its inhabitants the "personation of indolence, misery and filth." JESUS passed through it once MATT 20, honoring the house of Zaccheus. This once lovely spot, the "city of palm trees" DEUT 34: 3, lay desolate, with only a single palm now standing.

GILGAL—a wheel, rolling, was between Jericho and Jordan. Here the 12 stones were set up, circumcision renewed—"reproach of Egypt" rolled away, the passover kept, manna ceased, and Israel first ate of the fruits of Canaan JOSH 5. Here Joshua had his headquarters, and the tabernacle rested till the land was subdued, when it was removed to Shiloh, where Joshua divided the land 18: 1.

Here Samuel offered sacrifice, held his yearly courts and recognized Saul as king I SAM 11: 15. Here was a school of the prophets. Elijah and Elisha were probably often here II KGS 2: 1. Here Naaman came to Elisha, and Elijah threw his mantle on his successor, found "plowing, with 12 yoke of oxen before him, and he with the twelfth" I KGS 19 : 19. Here Ehud smote Eglon king of Moab JUD 3.

SHILOH is about 22 m N of Jerusalem, and N of Bethel. Here the ark rested about 400 yrs, till the time of Eli. I SAM 1–6. Here Samuel was dedicated to GOD, and trained for his great work of reformation ; and the few left of Benjamin, lay in wait to " catch every man his wife of the daughters of Shiloh," at their yearly feast and dance JUD 21 : 13–25. The last notice JER 7 : 11, is where Jerusalem is warned of the judgment which came upon Shiloh. Like Gilgal, this favored city was accursed for idolatry.

BEERSHEBA—Well of the oath GEN 21 : 14, was in the S of the land, 25 m from Hebron. "From Dan to Beersheba" (the N and S portions of Israel), is about 190 m. Two wells are here, the larger "12 ft across and $44\frac{1}{2}$ to the water, sweet and pure."——With what feelings Jacob must have come here GEN 46 : 1, to be escorted in the wagons sent by Joseph "the son of his old age," to carry him and his house down to Egypt! It was endeared to him by many associations GEN 22, 26, 31.

BETHLEHEM—House of bread, bread town, is *Ephrath*, fruitful GEN 48 : 7. Here Jacob buried his beloved Rachel. It is the city of Boaz and Ruth (See the romantic story of Ruth), David's native town I SAM 20 : 6, and forever memorable as the birth place of JESUS

"David's greater SON" LUKE 2: 4.

One of the most beautiful churches in Palestine, erected by the Empress Helena in the 4th cy, stands on the supposed spot where CHRIST was born. Its Arabic name is *Beit lahm*—house of flesh.

SHECHEM—SYCHEM. GEN 12 : 6, is about 40 m N of Jerusalem. It was one of the six cities of refuge, and of the 48 given to the Levites JOSH 20, 21. It was destroyed by Abimelech JUD 9, renewed by Jeroboam I KGS 12 : 25, and made the seat of his kingdom. Among its inhabitants are the remote descendants of the Samaritans—"all the Samaritans in the world 140–150, are here." BUCKLEY.

SAMARIA was built by Omri I KGS 16: 24, on the hill Samaria, and made his capital. It was enlarged by Herod the Gt and named *Sebaste*, now *Sebustieh*.

The people were a mixture of the heathen sent by Shalmanezer, and Israelites it is believed II KGS 17: 24. In their trouble ("The LORD sent lions among them" v. 25), they sent to Shalmanezer for a priest to "teach them the manner of the god of the land." They adopted the PENT (all the SCRIPTURES in the canon till Ezra), but continued in idolatry c 17. On the return from exile, they tried to unite with the Jews in rebuilding the temple, "claiming to be children of Ephraim and Manassah" Ez 4.

After Samaria was destroyed by Shalmanezer, Shechem at the foot of Gerizim, S of and across the valley from Mt Ebal, was made their capital.——After their rejection by Zerubbabel and Joshua, Sanballat by grant of Darius Nothus of Persia, built a temple on Gerizim (in allusion to DEUT 27: 11), for Manassah, who for marrying his daughter, was driven from Jerusalem NEH 13: 28, and instituted the rites and acts of Moses.

Josephus says that Sanballat obtained the grant of Alexander.

For such causes the prejudice and hatred between them increased, even to the denying by the Jews, especially, the offices of humanity JOHN 4: 9, 8: 48. For this wrong, the Jews were reproved and condemned, and their "neighbor" justified by JESUS. See LUKE 10: 33, good Samaritan. Their temple was destroyed by John Hircanus 129 B C. But to this day they hold the mount sacred, and go there 3 times a year to worship JOHN 4: 20. It is now a village —*Nablus—Neapolis.*

Like the Jews, they expected the MESSIAH, but unlike them, a spiritual king JOHN 4: 25, and so were more ready than the Jews to receive CHRIST v 39, and his apostles. Churches were early formed in Samaria (district) ACTS 8, 9: 31, 15: 3.

JOHN 4: 5, It is Sychar, probably a by-name, given in

contempt. As such, it might come from *Sheker* falsehood, or *Shikor* drunkard Is. 28:1. ROBINSON, HIBBARD.

OBS. How instructive is the BIBLE story of these cities, in the light of the past and present! It is the old story of GOD's faithfulness and man's failure. Had Israel kept their LAW—cleaned out the land of the wicked and idols, and hearts of sin, they would have remained to this day. "The memory of the just is blessed, but the name of the wicked shall rot." PROV. 10:7, is as true of a people as individuals. The curse seen and felt in our own land, is the more patent in the Holy Land, which JEHOVAH chose and honored above every other, in the revelation of himself—his work and ways. Jericho, Gilgal, Shiloh and Jerusalem above all, are examples, warning us that GOD's LAW is not a dead letter. For ages the topography of the most favored cities is lost, and regions flowing with milk and honey while they kept the commandments, lay desolate, appealing to heaven for redemption from the curses foretold. DEUT 28.

SEC 2 PALESTINE.

A notice of *Palestine* will illuminate many portions of SCRIPTURE. It is called the "world" LUKE 2, "the earth," and "land." Solomon Ps 72, reigned from the river (Euphrates) to the ends of the earth. But the reference to CHRIST's reign, has a universal meaning.

S of Judæa was Arabia, and on its border (from the sea) Sheba or Saba, whence the queen of Sheba came "from the ends of the earth" MATT 12:42.

The land was early settled by the sons of Canaan, grandson of Noah GEN 11. Hence called Canaan, and from the Philistines (*Pali*, shepherds), Palestine.

EXTENT and DIVISIONS. For 700 yrs after the dispersion, the children of Ham dwelt here, dwindling from 10 nations to seven GEN 15, DEUT 7:1, of which the Amorite was chief, so that Amorite was sometimes used for the whole GEN 15:16. The Philistines, Edomites, Amalekites, Ammonites, Moabites and Midianites were on the borders when Joshua came. It was about 43 m wide at the north by 90 at the south end.

On this chosen spot, little larger than N Jersey, was settled the chosen seed, in the purpose of GOD never to re-

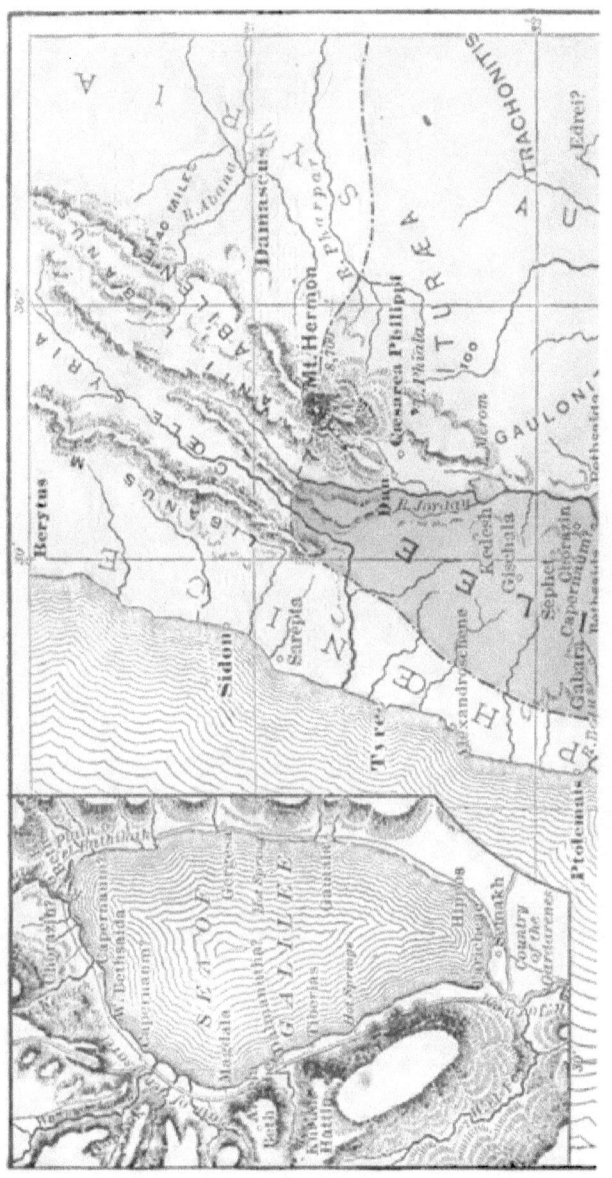

move, type of CHRIST's kingdom, the seat and **radiating point of learning and religion for all nations.**

On the N was Asher, Naphtali, Zebulon and **Issachar—Galilee.** Centrally were Ephraim and Manasseh—**Samaria.**

On the S settled Judah, Benjamin, Dan and Simeon—Judea. *E of Jordan* were Reuben, Gad and half tribe of Manasseh—Peræa.

On the death of Solomon, **10 tribes revolted from his son, and were, after 254 yrs, carried off by the Assyrians—723.**

When CHRIST came, the land consisted of the above four provinces and Idumea (Edom), not in the N T. Idumea comprised the part of Judah S of Hebron. Hircanus 129 B C, subdued the Edomites who had settled there, and the Romans added it.

Peræa (*pera* beyond), comprised all E of Jordan,—Iturea, Trachonitis, Abilene LUKE 3 : 1; also Auranitis, Gaulonitis, Batanea (Bashan), and Decapolis. Peræa *proper* lay S of Pella, between the Jabbok and Arnon.

Herod reigned over the whole, with a revenue of "$8,750,000," leaving his possessions Pt II c 1 Sec 1, to Archelaus, Herod Antipas and Herod Philip LUKE 3 : 1.

Palestine is broken and mountainous. The peaks of Lebanon and Sinai about 400 m apart, rise 10,000 feet above the sea. The Jordan springs from the sides of the former.

The mountains, hills and vales were by nature very fertile, yielding the productions of many climes. Its fruitfulness is ascribed to the favor of GOD, and its sterility to the "heat of his great anger" DEUT 29 : 23. In the time of David the population was probably ten millions II SAM 24 : 9. Compare with the returns I CHRON 21 : 5, 6, and 27: 24.

Beautiful allusions to the higher forms of Christian experience are taken from the fruitfulness of Canaan, as

"Rivers of milk and honey rise,
And all the fruits of paradise
In endless plenty grow"

THE DEAD SEA—Salt Sea GEN 14 : 3—(Vale of Siddim), Sea of the Plain, R V the *Arabah* DEUT 3 : 17, East Sea EZEK

47 : 18, Greek, *Asphaltites* from which our asphaltum, Arabic *Bahr Lut*—Sea of Lot, is 40 m long, from 8–9 wide and from 13 at the S end, to 1350 ft deep at the N end. It has no outlet. Nothing lives in it. The still, dark waters are so salt, that a man may float on the surface. Brimstone and salt abound; **but vegetation, only in a few favored places on its shores.** Desolation, **sterility and** silence, combine to make this region awfully sublime, reminding the visitor of the curse of GOD poured down 1897 yrs B C, on this lovely spot, for its proverbial wickedness. The Jordan before that event, flowed through the " plain " and valley *el Arabah* into the gulf of Akabah, an arm of the Red Sea.

Robinson and Lynch who explored this region, tell us the natural phenomena indicate that the plain was submerged with the cities, at the time this district **was overthrown, and the Dead Sea** thus formed.

It was near Hebron 25 m W, (and Hibbard says on the hill 5 m E of Hebron), where " Abraham got up early" to view the burning region, and " he looked toward Sodom and Gomorrah * * * and beheld, and lo! the smoke of the land went up as the smoke of a furnace" GEN 19: 27, 28.

Thus, **as** the smoke of their torment was a type of hell, so GOD has left this memorial for a sign and a warning of his hatred to sin, as long as the world shall stand.

CHAPTER VI.

INTERPRETATION CONTINUED.

WITH stately towers and bulwarks strong,
   Unrivalled and alone,
Loved theme of many a sacred song,
   GOD's holy city shone.   II. AUBER.

SEC 1 JERUSALEM.

THIS city, under its different names, from the time it was chosen to be the civil and religious seat and radial point of the Theocracy, began to be used as an eminent type of MESSIAH's kingdom in the church's sacred

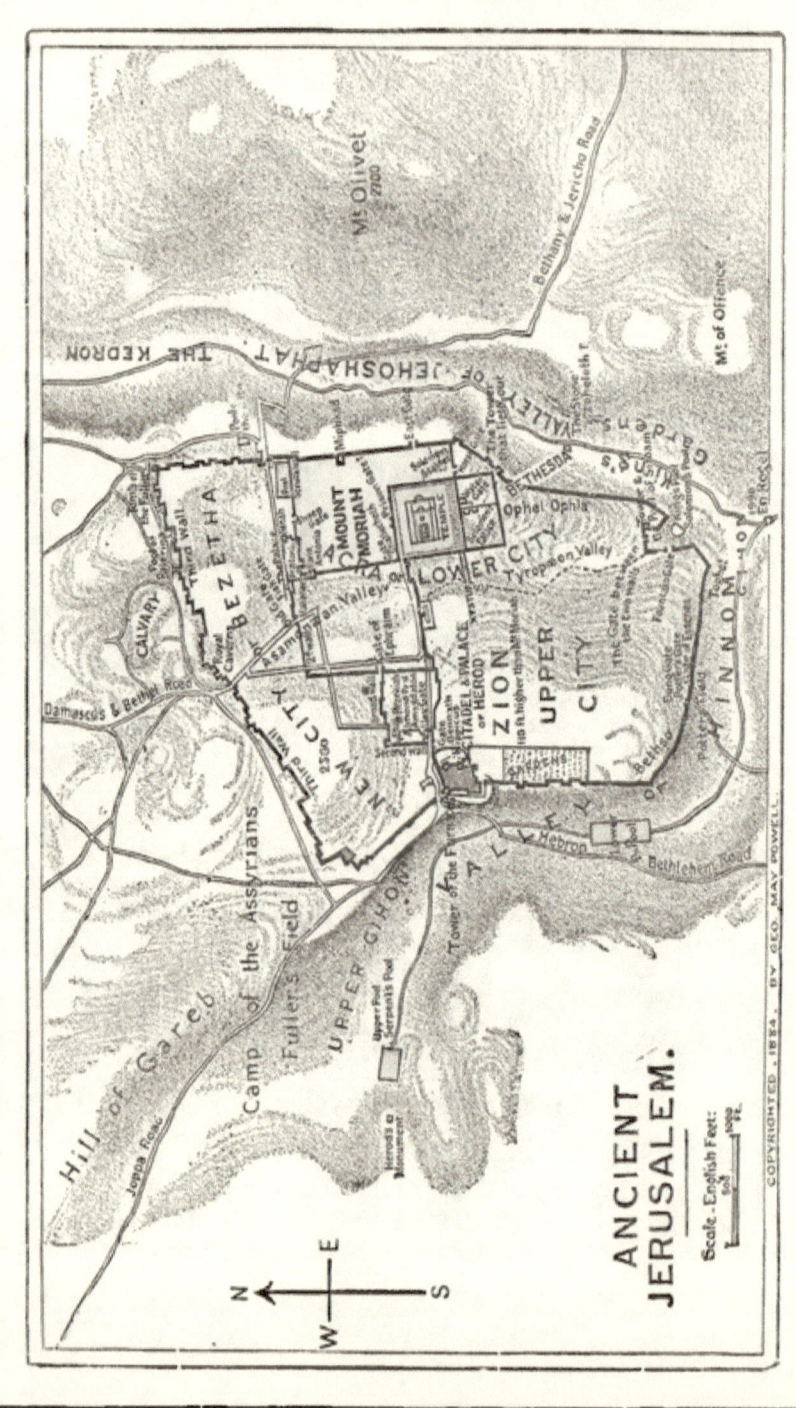

literature. The SPIRIT through the prophets (David and Isaiah especially), and apostles, adopted it as an impressive symbol of the security and blessedness of those under the reign of David's greater SON Is 40, 51, EZEK 40–8, REV 21.

JERUSALEM—"abode of peace," lat 32° N, 35° E from Greenwich, 19 m W from the mouth of the Jordan, is on a high rock, with four hills or heads, with a steep ascent on every side except the N. The soil is rocky, dry and barren round about. GEN 14: 18, where Melchizedek met Abraham, it is Salem. Next JOSH 10: 1 reads, "Adoni-zedek king of Jerusalem." (Adoni-zedek means lord of righteousness, Melchizedek, king of righteousness. It seems that the line of Jebusite kings took its name from their illustrious ancestor. He was both king and priest, and a type of our LORD HEB 7. The Rabbins say he was Shem). It seems that Jerusalem was from old time, the place of chief importance. JUDGES 19: 11, it is Jebus. Some think the name comes from Jebus and Salem, changed for euphony to Jerusalem.

JUD 1: 8, we read of Judah taking and burning it, though not able to take Zion, and Israelite and Jebusite dwelling together in the city v 21. JOSH 15: 63, JUD 19: 11, it is "city of the Jebusites." I SAM 17: 54, we read of David bringing the head of Goliath to Jerusalem.

When David took Zion from the Jebusites II SAM 5: 7, he assembled all Israel from "Shihor the brook of Egypt, to * * Hamath" I CHRON 13: 5, to bring the ark from Kirjath-Jearim, to place in the tent prepared for it 15: 1. Kirjath was 9 m N W of Jerusalem, and the ark had rested there from the day it was sent thither from Beth-Shemesh I SAM 7: 1, about 80 yrs before, (from the time the Philistines took it from Shiloh and death of Eli c 4).

The change of the royal residence and oracle (after a stop of 3 mos at the house of Obed Edom), to the "upper city," was an event of such importance as to cause great rejoicing to David and all Israel. Zion was called the City of David, and was thenceforth honored as the "place GOD should choose out of all the tribes to put his name there," **for** all to resort to worship. DEUT 12: 5, 14: 22, 16: 11, Ps 122. The Sweet Psalmist composed I CHRON 16: 8–22 (Ps 105: 1–15), Ps 68, 132, (and perhaps 24, 96, 105–6), commemorative of bringing up the ark. He says Ps 132: 6, " We **heard of** it at Ephrathah (Bethlehem), we found it in the fields of the wood" (mar *Jaar*, sing of Jearim. Kirjath-jearim is city of forests or groves. See I CHRON 13 : 5).

While Samaria or Shechem for example, would have been more convenient for assembling three times a year Ex 23 : 17, before the Lord, there were reasons (some re**vealed to** David no doubt), in favor of Jerusalem. Howbeit, GOD sanctioned the choice, so that it rose in **the time** of Solomon to be the most renowned city in the world.

GOD had rejected Ephraim (so long honored with his worship at Shiloh), for their failure, and chosen Judah instead. **See** the history recited in Ps 78: 9, 59–69. ZION—sunny mount (in connection with Solomon's temple which rose half **a mile N E**), was the glory of Israel. By *Synec'doche*, **it is put for** Jerusalem. It is associated with the most sublime and beautiful thoughts in the OLD and N TESTAMENTS, of GOD and **his** people. **It** has become the synonym of the church's strength, security and **perpetuity**, in her militant stage—wars, victories, defeats, **till CHRIST** shall come REV 14: 1.

It is the fairest type of MESSIAH's kingdom, and is used 59 times in the PSALMS and ISAIAH alone Her eclipse is celebrated in the most pathetic of inspired poems—LAMENTATIONS OF JEREMIAH, and her trials and triumphs are the experience of the body of CHRIST

"Till he come,"

to " sit on the throne of his glory " MATT 25 : 31. It was a new word, in **a** new, spiritual sense, of universal application, and adopted in the sacred annals, prose and poetry of all Christian lands.

By nature and art, she is the inspired symbol of beauty and strength.—" Beautiful in elevation, the joy of the whole earth, is Mount Zion * * * Walk about Zion, go round about her, tell the towers thereof, mark ye well her bulwarks, consider her palaces" Ps 48: 2–13.

It is the city of the great KING, where GOD is said to have his throne Ps 48, 132. In allusion to the typical king, it is made the seat of CHRIST's kingdom Ps 2: 6— "Yet have I set my KING upon my holy hill of Zion," and as emanating therefrom Is 59: 20, ROM 11: 26, * * "There shall come out of Zion the DELIVERER." And in allusion to CHRIST, Is 28: 16, says, "Behold! I lay in Zion * * * a precious corner stone." And "Out of Zion shall go forth the LAW" 2: 3.

Ideas of the blessedness of her inhabitants are given— "Her priests will I clothe with salvation, and her saints shall shout aloud for joy" Ps 132: 16. Is 35: 10, predicting the return of the exiles to "Zion," projects the event in spirit, and applies it to the GOSPEL and millenial times.

HEB 12: 22, Paul tells his Jewish converts in the SPIRIT they are not come to Sinai, but to "Mount Zion, to the city of the living GOD, the heavenly Jerusalem * * * and church of the first born which are enrolled in heaven."

>GLORIOUS things of thee are spoken,
>Zion, city of our GOD.   J. NEWTON.

No oriental traveller rests satisfied without seeing the holy city, and Christian and Mohammedan with Jew, regard Moriah as the spot which GOD chose for his house.

ZION (once DEUT 4: 48 for Hermon), is the southern and highest part of Jerusalem, rising 300 ft above the junction of the valleys Jehoshaphat and Hinnom, on the S 154, S W 104, and on the W 44 ft ab Hinnom. E is Ophel, the Tyropæon (cheesemaker's) valley between, deepening as it passess into Hinnom. The S end is without the wall, and according to MICAH 3: 12, is (to day) "ploughed as a field."

ACRA "the lower city" (a little lower than Zion), was N, and divided in David's time from Zion, by a wall.

MORIAH lay E of Acra, N. E. of Zion, connected with Zion

by a bridge and terrace. It occupies about one eighth of the city and is separated from Zion by the Tyropæon. Ophel, hill, mound, is a kind of continuation of Moriah, descending S toward Siloam over which it ends, from 40-50 ft high. Ophel is tilled, is "96 yds wide and 516 long." It was once an important point. See II CHRON 27 : 3.

The temple was built on Moriah, where Abraham is believed to have offered Isaac. The site was a rock, the threshing floor of Araunah (Ornan), the Jebusite king, and the spot chosen for David by direction of Gad, to offer sacrifice, to stay the destroying angel in the pestilence, II SAM 24. It cost about $2,000,000,000, was begun in the 4th and finished in the 11th year of Solomon's reign I KGS 6, II CHRON 3-5, was "exceeding magnifical, of fame and glory through all countries" I CHRON 22 : 5.

THE Taj Mahal—crown of edifices, built by Shah Jehan at the dying request of his favorite queen, Moomtaj-i-Mahal, as a monument of undying affection, is next to Solomon's temple, perhaps, the most beautiful building of any age. It is near Agra on the Jumna river, India. About 20,000 men were employed from 1630-1647. It is a masterpiece of genius and architectural loveliness. No lover of the pure and beautiful in art can read the description of the Taj and its surroundings (with engravg), without ideas and emotions in agreement with his ideal of a perfection not of mortals, and having the heart made better. See DR. BUTLER, in LAND OF VEDA, and L R, 1869.

N W of the temple was the fortress Antonia, built by Herod the Gt, and named after his Friend Mark Anthony. It was Pilate's court, called *Prætorium*. MATT 27.

BEZETHA—new city, lay N of Moriah and N E of Acra. Bezetha and Acra are not in the BIBLE. It looks like a country village. It was Herod ACTS 12, who extended the wall N, so as to form the "new city." Josephus says the wall was of stones, 10 cubits wide by 20 long.

Jerusalem varied in extent, but was largest when destroyed by Titus. The modern walls and towers were built by Sulieman in 1542. They are about 4½ m around, enclosing 210 acres and have 4 gates. The temple was

PLAN OF THE TEMPLE IN THE TIME OF CHRIST.

NORTH
N
WEST
EAST
SOUTH
A
B
C
D
E
F
G
H
I
J
K
L
M
O

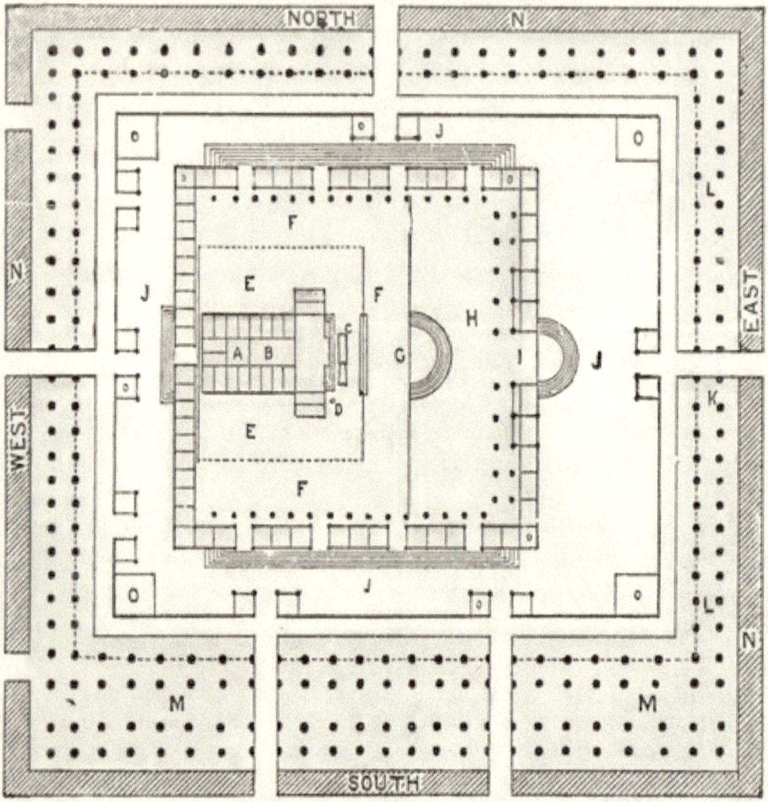

A. Holy of Holies. B Holy Place. C. Altar of Burnt Offering. D. Brazer Laver. E. Court of the Priests. F. Court of Israel. G. Gate Nicanor. H Court of the Women. I. Gate Beautiful. J. Court of the Gentiles. K. East or Shushan Gate. L. Solomon's Porch. M. Royal Porch. N. Outer Wall. O. Apartments for various uses.

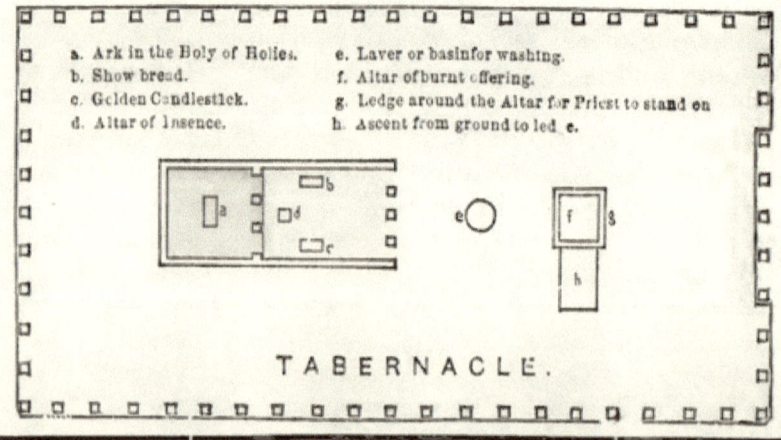

a. Ark in the Holy of Holies.
b. Show bread.
c. Golden Candlestick.
d. Altar of Insence.
e. Laver or basinfor washing.
f. Altar ofburnt offering.
g. Ledge around the Altar for Priest to stand on
h. Ascent from ground to ledge.
a
b
c
d
e
f
g
h
TABERNACLE.

under the smile of GOD only 34 yrs, when in the 5th of Jeroboam, Shishak carried off its treasures 972. "In the ruins at Karnak is seen sculptured *Joudmelek*—king of Judah, and Shishak at the head of his prisoners, commemorative of the event." In 826, Jehoash II KGS 14: 13, broke down "400 cubits" of the wall and pillaged the temple. After other profanations, it was burned by Nebuchadnezzar 584 II KGS 25, II CHRON 36.

The second was by Zerubbabel Ez 3. It was profaned by Antiochus Epiphanes 170. He slew 40,000, took 40,000 more as slaves, took "1800 talents of gold" out of the temple. Two yrs after, he sent Apollonius to massacre the males, and take the women and children captive. The daily sacrifice was taken away, the Sabbath, circumcision and LAW abolished, and their observance made a capital offence. It was rescued by Judas Maccabæus, 163, I Mac 4. See Pt III c V SEC 3.

Pompey in 63, took Jerusalem, massacred 12,000; and Crassus 12 yrs after, spoiled the temple.

About 16 yrs B. C, Herod the Gt (to court favor), began to rebuild the temple. He was a "man of magnificent tastes." 18,000 men were at work on it for nine yrs and a half. It was of white stones, with a roof of gold. The Jews continued to ornament and enlarge it, so that it had been (though not complete till a few yrs before destroyed), in the first of CHRIST's ministry, "forty and six years" in building JOHN 2: 20.

When the capital was taken, Titus tried to spare it. It was burned on the same day and month as the first—15 Lois (Aug) 73. It had no ark or mercy seat, Shekinah (divine presence), sacred fire, Urim and Thummim, nor prophetic spirit like the first. What a pretentious monument of worldly glory and pride, imitation of the true, the form without the power of godliness! Yet in *this* did the Jews *trust*, so that only when they beheld it burning, did they give up their hope of GOD's deliverance!

The arch of Titus has on it the golden candlestick, table of show bread, and trumpets to proclaim the jubilee, found in the temple. The Mosque of Omar built 636, now occupies the site of the temple.

Half a mile E of Moriah is **Mt** Olivet, rising 390 ft above the valley, 165 **above** Zion. The Kidron begins 2 m N W of the city, flows S a mile, then E and around the wall, and down the valley, into the Dead **Sea.** The valley of Jehoshaphat has been used as a burial place for 3000 yrs.

GETHSEMANE. On the side of Olivet, E of the temple, is where tradition locates this garden. It has a wall 150 by 160 ft about it, and 8 olive trees, scathed by tempests and gnarled with age. The monks tell us it was under this group that JESUS knelt. They are about 1000 yrs old, and probably the growth after those that witnessed our LORD's mysterious agony. The spot is retired, and endeared particularly to such as know the fellowship **of his suffering.** LYNCH.

The valley is Jehoshaphat JOEL 3: 2, 12, (mar, *the* LORD *judgeth*, or judgment of JEHOVAH). "Valley of decision" v 14, **seems** put for Jehoshaphat, where all nations v 2, 12, are to be gathered. It is from these **verses** that Jews, Mohammedans **and Catholics,** think the general judgment will be in this valley.

HINNOM **was** on the S, coming down till it united with Jehoshaphat. Here **Ahaz,** Manasseh and others sacrificed their children to Moloch. II KGS 16: 2, 3, 21: 1–6. It **was called** Tophet 23: 10, from tophet, a drum, used to **drown their cries.** Jeremiah **cursed the** place 7: 31. When Josiah reformed the religion, this valley was made the receptacle for filth and bodies of criminals II KGS 23: 10. Fires were **kept burning day** and night, and Hinnom thus became the **type of hell**—*gehenna* MATT. 5: 22.

When JESUS came to Olivet, Sunday, he wept over Jerusalem, and began to utter the series of retributive judgments culminating MATT 23, in seven woes against the "Scribes and Pharisees." And Tuesday on Olivet, after leaving their house "desolate," at the request of his disciples, he told them more fully 24 c, what GOD was about to do for their treatment of him.

He was taken from Gethsemane Thursday night to the palace of Annas on Acra, then to Caiaphas, (Sanhedrin on Zion), then to Pilate in Antonio, thence to Herod on Bezetha, back to Pilate, and thence led without the gate to Golgotha, where they crucified him.

To explain and illustrate how literal CHRIST's words MATT 24: 21, LUKE 21: 11, are, we give our readers extracts from a Jew who "held Iotopata in Galilee 47 days against Vespasian," and was afterwards in the siege—

A star like a sword hung over the city, and a comet a whole year. On the 8th of Nisan at the ninth hour of the night, a great light shone around the altar and holy house for half an hour. The Eastern gate which took 20 men to fasten, was opened the sixth hour of the night. On the 20 of Jyar before sunset, chariots and troops of soldiers were seen running about among the clouds, over the cities round about. At Pentecost, as the priests were going into the temple, a quaking came on them, and a great voice cried, Let us depart hence!! Some took these to be omens of good, but the wise, as tokens of evil. Jesus, a husbandman, 4 yrs before the war, coming to the feast, began to cry, A voice from the East, a voice from the West, * * from the 4 winds, from Jerusalem and the holy house, from the bridegroom, the bride and all the people! Day and night he cried in Jerusalem. He was beaten. Afterwards taken as one in a divine phrenzy, before the Procurator and beaten till the bones were bare. At every stroke he exclaimed Wo! Wo to Jerusalem! He kept on day and night during the siege, till on the walls a stone struck him.

Nearly 3000 towns and strongholds had been destroyed by Vespasian. Then John of Giscala, and after him (invited by some in hope of protection), Simon of Gadara, zealots and murderers, with their followers, got into the capital. These two factions fought each other, assassinated and plundered the citizens (joined by other fanatics and persons of their class), so that the city and temple were in a state of siege, while fear of death and suspicion began to fill the mind of the better class day and night, while the robbing and assassinating increased—a judgment of GOD, as some believed, for crucifying JESUS. Jew and gentile, priest and people, with them who came from abroad, were shot and killed while sacrificing, and the bodies of Greeks and barbarians mingled, lay around, their blood standing in lakelets in the temple courts.

Sedition, like a wild beast mad with hunger, eating its own flesh, was destroying Jerusalem. The noise of fighting and discord increased day and night, till the mourning and lamentation was heard above the noise of the strife. John robs the temple of its treasures, vessels and ornaments, for use or defence. So great is the distress, the citizens no longer mourn over or bury their relations. The sedition destroyed Jerusalem, and the Romans the sedition—a kindness compared to it.

THE SIEGE LASTED ABOUT 6 MOS. About 600,000 had come in to the passover. Then Titus came to Olivet with his legions and "eagles" MATT 24: 28. The fountains, and pool of Siloam had dried, but now flowed again, as if to help the Romans. The factions kept on killing from house to house, while a show of resistance was made. *Pseudo* prophets encouraged the people to expect deliverance. Famine begins. Parents snatch food from their children and children out of the mouth of parents. The feelings of modesty, justice and mercy are destroyed. People venture outside the walls for grass or offal, and these are snatched from them by others. Torture to extort food from the rich—where hid, was used, and others whipped and crucified. The heart sickens and eyes fill with tears at the recital. No city ever suffered such miseries, nor generation so degraded and wicked, since the world began.

Ons. JESUS had told the "daughters of Jerusalem" LUKE 23: 27, of this, while they led him forth to crucify.

After the trench and wall were made around the city, upper rooms, lanes and ways were choked with the dead bodies of men, women and children. Youth, age and beauty walked, and fell down black with famine. Silence dread and a deadly night seized the city, while the fanaticism within and against the Romans was at its height. Titus was moved with pity and offered a prayer over the city.

115,880 dead bodies in 2½ mos, were carried out of one gate. The dead were thrown over the walls also. Titus was told that 600,000 had been thrown out of the gates. During and after the siege, they were crucified till there were no more crosses nor space. The Romans in jest, nailing some of the fanatics in different ways—criss cross.

The city was taken on the 8th of Elul. 1,100,000 perished in the siege and 97,000 were taken alive. Jos Bk V.

The captives were sold for slaves, used in the conqueror's triumph, and to fight with beasts and men as gladiators.

About 60 yrs after, the Jews who returned were banished, and on pain of death forbidden to return, the temple site ploughed by Turnus Rufus and sown with salt. Titus had dug up the foundations Matt 24: 2. In 614 the Persians took the city, 90,000 Christians were slain. In 637 the Saracens conquered it till 1079, when the Turks took it. It has about 20,000, is a by word and reproach, "trodden down of the gentiles, till the times of the gentiles be fulfilled" Luke 21: 24.

Says Dr Olin, "The streets are only 8 or 10 feet wide, crooked, dirty, and some not named. The appearance of the city and inhabitants in public, is deceptive. Orientals unlike Europeans, take a pride in appearing abroad in their best clothes. But in most of the houses, one is displeased with the desolation, dirt and poverty. When one part becomes untenable, the occupants retire into another. While indifference, want of energy, due to the oppressive, deathly spirit of Mohammedanism, characterizes the people."

Obs. God in the geography as well as history of this land, is a subject of practical interest to us. The same providence is in operation in all time and places, proving from experience as from revelation, the sympathy and connection there is between nature and God's law. Paul Rom 8: 19-24, speaks of this sympathy, and Is 35, of this connection, in Christ's redemption. As one says of Ireland, a protestant county looks better than a catholic county. Happy Is. p 60.

Through the generations, so long as Israel kept their

LAW, the early and latter rains fructified hill and vale. When he backslid, the land became barren, as resenting the wrong. It is the smile of GOD that makes a land rejoice, his frown that makes it mourn.* The country and rocky portions (as some have seen exhibited in the "CYC OF JERUSALEM AND CRUCIFIXION"), impress one as being under the blast of GOD, while here and there a plant or shoot out of the crevices, reminds of him who in that region, was "like a tender plant and root out of a dry ground" Is 53 : 2.

After the destruction of Jerusalem, the Jews made Tiberias (S. W. of that lake), the seat of literature and religion.

"Sea" is often applied to great rivers. Nile is *sea* NAH 3: 8. The verse speaks of No-Ammon—Thebes, the ancient capital of Egypt, built on both sides of the Nile, 300 m from the Mediterranean. See Is 19: 5, 27: 1. JER 51 : 36, sea is Euphrates. The Nile is still called *el Bahr*—the sea.

The Jews called civilized nations Greeks ACTS 19 : 10, ROM 1: 16. "Barbarians" ACTS 28 : 2, is for a people of a strange speech, simply. The Greeks and Romans called other nations barbarians.

From LUKE 24 : 50, it would seem that JESUS led his disciples to Bethany, but from ACTS 1 : 12, ascended from Olivet. Bethany E of Olivet, included the mount adjacent as its "border," so the two authors are not inconsistent.

SEC 2 PHYSICAL GEOGRAPHY

Climate, weather, the seasons, etc, enlighten many portions of the BIBLE.

The heat in summer was intense. Many soldiers of Baldwin IVth's army died of heat at Shunem, where II KGS 4 : 20, the child died. CHRIST is as "the shadow of a great rock in a weary land." Is 32: 2.

In summer there was no rain, but the night dews were heavy, often wetting the traveller to the skin. It soon dried next morning Ps 133 : 3, Hos 6: 4. Philo says

* Bp Blythe of Jerusalem says, between 1841 and 1888, the number of Jews returning, has increased from 8000 to 70,000, and the latter rains withheld from the captivity, are returning.

there was no rain in Egypt. Hence, evidence of the miracle Ex 9: 18–26. The rainfall in Cairo is about 1½ inches a year. BUCKLEY.

OBS. The properties of water for cleansing, preventing and curing disease, are wonderful, but not known and appreciated as the CREATOR intended. It is not only its manifold virtues, that may explain why the SPIRIT employs it in the BIBLE as the symbol of his sanctifying, healing influence. The scarcity of living water in the East, makes the sign the more impressive and significant.

GOD *washed* the antediluvian world from the uncleanness of its inhabitants. Water was chosen for the sign of a new creature, in baptism. It was used by priest and people in temporal and spiritual things.

"In the wilderness shall waters break out, and streams in the desert" Is 35. "I will sprinkle clean water on you. From all your filthiness * * cleanse you" EZEK 36 : 25. JESUS at Jacob's well, and feast of tabernacles, uses water as the emblem of the baptism of the HOLY SPIRIT. And

"JESUS the water of life will give,
Freely to those who love him."

"Inasmuch as GOD has given water to drink, it must be better than any drink *man* has made."

The east wind is hurtful to vegetation. In winter, it is dry and cold ; in summer, dry and hot. It carries off the moisture of vegetation and withers it GEN 41 : 6, EZEK 17 : 10. Euraquilo—Levanter as sailors call it, which took the "ship of Adramittium" ACTS 27 : 14, was of this nature. The W wind brought showers LUKE 12 : 54 ; the S wind, heat v 55, and whirlwinds.

Caravans are sometimes buried under the sand by these dreadful winds. Connected with the hot, pestilential simoom, they are fatal. One says that in 1655, 4000, and in 1688, 20,000 persons were suffocated by two of them. Is 17 : 13, Hos 13 : 3, Is 32 : 2.

In summer, the nights are often as cold as in our March, and the days very hot GEN 31 : 40, JER 36 : 30, REV 7 : 16.

The BIBLE everywhere speaks of these phenomena whose laws are so mysterious, as under the control of the CREATOR JER 5 : 24, Ps 147 : 16, MATT 5 : 45, ACTS 14 : 17.

Wells are as valuable in the East as they are difficult to dig. Many are 160 or more feet deep, and some are only filled with rain water. Moses DEUT 6: 11, notices " cisterns " that Israel digged not, as a gift of GOD. Isaac and Abimelech's servants strove for wells. GEN 26. Jacob's well was " deep " Dr. Buckley says about " 3 yds across and 24 deep, filled up probably twice that depth." In 1697, one found it 105 feet deep. It was in the lot Jacob bought GEN 33, and gave 48: 22, on his death, to Joseph.

Travellers sometimes go 80 m without finding water. The mirage (*mirazh*) in the desert, the glowing, watery appearance of sand, is a symbol of disappointment JER 15: 18, mar. Is. 35: 7.

The " early " rains begin with the autumnal, and " latter," with the vernal equinox.

Israel crossed the Jordan in April, hence need of the miracle JOSH 3.

JESUS was crucified on the day the paschal lamb was killed and rose on the day of first fruits of early harvest— " First fruits of them that slept " I COR 15: 20.

3000 " out of every nation under heaven " were converted on Pentecost, the day the first fruits were brought to the temple ACTS 2: 5.

That feast of tabernacles prefigured, when *all* will be gathered, is yet to come.

" What a gathering that will be
At the sounding of the glorious jubile ! "

On GEOG AND HISTY of the BIB, HIBBARD'S PALESTINE is first class. Also HAND BK of BIB GEOGRAPHY, by G H WHITNEY D D.

CHAPTER VII.

INTERPRETATION OF ALLEGORIES, TYPES, PARABLES, SYMBOLS.

THE SCRIPTURES, written to the thought of man and succession of the ages, have in them infinite springs and streams of doctrine to water the church. BACON, ADVANCT OF LEARNING.
Our LORD teaches by parables rather than by the commonplaces of morality. SIR PHILIP SYDNEY.

IN seeking the sense of SCRIPTURE, we have thus far had to do with the meaning of the *words*. Hitherto, the verbal sense has been regarded as the BIBLE. In the above modes however, there is an allegorical or spiritual meaning also, for which we now give rules.

1 Seek for the one truth intended, and then compare or explain the other parts of the allegory, parable etc, in harmony with it.

Exs. The scope or purpose of Ps 80 is suggested in v 17. In parables it is often given, as MATT 22 : 14—many called but few chosen; LUKE 18 : 1, "And he spoke a parable * * * always to pray and not to faint."
Sometimes we turn to parallel passages, as LUKE 15 : 3. MATT 18 : 12—"a hundred sheep."
Sometimes we rely on the occasion or subject, as LUKE 13 : 6—the barren fig tree, or c 15—prodigal son, for the moral.
CANTICA, one continuous allegory, seems to teach the love there is subsisting between CHRIST and his members.

We are not to expect agreement between the words and things employed, and lesson, in every particular. In the figures, while there is but one meaning, there are in the allegorical portions two—a literal and spiritual sense.

Exs of wrong interpretation. In the good Samaritan, some explain the traveller to mean the natural man; priest and Levite, the moral and ceremonial law; inn, the church. In the prodigal son the ring, the everlasting love of GOD; younger son, man as a sinner, because after man as righteous; citizen, a legal preacher; swine, self-righteous persons; husks, works of righteousness; fatted calf, CHRIST; shoes, upright conversation; music and dancing, the GOSPEL.

1 We are taught, as said, to interpret according to the analogy of faith, comparing SCRIPTURE with SCRIPTURE.

2 We are not to find anything not agreeing with inspired teaching. Nor bring a sense into the WORD whose germ is not found there.

Exs. The high priest offered HEB 5, for his own sin, and then for the people. It does not follow that CHRIST had any sin to offer for. Nor because Dives prayed to Abraham, are we to supplicate glorified saints. Nor does LUKE 15:7, say that the Pharisees were righteous persons, needing no repentance. So David was in his office and descent a type of CHRIST, but not in his sins.

3 We are not to use allegorical portions as teaching, but illustrating doctrines.

Exs. From the ten virgins, we are not to think half will be saved and half lost. In the parable of the lost sheep, one in 100 went astray; in the ten pieces of silver, one was lost. "These parables —the lost sheep, pieces of silver and prodigal son, are designed to show how GOD receiveth sinners." WESLEY.

By the "man who had not on a wedding garment" MATT 22:11, CHRIST by the finger of GOD, seems to point out the self-righteous Pharisee. So WHEDON.

PARABLES OF THE O T.

Jotham's—trees making a king	JUD 9
Nathan's—the poor man's lamb	II SAM 12
Two brothers striving	II " 14
Prisoner escaping	I KGS 20
Micaiah's vision	I " 22
Thistle and cedar	II " 14
The vineyard	Is 5

Parables of the Gospels.

The sower	....	Matt	13, Mark 4, Luke 8
" tares	....	"	13
" mustard seed	....	"	13, Mark 4, Luke 13
" leaven	....	"	13 : 33, Luke 13 : 20
" net	....	"	13 : 47
" hidden treasure	....	"	13 : 44
" pearl of gt price	....	"	13 : 45
" lost sheep	....	"	18 : 12, Luke 15 : 4
" unforgiving servant	....	"	18 : 23, " 7 : 41
" man and two sons	....	"	21 : 28
" wicked vine dresser	....	"	21 : 33
" ten virgins	....	"	25
" feast	....	"	22 : 1, Luke 14 : 16
" laborers and vineyard	....	"	20 : 1
" talents	....	"	25 : 14, Luke 19 : 12
" wedding garment	....	"	22 : 11
" good Samaritan	....	Luke	10 : 33
" friend on his journey	....	"	11 : 5
" barren fig tree	....	"	13 : 6
" strife for place at feasts	....	"	14 : 7
" tower, and king going to war		"	14 : 28
" lost piece of money	....	"	15 : 8
" prodigal son	....	"	15 : 11
" unjust steward	....	"	16 : 1
" rich man and Lazarus	....	"	16 : 19
" importunate widow	....	"	18 : 1
" Pharisee and publican	....	"	18 : 9
" true vine	....	Jno	15

The rules employed for allegories and parables apply to the historical Scriptures also. The Jews were related to Jehovah e g, as the church and each Christian is now. Their bondage, deliverance, wanderings 40 yrs, entry into Canaan, all prefigured Christian experience. I Cor 10, Heb 4: 1, I Pet 2: 10.

Also the relation of Israel to the heathen was typical of Christ's kingdom and its foes. Sodom, Ishmael, Egypt and Babylon, have their representatives in the true Israel. Gal 4: 25, Rev 14: 8.

Again, while Israel as the son represented our Lord, so eminent ones among them as Moses, Joshua, David and

Solomon, were types of him. And hence, expressions used of the type, are applied to CHRIST as antitype. Hos 11: 1, MATT 2: 15, compare.

Also the rites and worship of the people were "copies of the things in the heavens" HEB 9: 23, "the shadow of good things to come" 10: 1. The substance is CHRIST.

Thus from the beginning, there has been a connective series, adumbrating the coming of MESSIAH and his reign. "The O T," as Augustine says, "is the NEW veiled, and the NEW is the O T unveiled."

In interpretation of the typical and also historic SCRIPTURES in their spiritual allusions, we use the same rules as in the allegorical portions—compare the type or history with the general truth, type and antitype embody; expect agreement in some things, let each part harmonize with the whole, and Scriptural teaching elsewhere.

The writers do not destroy the historical sense to establish the spiritual, as some readers do; nor find a hidden meaning in the words, as the Jews; but in the *facts*, so easy and natural, confining to things of practical importance HEB 5: 11, 9: 5. In quotations out of the O T e g, they have reference to the history, office, character and doctrines of CHRIST and his Church.

As these rules have been much abused by Jews and Christians, some illustrations may interest the reader—

Exs. GEN 1, in the Heb for *created*, some Jews find their first letter for FATHER, SON and HOLY SPIRIT, and so infer the doctrine of the trinity. Ps 21: 1, in *shall joy*, they find by transposing, MESSIAH, and so refer it to him.

Some have allegorized by destroying the facts.

Exs. John Baptist is only a mythic representation of the prophets in their relation to our LORD. The seven days of creation are not real—simply teach the perfection of GOD's work.

Again, many have refined on the WORD, admitting the historic truth, but basing on every part a doctrine, as if intended by the HOLY SPIRIT.

Exs. The division of animals into clean and unclean, taught virtue

ALLEGORIES, TYPES, PARABLES, ETC. 153

and vice in man. Heaven and earth in the LORD's prayer, says Tertullian, refer to our soul and body. The 5 loaves JNO 6: 9 says Clement, are the 5 senses. Justin, that Jacob's wrestling with the angel and hurt, refer to CHRIST's temptation and death on the cross. Athanasius expounds MATT 5: 29, teaching that the body is the church; the hands and eyes, Bishops and deacons, who ought to be cut off if offending. Hilary, that the mother of Zebedee's children means the LAW; the children, the believing Jews. Cyril, that Malchus, whose ear Peter cut off, was a type of the Jews, who were deprived of right hearing.

Such interpretations came from ignoring or treating the literal, historic sense lightly, regarding the allegorical or spiritual sense only, as worthy an enlightened mind. Hence, Origen taught that creation, Lot's incest, Abraham's two wives, Jacob's Rachel and Leah, are allegorical—mythic story!

How do wrong premises lead to wrong conclusions! Such examples were copied among the sects in the early church, and thus the meaning of much of the BIBLE with the lessons intended, was either obscured or denied. Intelligent piety will reject such modes of teaching as the result of a vagrant, morbid fancy, and rightly take in the sense the divine wisdom intends.

OBS. THE BELIEF and tradition from time immemorial, that the "millennium" REV 20: 1–3, will begin at the end of 6000 yrs, has support from analogy of SCRIPTURE, is a pleasing view, inspiring to faith and Christian workers in "desiring (hastening) the coming of the day of GOD" II PET 3: 12, has a boom in our hearts and signs of the times, and comes in here.

These thousand years bring a * * * lasting immunity from outward evils and affluence of blessings. Such a time the world has not yet seen. It is followed by the loosing of Satan, who is soon thrown with the beast and false prophet, into the lake of fire. In a short time, those who assert that these things are at hand, will appear to have spoken the truth. The binding and loosing of Satan will be in the invisible world. WESLEY on REV 20. See also WHEDON.

In the creation of the world in six days and appointment of the seventh day—sabbath, (considering the typical nature of everything in the O T), there is much in favor of this view, strengthened by the lessons of the Sabbatic year and general jubilee LEV 25.

In both TESTAMENTS "One day is with the LORD as a thousand years and a thousand years as one day;" day seeming to be in allusion to "day" in creation GEN 1.

As GOD finished all his work in six "days" and ordained the seventh to be a day of rest to the end of time, so this view implies that there are to be six thousand years, and the seventh thousand, to be a Sabbatic age.

Sabbath means rest, perfection etc., and is the expressive type of CHRIST's reign on earth. The seven days—week, is a complete circle or portion of time, the seventh reminding of the "Sabbath rest" HEB. 4 : 9, the millennium.

This view regards the creation and Sabbath as intended to be a pattern and type of the duration and end of this, our earthly stage. This has further evidence, when considered in connection with the Sabbatic year and jubilee. (It is instructive that SCRIPTURE is silent as to whether at any period the people were obedient, in their observance.) Also, there may have been more in these institutions than is known to us. Both of these ordinances are from the order of creation and Sabbath, both years of rest (slaves were freed and lands reverted to their owners), and spiritual things, and both foreshadowed CHRIST's reign.

CHAPTER VIII.

PROPHECY, INTERPRETATION OF.

HISTORY is to us the interpreter of prophecy ; but to the Israelite, prophecy was rather the interpretation of history, giving notice of coming events. DAVISSON.

THE prophetic SCRIPTURES have come to us in oriental style—abounding in figurative words, allusions to the customs, worship etc, of their times.

As to time, the prophets (often called seers and their

revelations visions, II CHRON. 9: 29, NAHUM 1: 1), speak of the future as present.

"Unto us a child is born." Is 9: 6.

2 *They speak* of the future as past.

In Is 53, much of the work and suffering of CHRIST are spoken of as past. The prophet in spirit, stands between his death and coming glory.

3 They describe events as continuous when order of time is not revealed. They saw the future in space rather than time, and foreshortened ; or as one ignorant of astronomy groups and speaks of the stars—as they *seem* to him.

" As in perspective, a range of hills seems like a range of distant mountains, so prophecy sometimes speaks of events; some as nigh, and others on the distant horizon."

In Is. 10 the deliverance from the Assyrians is connected 11, with the coming of MESSIAH.

Isaiah, Micah, Hosea, Ezekiel and Jeremiah connect these two events, yet without intimating MESSIAH was to take part in both.

Joel synchronizes Pentecost and effusion of the HOLY SPIRIT in after times. 2: 28.

In the humiliation and glory of MESSIAH, there is scarce any notice (as in ZECH. 9: 9, 10), of the ages between.

Sometimes the date is shown, as the sojourn in Egypt, 430 yrs GEN. 15: 13. The 65 yrs Is. 7: 8, in which Israel was to be broken.

Again, events are blended, as the latter parts of Isaiah and MATT. 24: 28-9, where JESUS foretells the destruction of Jerusalem and day of judgment.

As to language. If prophecy had been given in literal style, it would have defeated its object.

It would have prevented fulfilment, or if fulfilled, weakened faith in its divine original.

As earthly, are images of spiritual things, so is the whole Jewish economy. Language therefore, borrowed from nature and the LAW, is as appropriate as it is necessary.

Thus MESSIAH (after the reign of Saul), is to be king, and possessed of the most exalted regal attributes, being sometimes called David, who himself was an ideal of kingly authority. HOS 3: 5, JER 30: 9, Acts 13: 34. His kingdom is to be the perfection of the Theocracy, and is called Jerusalem or Zion. Is 62: 1, 6, 60:

15-20, GAL 4 : 26. As prophet and priest, he is spoken of in the highest strains. Ps 110. The glory of his days is compared to the prosperity of David and Solomon. ZECH 3 : 10, 1 KGS 4 : 25. Note the connection.

Such figurative language is found through all the dispensation, beginning with Abraham. His children were to be as the stars of heaven, and all nations blessed in him. Ex 32 : 13, ROM 4 : 16, GAL 3 : 16.

Next comes the deliverance from bondage, and in connection, remarkable expressions of favor GOD bore to them; all of which in the N T, are applied to the Church.

GOD *chose* them DEUT 10 : 15, EPH 1 : 4. *Delivered* and *saved* Ex 3 : 8, GAL 1 : 4. *Created* and *called* Is 43 : 1, COL 3 : 10. Both are *sons* and *dear* EZEK 16 : 3, I PET 1 : 3. *Brethren* DEUT 1 : 16, COL 1 : 2. *Fellow citizens* with *aliens* around EPH 2 : 19, and both *heirs* to the *inheritance* NUMB 26, HEB 9 : 15. Compare in this way "servants," "husband," "wife," "mother," "children," "adultery," "priests," "saints," "holy," "shepherd," "flock" etc, under the two dispensations, and the duties and privileges implied.

In the first, the relations and blessings are temporal; but under the GOSPEL, spiritual and eternal.

Next comes the LAW—ritual, sacrifices, priesthood, mercy-seat, tabernacle, temple and worship. These are by the prophets spoken of as restored in the latter days; but in the GOSPEL, each expression is used of our LORD or his church. CHRIST is priest, propitiatory, tabernacle (*skana*), and temple (*naos*) JOHN 1 : 14, 2 : 19; as, since his ascension, is his church I COR 3 : 16, "a royal priesthood, a holy nation" I PET 2 : 9.

The next (prophetic) era, revives with Samuel beginning the kingdom. To David is foretold that his line should have the throne forever—to the end of the kingdom literally; and spiritually (in the person of his SON), to the end of time. Of *this* sense Samuel says nothing, nor Nathan. But David understands, and applies it in part, to himself I KGS 2 : 4; but its fulness to his LORD Ps 2, 72, 110. All these PSALMS are HEB 1 : 5, ROM 1 : 4, referred to CHRIST's birth, resurrection and kingdom.

This era is closed with Amos, Hosea, Isaiah and later

prophets. Their theme is the restoration of GOD's people and worship, and in a twofold form they speak of it. Those before and in the captivity, speak of a restoration, and borrow from it terms descriptive of a new kingdom. Haggai and Zech foretell the second temple, and under that figure, the church. Under the second temple, worship was selfish and insincere. *Ichabod* was written on Judaism, and Malachi speaks of the ONE who should come and "purify the sons of Levi" SEE HAG, ZECH, MAL, Pt III c V.

As the Jews foreshadowed the church, so prophecy, the experience of both.

The first and proximate sense was limited to and by the O T times; but the second or application, was immeasurable in purpose and duration.

To David e g, the promises of perpetuity and good, as " I will establish * * his kingdom *forever*. * * If he commit iniquity, I will chastise him * * but my mercy shall not depart from him as * * from Saul" II SAM 7 : 13–15, were conditional and absolute; conditional to David, but to CHRIST absolute. The condition is repeated I KGS 2 : 4, 9 : 4. The "forever" to David meant about 400 yrs and through 20 of his line (Revolted Israel it may be noticed, lasted but 254 yrs, had 19 kings from nine different families). The "forever" therefore, is absolutely intended for Great David's greater SON, of whose glory and worth, all types are inadequate to speak.

Interspersed with the typical, are prophecies of universal application. As, " The curse of the LORD is in the house of the wicked, but he blesseth the habitation of the righteous" PROV 3 : 33. "Say ye of the righteous * * well with him, for they shall eat the fruit of their doings. Woe unto the wicked" etc. Is 3 : 10. In such teachings—promises and threatenings, the prophecies abound and are repeatedly fulfilled. Thus as Abp Leighton says, "The sweet stream of prophecy did, as rivers in dry places, make its own banks fertile and pleasant, as it ran on and flowed forward to after ages."

Ons. To the humble, trusting soul, "JEHOVAH-*jireh*" GEN 22: 14, is as new and living as to Abraham. To the spiritual mind, the two marginal notes in R V, add suggestional interest.

Such being the structure of prophecy, the following rules of interpretation are suggested—1 *Ascertain* the prophet's place in relation to his time and predictions—

As each was a messenger in and for his own times, so from the circumstances of his people, he borrowed his imagery; and to the state of the country around as existing or foreseen, he adapted his message. Take your place at his side, and look with him on the past and future. If the land lay desolate around him, realize its condition. If he be in vision in GOSPEL day, get with him at the birth or death of CHRIST, or in his kingdom.

To understand ISAIAH e g, read II KGS 14-21, II CHRON 16-22.

2 *Distinguish* between literal and figurative language.

From the words themselves Is 11: 15, 16, 4: 5, ZECH 10: 11. Here the figures are in allusion to early events in Israel.

From the context.

To explain Is 66: 20 literally, requires that 21, 23 vs be so too, thus re-establishing the Jewish worship, which is inconsistent with HEB 10. In EZEK 47, the stream of water from the temple, prefigures the GOSPEL.

Parallel passages

In Is 11, MESSIAH is spoken of as a prince of peace, but c 9 speaks of his wars and victories. Parallel passages and the N T, explain the nature of the peace and war of c 9 to be spiritual.

3 *It is a golden rule,* that as prophecy is not self-interpretative—of private interpretation II PET 1: 20, predictions should be compared with others on the same topic, and history, profane and sacred.

Instances of fulfilled prophecy from history are given CH IV PROPHECY, and PT II c VI, JERUSALEM.

4 *As the* N T gives the meaning of the OLD in part, so it also suggests rules applicable to all, of which we notice but one, suggested in almost every chapter.

The great theme of prophecy is CHRIST and his kingdom, some of which is fulfilled, some fulfilling and some future.

PROPHECY, INTERPRETATION OF.

In Paradise, it foretold a REDEEMER. In Abraham, it connected the covenants of Canaan and CHRIST. In the LAW, foreshadowed the "Prophet" and doctrines of Christianity. To David, the kingdom of his SON. In the later prophets, the change from Moses to MESSIAH, and destiny of the nations. After the exile, it gives clearer light on the change from Judaism. JESUS brings life and immortality to light in the GOSPEL, and in the APOCALYPSE, he signifies in dark, symbolic words to John, the history of his church "Till he come."

"The testimony of JESUS is" truly, "the spirit of prophecy." JOHN 5 : 39, ACTS 3 : 18, 10 : 43, ROM 1 : 2, 3 : 21, REV 19 : 10.

This fact proves and illustrates the general scope of ancient predictions and limits them, teaching us to seek CHRIST everywhere, under both dispensations.

While most interpreters agree in the above teachings, they differ in their application; one class viewing them in a more spiritual light than the other.

POINTS OF AGREEMENT

1 All admit the literal fulfilment of predictions in our LORD'S advent, as riding upon an ass ZECH 9 : 9, casting lots on his vesture Ps 22 : 18, Grave with the wicked and rich Is 53 : 9.

2 *Most agree* as to the literal fulfilment of prophecies in the history of the Jews and other nations. And while both sides alike use this as evidence of SCRIPTURE, one uses it also as a rule of interpretation for prophecy *to be fulfilled*.

3 *As to the scheme* of prophecy, most agree there are two centers or eminences from which it radiates, and around which the destinies of this world and the church revolve, and may be surveyed—the advent of our LORD to suffer, and his advent to reign (millennium); followed after the "little time" Rev 20 : 3, by the judgment.

4 *The conversion* of the Jews and prevalence of truth spoken of in both TESTAMENTS, ending in the final overthrow of CHRIST'S enemies, are admitted by most. Some from both sides add the return of the Jews to Palestine.

The spiritual blessings foretold are, by both parties, applied to the church, and the reign of CHRIST to be *visible*, affecting all human relations. So far, there is substantial agreement.

Points of difference

The above then in brief, is what one class finds. Finding that the Jews were types, and distinction ("middle wall") between them and the gentiles abolished, and our dispensation spiritual; and that predictions if read literally, would restore Judaism and a system only to the church's infancy; and that they are not repeated in the N T, and that predictions of them as a nation are referred to the church, or their conversion Acts 2 : 17-21, Rom 11 : 26, they conclude the spiritual sense to be the design of the series—the mind of the Spirit.

The other class agree to much of this, deeming it however, not the whole truth. Inasmuch as the Jews in both Testaments are spoken of as beloved for their father's sake, and that prophecies as Is 11 : 12, Hos 3 : 5, Zech 14 e g, inapplicable to, or written after the first return, remain unfulfilled, and cannot be applied to the church without violating the rules of language; that prophecies seeming to have early fulfilments in Jewish history or the church as Is 13 : 9, 10, 25 8, Hag 2 : 6, in the N T, seem also referred to as future Matt 24, I Cor 15 : 54, Heb 12 : 26, they conclude that much remains to be fulfilled in a literal and more extended sense. They hold the principle of literal interpretation, whether it applies to the restoration of the Jews, Christ's *pre*-millennial advent, or establishment of his reign.

To give our readers a better idea of this view, we tabulate the part relating to the *Jews* (omitting most of the texts), as found in Isaiah, Ezekiel, Jeremiah, Daniel, the minor prophets and Revelation.

They are to be gathered and brought to Palestine Is 11 : 11, 27 : 12, 13.

Be carried by the gentiles, who shall join with them and be one Is 49 : 22, 14 : 2, 66 : 18, 20.

Miracles wrought when Israel is restored; as

> Drying up of Euphrates Is 11 : 15, 16, Rev 16 : 12,
> Rivers in desert places   " 41 : 17–19,
> Christ as their head   " 52 c.

Have judges and counselors, with Christ their king, who is also acknowledged by the heathen Is 1 : 26, 60 : 17.

They are to rule over all nations Is 11 : 13, 14, 14 : 1, 2.

Live peaceably, be numerous, prosperous, a blessing to all the world Is 11 : 13, 14, 14 : 1, 2.

Land again to be fruitful Is 29 : 17, 35 c.

Jerusalem rebuilt, never to be destroyed Is 26 : 1, 52 : 1.

Wars and desolation just before Is 34, Ezek 28 : 25–6.

The other class, regarding the Jews and prophetic language as typical, think such Scriptures to have reference to the first return, or return of Christ after his first advent, or the time Rom 11 : 26, when "all Israel shall be saved" and adopt that system their LAW prefigured.

A synopsis from Bickersteth's tables may illustrate this view.

As the times of the gentiles are passing away, their power is broken, many having been converted Rev 7 : 9–14, Rom 11 : 25–32. The Jews are visibly recalled Dan 9, Ezek 20, Is 62. Are restored to favor, and their own land Ezek 36, Is 11 : 11, persecuted by gentiles under the last antichrist Ezek 38 : 1–16.

Soon, signs in the sun and stars appear Matt 24 : 29, and sign of the Son of man 24 : 29, 30.

Christ raises his dead, changes his living, who rise with him in the air Matt 24 : 31, I Cor 15 : 51–4.

The wild beast and kings combine against Christ Rev 16 : 14, 19 : 19.

He pours judgment on antichrist, pleading with all flesh by fire and sword Rev 19 : 10–21, 15 : 1.

This dispensation is discriminating, purifying I Cor 3 : 12–15, Mal 3 : 3. The fire and tribulation have a crisis at the beginning Ezek 38 : 22, 39 : 6, Is 66 : 15, 16, also at the end of the millennium Dan 12 : 1, Rev 19 : 20, 20 : 9.

Christ descends on Olivet, Zech 14 : 4, 5, welcomed by Israel Zech 12 : 10–14, Acts 3 : 19–21. Satan bound, and the millennium begins Rev 11 : 18, 20 : 4, 6, Dan 7 : 18, 27. Rebellion still in the world, Satan loosed Rev 20 : 9. Final judgment Rev 20 : 10–15.

New heavens and earth, the new Jerusalem descends from heaven, and the saints reign forever Rev 21 : 10–15.

"Lo! he comes with clouds descending

* * * * *

Halleluiah!
God appears on earth to reign."

That the *details* as *above* are to be fulfilled in their order, is neither agreed, nor contended for.

Christ and the inspired writers speak of his "coming" in different forms, ways etc.

At birth—in the flesh John 16 : 28, I John 4 : 2, 3.
Beginning his ministry Matt 3 : 11.
In any great interposition Rev 2 : 15, 16.
Pentecost John 14 : 18. Destruction of Jerusalem, Matt 24 : 27.
To judgment Matt 16 : 27.

His reign began after his resurrection and Pentecost Mark 9 : 1, Heb 1 : 5. And "he must reign till he hath put all his enemies under his feet" I Cor 15 : 25.

It is not for us to decide on the merits of either of the above systems. The reader will do that. We simply mark the points of agreement. The spirituality and blessedness of Christ's reign are common to both. The difference is rather in the mode or accompaniments. And in respect to these, we commend the reader to the disclosures of the N T and rules sanctioned in its "quotations" Pt III c III.

In prophecy, it is generally agreed that where years are not mentioned, days are for years. This rule is founded on analogy. See Numb 14 : 34, Ezek 4 : 5, 6, where God appoints "each day for a year."

Again, "Time, times and half a time" seems to mean three and a half prophetic yrs of 360 prophetic days—1260 yrs, the period for the rise and fall of antichrist Dan 7 : 25. See Rev 11 : 2, 3, where the same period seems meant—1260 days or 42 months. In Gen 15 : 13, 400, Ex 12 : 40. 430 yrs (the sojourn in Egypt), the 65 Is 7 : 8, the 70 of the exile, and the 70 weeks Dan 9 : 24, when Messiah was to be cut off, the time is given.

As said (*vide* Chronology), God has permitted uncertainty as to the past, as he veils the "times" and "seasons" future, from us, applies to prophecy as well. Prophecy assures us of his purpose, and lays down prognostics of what he will do; adding, the wicked shall not, but the wise (marg teachers), shall understand, DAN 12: 10. Even in fulfilled prediction, the dates are often uncertain, suggesting modesty in setting the time of coming events.

EX. While *we* begin the exile with the carrying away of Daniel 606, and end with the decree of Cyrus II CHRON 36: 57, 22, EZ 1, some date from the burning of the temple to the decree of Darius, II CHRON 36: 14-21, EZ 6.

IN CON. The subject of this section is fruitful, and suggestive of sublime and beautiful ideas of the glory—the character and attributes of GOD, as the MAKER and RULER of the natural and moral world. His omniscience and prescience are opened to our view. Foregleams of his plan and purpose, impress us. Fore-known are all things to him, good and evil, down the stream of time to eternity. And all events are present and certain, without alternations of time or contingency of happening, as with us, through the conflict of the ages. And that without any decree affecting our own responsibility.

2 It suggests that he knows what is in our heart, what we will be and do, and has judged already, to give us according to our ways; yet in such manner as not to interfere with our free agency. This thought, in connection with the doctrine that the hearts of all men are in his hands, is an inspiration to the faith that overcomes, to live in GOD's order, and SPIRIT of JESUS, in order to get the desire of our heart fulfilled.

"Whate'er we hope, *by faith we have*,
Future and past subsisting *now.*"

3 The prophet was also a teacher of his times as well as a revealer of the future. Hence in the N T, their successors, the apostles, are called prophets, and their preaching "prophesying." ACTS 13: 1, Barnabas and others at Antioch, are called "prophets and teachers" In ACTS and the EPISTLES, to preach is the same as to prophesy. "The

spirit of prophecy " and office culminated, and has its ideal, in the person and revelation of JESUS *our* PROPHET. So after the SPIRIT was poured out on Pentecost, JOEL 2: 28. quoted by Peter ACTS 2: 18, the apostles, even "servants and handmaidens," prophesied. So Philip's four daughters, ACTS 21: 9, "did prophesy." While the apostles and others had the gift of foretelling things future, ending perhaps with John, it does not seem so much to have been lost, but blended with—merged in the clearer light of GOSPEL day; dispensing with its ancient form.

> Come HOLY GHOST, for moved by thee
> The prophets wrote and spoke;
> Unlock the truth, thyself, the key,
> Unseal the sacred BOOK.   C. WESLEY.

PART III.

CHAPTER I.

SYSTEMATIC AND INFERENTIAL STUDY.

No science is more inductive than theology. The BIBLE is a record of words and facts, and it is our duty to analyze, reducing them by a method inductive, into order, and then deducing—gathering, the general truth.   BP OF KENTUCKY.

SEC 1   DOCTRINES.

THE texts of SCRIPTURE form the basis of theology, as the facts in nature do in natural science. While the inductive philosophy is used in both, in revelation there is a guiding light for systematizing and inference, not found in nature.

The systematic study of the BIBLE differs from interpretation, as systematic theology does from the meaning of the words.

DOCTRINES. 165

Truth is revealed in the form of doctrine, precept—command, promise and example. Doctrine (what is taught), implies command; this promise, and both duty corresponding.

Now the careful student will not only classify doctrines, under their respective forms; but the various forms under their respective SCRIPTURE truths also. It is in finding the true sense and assigning to every part—every truth and duty its place in order, according to its importance, so that each will honor the rest, that makes the true *system* of *divinity*.

When we say doctrine implies precept, we state an important truth. Doctrine embodies command, and is by GOD intended to enlighten, convict of sin, and lead to holy living. Many put asunder what GOD has thus joined, or explain truth so as to weaken its effect on the conscience—making void the LAW, or "hold down the truth in unrighteousness."

While there are a few partial summaries of truth as EPH 2: 4-10, TIT 2: 11-14 in the BIBLE, so that one may gather in part a system of sound doctrine, yet without systematic study, it tempts us to overlook the proportion and connection of doctrines; the more dangerous when a part (as noticed c VI. SEC. 2, OBS), is taken to be, or taught for, the whole truth. Getting and resting in favorite doctrines unduly, is one cause of so many weak, cranky people, and "wood, hay, stubble" in GOD's building. Our spiritual man is so constituted (made in the image of GOD), as to require the *whole* truth as in both TESTAMENTS, for its satisfaction and perfection. SEE COL 3: 10.

SCRIPTURE may be studied to ascertain its doctrines, or its rules of morality and holiness. The system of doctrine thus framed is *dogmatic*—doctrinal, and the system of duty, moral or *practical theology*. The articles of our creed may illustrate the first, and both are interwoven in our BIBLE and religious experience.

RULES FOR FRAMING A SYSTEM.

This is done by gathering all the texts on the same subject under one head; then compare, restrict and explain the whole consistently.

1 *As said*, the N T is the key to the O T mysteries chiefly.

2 AMBIGUOUS, figurative or unexplained portions, are illuminated by those that are clear, literal or enlarged on.

3 *As* SCRIPTURE does not contradict itself, explain doctrines consistently.

Ex. Repentance, faith, obedience, are the gift of GOD ACTS 5:31. Yet the guilt of impenitence is charged to us MATT 11:20, 21, and not to obey, the ground of condemnation JOHN 3:18. So the gift implies the gracious ability, and our responsibility.

4 *Explain* and *apply* doctrines to the purpose intended, often personally.

Ex. "Election," however it may be regarded, it is agreed involves no capricious fondness, but is founded in wisdom. It is a revelation of the divine character, in agreement with GOD's foreknowledge. As said, prescience alters not man's freedom. Hence good and bad are "predestinated" to life or death from the first, "according to the foreknowledge of GOD." I PET 1:2, EPH 1:11.

The doctrine is introduced for such purposes as 1. To show salvation is through *charis*—grace, not of works ROM 11:5, 6. 2, Account for the stumbling of the Jews without excusing them c 9; or certainty of CHRIST's kingdom in spite of opposition MATT 21:42, I COR 15:25. Explained and applied to the purpose intended, it is not capricious, and does not alter man's responsibility, and personally, it illuminates and confirms our faith.

OBS. As in faith, there is the *grace* and the *gift* as Daniel Steele says, so in election, there is the *conditional* and *unconditional*.

Again, in the connection between the first offense and condemnation of *all* ROM 5, is used to illustrate CHRIST's redemption.

5 *We may* not make deductions by reason from revelation. They may be false. The **Jews and Papists** illustrate the folly and wickedness of this.

The BIBLE says, man is totally depraved; but it is not deducible that every one is, in the same degree.

"No man is to be pressed with consequences from the SCRIPTURES, unless the transcript be by the hand that wrote the original." JEREMY TAYLOR. And the martyr Ridley says, "In these matters I am so fearful, that I dare not speak further * * * than the text leads me by the hand."

6 *Relative importance.* a. What is omitted in one book, several or many, is not thought so important as what is named in all.

b. Mark what is oftenest spoken of by CHRIST and his apostles.

Thus the commemorative element in the supper, is found to be primary, for it is thrice named I COR 11 : 24-26. So of the divine procedure, CHRIST admonishes three times MATT 13, 25, LUKE 19, that gifts unused are taken from us; but if improved, are increased. Humility is recommended seven times in the first 3 GOSPELS.

c. Note what is common to both dispensations.

Thus the sacrifice of CHRIST, as typified through 4000 yrs, "Once offered to bear the sins of many," suggests its great value, and the feelings we ought to nourish in reference to it HEB 9 : 28.

d. Note the value given to any truth or precept. Unbelief is spoken of as the great sin and ground of condemnation. "Without faith, it is impossible to be well pleasing" to GOD. Sometimes one quality is set above another. Love is greater than faith and hope I COR 13.

Applying the above rules to the finished work of our LORD, in its connection with our justification and sanctification, we find it set in the foreground in all the N T. And his resurrection and ascension, as evidence of his divinity and our resurrection, are mentioned in the LETTERS alone more than fifty times.

CANONS ON THE APPLICATION OF THE RULES—

1 NOTHING may be made an article of faith, not found in the BIBLE.

2 THERE must be an indifferent judgment till the truth itself decide. Bias, inclination, fancy, like stained glasses, will reveal truth in a false light.

3 GIVE every doctrine its relative value, as in the WORD.

4 SCRIPTURE is full and clear in cardinal doctrines.

Where not, it is because not important, or the knowledge thereof, not for this life.

5 Of apparent contradictions, some are only verbal. In such as the following (affecting doctrines), as when the same act is affirmed of different persons, or contradictory qualities ascribed to the same person or object, there is a sense in which both assertions are true.

Exs. It is said ten times, Pharaoh hardened his heart, and ten times, GOD hardened it. What the sense is *not*, may be gathered from revelations of GOD's character; what it *is*, may be told or may not. If not, it is one of the "secret things" which belong to GOD.

The BIBLE says that all men are sinners. Also, that some (born of GOD I John), do not sin. In Ex 20, we read that God visits the sins of the fathers on the children, but in EZEK 18: 20, the children do not bear the iniquities of the parents. "Either the parent's sin falls temporarily on the child * * * or the first may be limited to those who hate GOD. The fruit is good or bad as the stock is. Children of drunkards run out in the third and fourth generation.* In such texts, there is a sense in which both assertions are true.

SEC 2 PRECEPTS.

DOCTRINE has been put first, because at the basis of all morality; also, because most of the rules are alike applicable to precepts, promises and examples. The GOSPEL opens with the "story of peace" and pardoning mercy of GOD. CHRIST then teaches the sense of GOD's law, as in the sermon on the mount, freeing it from the glosses of the Jews, convicting us for a higher life—"in newness of the spirit, and not in oldness of the letter." Knowledge of truth precedes goodness. Or in SCRIPTURE phrase, we are sanctified by faith through the truth, or operation of the HOLY SPIRIT.

The preceptive parts are rather principles of action or life, than directions; appealing to the motives, the conscience, that our words and acts may be right. For intentions are the beginnings of words and actions.

---

* It is in the reverse of this law—the generation of the godly, that we have one pledge of CHRIST's reign, and of the righteous filling the land.

Thus the commandments are taught by our LORD to be love to GOD and man—going forth in right words and conduct to GOD-ward and our kind, MATT 22: 40.

And on these again, "Hangeth the whole LAW and the prophets." Such teaching accounts for the opposition it met with. The Scribes and Pharisees had been giving the *letter* of the law and their own traditions, instead.

<small>Even when in specific form as MATT 5: 40 - (about letting have the "cloak"—inner garment, compare JOHN 18: 22-3, JESUS's reply when struck), it is the spirit which leads to the duty, rather than the letter that is meant, without which it could not be kept.</small>

The precepts come to us generally in comprehensive terms, to be explained and applied by the reader according to his own mind and heart. While in most cases they are plain, still are they taught in such a way as to suggest that GOD means "to prove thee, to know what was in thine heart, whether thou wouldest keep his commandments or no," DEUT 8: 2. Precepts are therefore of such a nature as to be best understood and applied by the pure in heart.

To apply the moral LAW.

1 WHAT is forbidden in the highest degree, is forbidden in the lowest degree also:—as murder, and the passions which lead to it; adultery, and even inordinate desires, appetites etc, are sins of the flesh.

2 When sin is condemned, its opposite is enjoined; and when a duty is enjoined, the opposite is forbidden. It condemns images, teaching us a spiritual service. Love supreme to GOD, forbids love to persons and things, except as it may lead to him. (Yet there is a love pure, that regards the creature for GOD's sake, that neither takes nor gives harm.) It surrounds the parental relation with sanctity and honor, also forbidding neglect and disobedience in both parent and child.

OBS If we are to love GOD with all the heart, is not partiality to relations and friends, to the prejudice and harm of others; that parental fondness which indulges children (this finds an expression in the doll—*idol*, an image of corruptible man, or other creature), ministering to the lower nature; that favoritism—thought, time, money bestowed on pet birds and animals, a kind and degree of worship, a vitiation of the first commandment?

There is a book—HEART AND ITS INMATES, which illustrates the state of man's heart, under the symbol of the various creatures, in it—"Most people think that if they keep the best rooms of the heart swept and garnished for CHRIST, they may have a chamber for Belial for occasional visits, a stool in the counting house, or corner in the scullery, where he may lick the dishes." RUSKIN.

As the heart controls all, so GOD in "the great and first" commandment, aims to sanctify, regulate and direct the whole life. Not to love is to hate, and he "that hateth his brother is a murderer" I JOHN 3 : 15.

SEC 3 MORAL AND POSITIVE PRECEPTS.

THOSE commands (according to Doddridge and Bp Butler), are moral, the reasons for which we see, and those positive, the reasons for which we do not see. The moral are founded in reason, justice, mercy, as the decalogue. Positive precepts are incidental, and may be temporary, as for an occasion, person or nation. These refer to acts not necessarily implying a good, obedient heart. Those have reference to and imply actions, as the expression of holy feeling.

Some precepts are mixed—both moral and positive, as the Sabbath. That man requires one day in seven, is the moral part; while the law fixing the day, is the positive. And moral duties become positive, as being commanded, and positive moral, as requiring holy motives.

Positive laws differ from the moral—

1 *In* their *nature* They are indifferent till given. To look at the brazen serpent, or sprinkle the door-posts with blood, was not a duty till enjoined, and was also temporary. The moral law is spiritual and eternal.

2 *In* their *evidence.* The one is in the BIBLE, is matter of revelation; and differences of opinion therefore, with regard to their observance, may be excusable. The moral is written (though often nearly effaced), in the heart.

MORAL AND POSITIVE PRECEPTS. 171

3 *In* their *grounds*. Positive precepts are founded in the will of GOD, and the design of some is obvious, as baptism, the LORD's supper and Sabbath. But why these rather than others, is not revealed. The other is founded in the nature of GOD and of man, and the relation subsisting between them.

4 *In* extent of *obligation*. The positive are specific: e g, the ceremonial law was for the Jews, not gentiles. Worship in the grove GEN 21 : 33, was right for the patriarchs, forbidden to Israel DEUT 16 : 21, under the GOSPEL, indifferent JOHN 4 : 21–3.* The moral part is universally binding, and in every relation of life.

5 *In* their *observance*. The first, addressed to outward actions, are to be observed according to the letter; the moral law, controlling motives, is obeyed in many different ways.

6 *In* their *connection*. The positive are not necessarily connected. The moral are: e g, faith is the parent of many virtues. And love to GOD increases sorrow for sin and fear to offend. But circumcision did not imply a clean heart. "Institutions may be observed apart, but virtues go in troops." BP HALL.

GOD rejects positive institutions when made an end Is 1 : 11-17. The outward rite should yield to the dictates of mercy—keeping a sabbath, to the law of love MARK 2 : 23-8.

OBS 1 On the 4th commandment, let no one think of keeping it according to its nature and design, without preparation for it in all things, on the day before. The pious Jew did thus.

2 They are wrong whose conscience obliges them to keep the seventh day.

---

* Our woods and camp meeting, have their earliest reference to the "grove" and feast of tabs—"booths" LEV 23 : 33.

CHAPTER II.

SYSTEMATIC AND INFERENTIAL STUDY CONTINUED.

Sec 1 Promises. (About 3000)

IN general, the promises of GOD are the expression of his immutable counsel. Counsel, not in the sense of secret purpose, as some teach. They are the revelation of his purpose "before times eternal" TIT 1 : 2, and quoted HEB 6 : 17, 18, in proof of his immutability.

Faith in the promises is the great medium of man's restoration and holiness. "As the threatenings awe and tend to check irregular inclinations, so the promises excite to and encourage universal holiness."*

Of the promises, some are peculiar, as to Noah, Abraham, Moses, Peter. Such are personal in their application.

SOME are TEMPORARY, as those to Israel in worldly good. So of the gifts promised in the first age—miracles, and inspiration of the SCRIPTURES, which are now withheld or greatly modified.

SOME are UNIVERSAL, as the GOSPEL of CHRIST, which is become the ground and measure of faith for all people and times.

To this class belong those promises which refer to the things of this life. Under a typical dispensation, where eternal things were less clearly revealed, riches, honor, power, seem to have been promised to and motives for, obedience. While "the hand of the diligent maketh rich," this law seems modified under the GOSPEL—1 Persecution for CHRIST's sake is foretold, but has in it promise of greater good. 2 CHRIST's kingdom in its very nature, implies a life of *faith*, not of sight. 3 Temporal things

---

* CLARKE ON THE PROMS, INTRODUCTION. CLARKE'S INT might be read with interest here.

are to be used in promoting our spiritual life and the kingdom of God.

Providence seems to have been a teacher to Israel and the world. And Providence and promise, as C. H. Yatman says, go hand in hand. The prosperity of God's chosen was, it seems, for a sign to the nations—proof of the one true God and his providence. But now, the Bible complete, God is free so to speak, to deal with us as seemeth him good. In seeking therefore in the temporal promises, we are to remember that prosperity, health etc, have ceased to be the uniform expression and evidence of the divine favor.

<small>Obs. The poverty of Christ is in the gospel, held up for our imitation. Socrates chose poverty as the more excellent form of life. Mr. Wesley said if he left over £10 behind, the world might call him a thief and robber.*</small>

Some are *absolute,* as of the Messiah and call of the gentiles. Of these are "The gifts and calling of God, (which) are without repentance" Rom 11 : 29.

Others are *conditional.*

The spiritual life e g, through its different stages, is conditioned on keeping the commandments—pleasing God in soul and body. So of the physical life—health and freedom from chastisement Ex 15: 26, Deut 28: 60. Such is the connection of soul and body, that the vigor of both alike depends on the observance of God's ordinances, on which the laws of our being are founded. To such a life, is suffixed that remarkable promise Ex 15: 26 * * * "For I am Jehovah *rophi*—the Lord that healeth thee."

This class of promises then, is to *character.* "If ye be willing and obedient, ye shall eat the good of the land" Is 1: 19, has both prem'ise and promise of both temporal and spiritual good.

While we cannot claim the promises on the ground of sorrow or distress, we do on the ground of Christ's atonement. The means and order are given Ps 50: 14, 15,

---

<small>* Put not your trust in money,
But put your money in trust.   O. W. Holmes.</small>

" Offer unto God thanksgiving, pay thy vows * * call on me in the day of trouble, I will deliver thee, and thou shalt glorify me."

Faith and *patience* are a condition to reap the promises. We are to keep in mind that a thousand years are with the Lord, as one day. This doctrine is an occasion of failure to some. The promise JOHN 14 : 3, to come and take us to himself, CHRIST spoke over 1800 yrs ago.

" No time is too long nor labor too severe, when the glory of eternity is the mark we level at " CAUGHEY.

" He that believeth shall not make haste " Is 28 : 16, is iterated " By patient continuance in well doing " ROM 2 : 7.

OBS. GOD keeps us out of our suit in some things, till compelled, as it were, by " importunity," to yield. See this illustrated in the parable of the unjust judge, three loaves LUKE 11, 18, and Syrophœnician woman MARK 7.

> Quietly wait, if blessings sought
> Are found within what CHRIST hath bought;
> If found within the boundary line
> Of real good, they shall be thine.
> Though suns may rise and suns may set,
> The LORD his word can ne'er forget.* S. S. TRS JOUR.

While GOD'S promises are in a sense his debt, they are to be used as incentives to prayer.

He had promised David that he would establish his kingdom, and David pleads with him to fulfill it II SAM 7 : 18–25.

He told Elijah he would send rain I KGS 18 : 1, yet Elijah v 42–4, prays earnestly for it.

Daniel knew that the captivity was ending, when he *set his face* to pray for the Restoration 9 c.

OBS. In Daniel, we have an illustration of the maxim that *he who prays most and best, does most and best work.* It pays to " keep prayed up," and also done up every day.

And

---

* Faith and trust may be compared to the pioneer and settler. The first explores, the other settles and dwells in the land. REV. J. R. T. GRAY, D. D.

"It was while they all were praying,
Expecting it would come,
Came the power
That JESUS said he would send down,"
on Pentecost.

A few extracts out of our FATHER'S WILL, as the experience of some of his children, are appended.

Ps 25 . 9, 14, The meek will he guide in judgment
   34 I will bless the LORD at all times
   37: 3-6, Trust in the LORD and do good
   41: 1-3, Blessed is he that considereth the poor
   50: 14, 15, 23, Offer unto GOD thanksgiving
   91, He that dwelleth in the secret place
   92: 11, 14, Mine eye also shall see my desire
   103, Bless the LORD, O my soul!
   107: 43, Whoso is wise. Com A V
   122: 6, Pray for the peace of Jerusalem
   126: 5, 6, They that sow in tears shall reap in joy
PROV 3: 13-18, 33, Happy is the man that findeth wisdom
MATT 5: 3-12, The beatitudes
MARK 11: 20-5, Lesson of the barren fig-tree
JOHN 3: 16, For GOD so loved the world
   15: 7, If ye abide in me * * * ask whatsoever ye will
ROM 8: 28 to the end,—And we know that to them that love GOD
I COR 10: 13, There hath no temptation taken you
HEB 13: 5, JOSH 1: 5, "I will in nowise fail thee"

What a thesaurus of unrealized blessedness is found in Ps 81 for Israel, had he not failed to meet the conditions! DEUT 28 gives a *symposium* of what was for that nation, most of which also, is applicable under the GOSPEL.

On FAITH, to which the promises are given, the masterpiece is HEB. 11.

On LOVE (so fraught with promise), the ideal is sketched I COR 13.*

As the ordinances of heaven—sun, moon and stars, run on from age to age unvarying, so the counsel of GOD is in full, undiminished force to the end—"an everlasting covenant, ordered in all things and sure" II SAM 23: 5.

Also as in oratory, the chief element of power consists

Vide THE GREATEST THING IN THE WORLD, LEC, PROF HENRY DRUMMOND.

not so much in what is expressed, as suggested and implied, so in REVELATION, there is a *plethora*—a length, breadth, depth and height no man has ever realized. "And there was the hiding of his power," HAB 3: 4. And hence, in the experience of individuals and the church, its doctrines, precepts and promises have been growing more important and full of meaning from generation to generation. e g, The first promise GEN 3: 15 to Adam, and JEHOVAH *jireh* 22: 14 on Moriah, have a meaning and evidence to-day as never before.

This has a striking illustration in the atonement on the †. Once the sign of reproach and suffering, GOD has honored the cross of JESUS, making it the symbol of his faith, conflicts and triumphs, throughout the whole Christian world.

"All the light of sacred story
Gathers round its head sublime."

IN CON. To the good, the promises come in every relation and state, from the king, to them that are subject. To the minister and his flock. Parents, "to you is the promise and to your children" ACTS 2: 39. To filial obedience, "length of days."

To the widow and orphan, GOD is a "husband" and "father." To the aged, weak, afflicted, poor, prisoner, persecuted; to the merciful, peacemaker, meek, are blessings *peculiar*, in reversion. And the time of man's extremity, is GOD's opportunity.

The preceptive part complied with, GOD, no respecter of persons, here meets man as it were, on one common, holy ground. And the PROMISER is more concerned in the fulfilment, than the promisee. These SCRIPTURES ring with a challenge to faith, to prove our MAKER's power and faithfulness.

In this *Magna Charta* of rights and privileges, GOD gives us so to speak, a *carte blanche*—a note signed, to be filled with whatever the receiver may desire,

EXAMPLES.

"Standing on the promises of CHRIST my SAVIOR,
Through eternal ages let his praises ring."

CLARKE ON THE PROMS (about 2000), in plan and fulness, is the best on this subject.

SEC 2 EXAMPLES.

As said, our BIBLE abounds in this mode of teaching. Examples illustrate truth and duty, and exert a potent influence on life and character. This, in application to goodness, is spoken of PROV 13: 20, II COR 3: 18; and the power of bad example (personified), by a poet—

"SIN is a monster of so frightful mien,
That to be hated needs but to be seen;
Yet seen too oft, familiar with her face,
We first endure, then pity, then embrace."

It is well to know also, that the unconscious influence exerted by us and upon us, is greater than what we are conscious of. "If it were not for bad example, people would be ashamed or afraid to do wrong." DEMPSTER.

In order of time and importance, it is before precept. The living teacher impresses us more than his posthumous works. See this referred to in the case of the great TEACHER c IV SEC 1.

HOLINESS (which is at the basis of goodness), as it is the most important quality in man, so also it exercises the greatest influence over us. Holiness is the most glorious attribute of GOD. And if to be good is to be great, it is a laudable ambition for a person to aspire to be *great as he is good*.

To illustrate the effect of example in its more amiable forms, we quote an excellent writer—

A selenium cell connected with an electric bell, has been attached to the Lick Telescope, so that when a comet comes within the field of the instrument, though invisible to the eye, it announces itself in ringing the bell.

More sensitive than selenium to light, is the pure mind to purity. Paul tells us, "we are come unto mount Zion and unto the city of the living GOD * * * and to innumerable hosts of angels, to the general assembly and church of the first born * * * and to JESUS the MEDIATOR" HEB 12.

In the toil and moil—the dust and sweat of daily life, the sweet peace bells ring to unhearing ears. But when alone with GOD, we see and hear things which set them ringing in our heart.

A pure, gentle soul cannot come within the radius of any circle, but his quality and influence are felt; and by some, more than others. His look, tone, voice, gesture, pose—that undefinable thing we call "patience," impresses every one.

The pure in heart shall see GOD. How long it took to polish the lenses of this telescope, and so much money, before it could sweep the zodiac, above the mists and tremors of earth and air! How long it takes *us* under discipline —in the hands of our MAKER, to be made pure! Are we co-workers with him to have his will done in us? ANNUNCIATION C ADVOCATE.

The most lovely of our kind are human, and do not fill our idea of virtue incarnate. It is only in the life of our LORD that we read (in the GOSPELS especially), and contemplate a character unique—alone in kind and excellence. There is no virtue—physical, mental or moral feature in excess or defect, as with man. In him the human blends with the divine in a perfect harmony, suggestive in a holier sense of the first Adam, reminding us of what we were in him, when fresh from the hand of GOD.

And through and above all, we are to fix our eye upon JESUS, and esteem others only in so far as they "have been with Jesus." And this, we are also taught to do, for his sake alone. It is CHRIST only, who authoritatively says, "Follow me" MATT 8 : 22. It is a good rule in the imitation of CHRIST (as one said to the writer), to live as you think *he* would, if in your place.

To that one who, like the subject of ST. JOHN the AGED c IV SEC 1, has had the MASTER'S look and word to

"Light and break the silence of his heart forever,"

Christ has become *the* object of love and worship; and his most valued teachers and friends, are but of relative importance.

He who has learned of Christ ceases from man Is 2: 22, and finds in his life, teaching and finished work, both motive and means for the highest state of holiness and happiness. Indeed, every form and degree of the higher life experience is summed up and centered in the knowing and being united to him.* See closing par.

That so many of Christ's "followers" seek rest for their souls in ordinances, going far and near after popular teachers etc—trusting in man, is a proof both of the ignorance and deceitfulness of the heart—its enmity to God. Jesus is the last resort. Until we take him, we may be "ever learning and never able to come to the knowledge of the truth" II Tim 3: 7.

1 *There* are *actions* recorded in Scripture, as of injustice and idolatry, with censure. They illustrate human nature, and other important ends.

2 *There* are *actions* of the good noticed without censure, as Abraham's equivocation with Pharaoh Gen 12, and the father's example followed by the son's, with Abimelech c 26, and Rebecca's weakness and sin, in getting the blessing for Jacob. To this class belong such customs as are forbidden in the GOSPEL, as the taking of more than one wife and putting away of wives, suffered by Moses.

3 *Others* (in the O T), were by express command, as the offering of Isaac, destruction of the Canaanites, killing of the idolaters in the camp. Abraham's offering was for an example and test of faith, the Canaanites were irretrievably wicked and their probation up. The Levites slew the idolaters because it was treason against the invisible King.

4 *In judging* Scripture examples, ascertain the principle on which the acts were performed. This is suggested in Heb 11, where some things are imitable only by the law of faith, whence they spring. Elijah mocked the

---

* On the imitation of Christ, Kempis and Imago Christi are without rivals.

priests of **Baal**, to make the exposure, and sin of the god and his worshippers, appear the greater. He called fire from heaven II Kgs 1, not to avenge himself, but for a sign against Ahaziah. But when James and John desired our Lord to do likewise, they were reproved, both as to the example and spirit manifested. Luke 9: 54, A V.

From the above, we deduce the following general *rule of judgment*—Estimate each act, as the person who performed it, was bound to by the law under which he lived, but not to copy if inconsistent with the gospel.

Principle of *imitation*—If the matter be of a *moral nature*, we are to copy the example of inspired men, so far as the reasons are the same in their case and ours. If not similar, we keep the command by cherishing the spirit thereof.

We are taught "through love" to "be servants to one another," and if one portion of the church is in need, we are to give as the churches did Acts 11, I Cor 16. But if we follow the example of washing one another's feet, we apply the exceptive rule above. The sandal, heat, sweat and dust in that land, made it a necessary refreshment. A kiss was the form of salutation and affection. The principle—the expression of affectionate feeling, is still binding, but shown in other forms also.

If the example refer to a *positive institution*, we do not copy in the mere circumstantials. Our Lord instituted the holy supper in an upper room, Thursday, in the evening, with unleavened bread, all reclining. But we do not deem *one* of these five accidental means necessary to the observance.

In all cases the duty is founded on the command, the application to be fixed according to the phraseology and example of inspired men, subject to the rules given above.

1 *Examples are helpful in interpretation.* If by men at the time inspired, and according to the above rule, we have an inspired interpretation of its meaning. The conduct of Paul Gal 2, in opposing Peter on circumcision, and practice of the apostles, decides the significance of many passages of Holy Writ.

NOTE. The prejudice of Peter in respect to the gentiles, viewed in connection with the time—10 yrs after Pentecost, and means used—the two visions and Cornelius's messengers (ACTS 10), to destroy the *caste*, may suggest the mysterious power, and also evil of both false teaching and ignorance. Peter had **not** so learned of CHRIST.

2 *In practical application.* If it be asked whether it is the duty of all Christians to *work* for JESUS, we learn (and in agreement with the moving of the SPIRIT), to apply the precept in Abraham GEN 18 : 19, the captive maid II KGS 5 : 3, Demoniac MARK 5 : 20, Andrew and Philip JOHN 1 : 41, 45, Samaritan woman 4 : 29.

Is it a question whether I can be as holy in business as in retirement or public service of religion? I find that Enoch had sons and daughters, Abraham great possessions, Joseph was governor of Egypt; Moses king in Jeshurun DEUT 33 : 5, Daniel was next to the king in Babylon, and JESUS was perhaps not less holy as a mechanic than

"When listening thousands gathered round"

(in the sermon on the mount), or the sacrifice on the cross.

We are instructed, warned, inspired to do and dare by the lives of men and women eminent for virtue or vice. And the BIBLE is like a vast picture gallery, where every one may find his ideal.

Some are impressed with the obedience of faith in him who is honored as the "father of many nations;" or the gifts and inspiration of the babe found in an ark of "bulrushes" and "wept," who rose to be as in the place of GOD to Pharaoh, Aaron and Israel—the Heb prophet and legislator; others are inspired with the patriotism, faith, zeal, chivalry of Moses' minister Joshua, or the character of the judge, prophet and reformer Samuel; while the devotional spirit, the varied enduements personal and regal, and great life of the youngest of Jesse, the "man after GOD's own heart," or the wisdom and statesmanship of him who in Babylon

Dared to have a purpose firm and
Dared to make it known.

With the womanly virtues of such as Ruth and Hannah, all are pleased.

We look on the portrait of Saul with feelings of pity and sorrow; on that of Ahab, with execration as a masterpiece of weakness and wickedness. From that of Jezebel and her daughter Athaliah, we turn away with horror and disgust.

Of the kings, Josiah impresses us above all, both for goodness, and as *the* reformer. He seems to have been beloved in life and mourned in death, above all; perhaps above any in the world. In childhood it is said " Like unto him was there no king (Jehoshaphat nor Hezekiah), * * * neither arose there any like him." And in death (at Megiddo), " All Judah and Jerusalem mourned for Josiah. And Jeremiah lamented for Josiah. And all the singing men and singing women spake of Josiah in their lamentations to this day. And they made them an ordinance in Israel."

What consecration to GOD is suggested ! What zeal, courage, firmness it took to destroy Baal and his priests, and restore the temple and worship of GOD ! ! (The LAW was lost, the sanctuary dedicated to "Asherah," and the nation at its lowest, darkest state, sunk into idolatry.) And what a lesson and inspiration to reformers in church and state, does Josiah present ! * * * But such a life we feel better able to contemplate, than adequately describe. None can read the story inspiration has given—II KGS 22-3, II CHRON 34-5, and not feel that *goodness is true greatness.*

Of N T heroes, John Baptist, the beloved disciple and Paul, are beloved and honored of all, while Mary who sat at JESUS' feet, may be regarded as a better type of womanhood than Martha. The history of the three Herods, Herodias and daughter, Judas and Simon Magus, give exhibitions of human nature in some of its most hateful aspects, full of warning, and sense of GOD's retributive justice.

How affecting is the humility of the true teacher JOHN 3 : 29 (before imprisoned in Machaerus), when his ministry was waning and CHRIST'S waxing!—"He that hath the bride is the bridegroom ; but the friend of the bridegroom * * * rejoiceth greatly, because of the bridegroom's voice; this my joy therefore, is fulfilled. He must increase, but I must decrease."

All that philosophy and wise men * * * can teach, says Luther, history presents by examples and cases. And thus CHRIST * * * is preached from the annals of his own kingdom. NEANDER.

OBS. Intelligent piety will not regard with superstitious reverence, nor worship eminent saints as some do. Nor are we to confound the real with the typical character of some—Jacob for example. For it seems to be in spite of their weaknesses, rather than holiness (above all others at least), that GOD chose and honored them so. As the progenitors of MESSIAH, there was a kind and degree of honor due from GOD (so to speak), and man, even in the case of the "supplanter." See SCRIPTURE DIFFICULTIES, PT III, c IV. "I am the GOD of Abraham, Isaac and Jacob" often occurs in the O T, and CHRIST uses their names MATT 8: 11. But we understand this honor as official, rather.

2 While we think of some as greater in word and deed than any after their times, we know whom GOD chooses for extraordinary occasions, he works with to "see them through." "By faith," the secret of power, is suggested HEB 11. Now true greatness consists not in doing extraordinary things, so much as in the attention paid to the ordinary, and things this world calls trifling or foolish even.

3 Let us not in the extent of our obligations, graduate ourselves by the duty and privilege of servants under the LAW. But consider the purport of the TEACHER's words spoken of John Baptist—" He that is but little in the kingdom of heaven, is greater than he."

Hence, while there are examples in and out of the BIBLE, dead and living, we think of as more favored by nature and grace, let us remember that they are of like passions with us, and even more conscious of their weakness and dependence, than we are. And both teacher and lesson would be a failure, if JESUS (of whom inspired examples wrote and spoke—

"The MAKER, and MONARCH, and SAVIOR of all,"

as the ALPHA and OMEGA), be not put in the foreground.

It is he who shines forth as the "way, the truth and the life." O that I could with John (when he looked on JESUS walking, now revealed to him as the SON of GOD, and called to his disciples "Behold the LAMB of GOD!") point him out to some, as the one only pattern for holy living! Such a spiritual view of JESUS as the DIVINE MAN, meets our ideal of virtue in a bodily form.

> "As by the light of opening day
> The stars are all concealed,
> So earthly glories fade away,
> When Jesus is revealed."

With the fairest types of our kind, we are disappointed. But in CHRIST, is perfection of power, wisdom, goodness, LOVE, patience, humility, compassion. And it is daily looking to him, in the GOSPEL glass, "with unveiled face, reflecting as a mirror the glory of the LORD, we are transformed into the same image" II COR 3 : 18.

We count them happy who, like the chosen three in the transfiguration, see " no man save JESUS only." And there are those like John the Baptist, the beloved disciple and Mary, to whom the MASTER reveals himself as not to others.

> "O could I speak the matchless worth,
> O could I sound the glories forth
> That in my SAVIOR shine!"

* * * CHRIST is himself in truth, the GOSPEL. His coming and work, apart from what he taught, constitute the " good tidings of great joy" to all people. Did man need a sacrifice for sin, in which the rights of the LAW find their explanation and end? That sacrifice he offered. Did he need a perfect rule of life? This he gave when he dwelt among us. Immortality he brings to light, not by teaching so much, as by rising from the dead in our behalf. There is no question essential for us to know in religion, which CHRIST's life does not solve. In him, we see GOD revealed —his justice, mercy, faithfulness, power. In him, we see our nature—our sin in his sufferings, duty in his example, and dignity in his ascension and glory. ANGUS, p 550.

CHAPTER III.

QUOTATIONS OUT OF THE OLD IN THE N T, CLASSIFIED AND EXAMINED WITH REFERENCE TO THE TEXT, TRUTHS AND EVIDENCES OF SCRIPTURE, AND PRINCIPLES OF INTERPRETATION.

AS *these quotations* illustrate the original text, evidences, explain types, history, prediction and principles of interpretation, they are important and belong here.
This branch we take up—
1 To ascertain the variations between the OLD and N TESTAMENTS and lessons suggested. 2 The truths these lessons involve.

There are 263 quotations and 376 references. From the PENT 90, refs 100. From the PSALMS 71, refs 30. From ISAIAH 56, refs 48. *Minor prophets* about 30.

Quotations are—
1, *Prophetic,* as of CHRIST directly, MATT 4: 15, or of some typical person or event and then other person or event under GOSPEL JOHN 19: 36. 2, *Demonstrative,* as of or to prove, something JOHN 6: 45. 3, *Explanatory* of some fact or statement HEB 12: 20. 4, *Illustrative,* quoted and given a new sense ROM 10: 18. Some are both demonstrative and explanatory, as GAL 3: 11.

Quotations are oftener from the LXX than the HEB, sometimes verbal, but often abbreviated or paraphrased, yet without violence to the sense.

The N T having been better guarded than the LXX, quotations are here and there used to correct that version.

Again, they are used to correct the Heb text—

Exs. HAB 1: 5 "Among the nations," is changed ACTS 13: 41, to "ye despisers." So Is 29: 13, MATT 15: 8 is, "This people honoreth me." GEN 47: 31 "beds head," HEB 11, is "top of his staff." Ps 40: 6, "ears * * opened" (marg digged), HEB 10: 5 is, "a body didst thou prepare for me." Compare AMOS 9: 11, 12, ACTS 15: 16, Ps 16: 10, ACTS 2: 27. HOS 13: 14, "O death, where are thy plagues?" I COR 15: 55, is "O death, where is thy sting?"

Thus (as shown), several passages in the HEB may be

rendered as found in the N T. The LXX takes in these instances the secondary, the English the primary meaning of the words.

Ex Ps 19: 4, the LXX translates "sound," Eng "line." The word means string or cord; thence, musical sound. Notice how Paul Rom 10: 18, renders and applies it.

After the above corrections, there remain many quotations not agreeing with the exact words of the original. About one half the quotations give the sense rather than words, as Is 11: 10, Rom 15: 12 is, "There shall be the root of Jesse."

The principle on which the quotations are made, seems to be the same as a scholar would adopt in taking from our version. Where the SEPT is accurate, they use it; otherwise the HEB. Matthew often uses the SEPT, but in things relating to MESSIAH, he adopts the HEBREW. Paul in HEBS, quotes mostly from the SEPT, and often verbatim.

Again, a new, limited, or enlarged sense is given in a quotation——

Exs. GEN 22: 18, "nations" Peter ACTS 3: 25, changes to "families," suggesting to the Jews that the gentiles are now "brethren." HEB 5: 10, Paul translates *cohen* (which v 6 he renders priest) *high priest*, as better suited to his argument. Gods Ps 97: 7, he changes to angels HEB 1: 6,—the limited sense. Gods means mighty ones, is applied to GOD, false gods, angels and persons in authority.

But the *truths* taught in these quotations, are the chief lesson. They illustrate the doctrines and ethics of the ancient SCRIPTURES, confirm their divine original, and supply aids in interpretation—

1 *Salvation* by faith, and through CHRIST, is proved by quotations ROM 1: 17, GAL 3: 6-9, ROM 4: 10, 11, I PET 2: 6, 7. Faith, from its relation to Christ's righteousness, is counted to *us* for righteousness ROM 4: 3-8.

Election of grace and promise wide as the fall ROM 11.

Holiness essential, consists in love, and is enforced by example. MATT 22: 37-9, "Thou shalt love the LORD" I PET 1: 16 * * * "ye shall be holy."

Grace to the humble JAS 4: 6 * * * "God resisteth the proud, but giveth grace to the humble."
Temporal good to obedience EPH 6: 2, 3—"Honor thy father and mother." I PET 3: 10, 11—"For he that would love life" etc.

The divinity of MESSIAH and agency of the HOLY SPIRIT, are proved by these quotations. Compare c VI, SEC 3 and apply here and connect with the following—

Exs. Is 8: 14 "JEHOVAH * * * a Stone of stumbling and for a rock of offence" is ROM 10: 9, 11, 9: 32-3 applied to CHRIST. So Is 45: 23—"every knee shall bow, every tongue shall swear." JEHOVAH (LORD), is ROM 14: 11, spoken of as CHRIST.
The vision Is 6 3-10, is spoken of JNO 12: 41, as a sight of CHRIST's glory; and the "voice of the LORD" is ACTS 28: 25, called the HOLY SPIRIT.
In HEB 1: 6, 8, 10, Paul applies to CHRIST Ps 97: 7, 45: 6, 7, 102: 25-7, where the person spoken of is the CREATOR and RULER of all things.

That the ancients believed in immortality, the resurrection and future judgment, we may learn from MATT 22: 32—"GOD is not the GOD of the dead." HEB 11: 5, 13, 14, "By faith Enoch was translated." I COR 15: 55, "O death, where is thy victory?" and places where the day of the LORD is spoken of, as I THESS 5: 2, * * * "the day of the Lord so cometh." REV 6: 17—"the great day of their wrath is come." JOEL 2: 31, "The sun shall be turned into darkness. Ps 17: 15 * * * "Satisfied when I awake with thy likeness." JOB 19: 26 * * * "Yet from (mar *without*), my flesh shall I see GOD." DAN 12: 2—"And many * * * shall awake." HOS 13: 14—"I will ransom them from the power of the grave."

2 *The quotations* relating to our LORD and his kingdom are over 120. They supply what is called prophetic evidence.

3 *They supply rules* of interpretation.

The whole GOSPEL may be illustrated and proved from the O T—

Exs From DEUT 25: 4, Paul teaches that the laborer is worthy of his hire, and that they who proclaim the GOSPEL should live of the GOSPEL I TIM 5: 18, I COR 9: 9, 14.

So from Is 55: 3—"I will make an everlasting covenant with you, even the sure mercies of David"—(the favor pledged to David that his seed should sit on the throne for ever), Paul concludes that CHRIST to whom it refers, must have risen from the dead Acts 13: 34.

4 *Some predictions* have a double fulfilment, as where the persons or things are types one of another, as DEUT 1: 10, where Moses speaks of the promise to Abraham in its literal sense, and ROM 4: 18, where Paul speaks of it in its spiritual sense.

Sometimes they are in some respects identical, as GAL 3: 16, where the "seed" is shown to be CHRIST, and then v 29, is applied to them who believe in him.

Sometimes they seem to be blended as Is 40: 3–5, where the coming of our LORD and his kingdom have scarce any time between. So in JOEL 2: 28–32—"And it shall come to pass * * * I will pour out of my SPIRIT." So MATT 24: 29–30, where the destruction of Jerusalem and judgment day are connected by "immediately."

IN CON. If it be said that this double reference weakens the evidence of prophecy, it is answered, The facts on which they are founded—the typical nature of the O T and identity of MESSIAH with his church, supply both *evidence* and consolation; while many Psalms and predictions in the prophets, apply to CHRIST *exclusively*.

CHAPTER IV.

ORIGIN, NATURE AND USE OF SCRIPTURE DIFFICULTIES.

IN divinity, there are things we must leave, or conclude with O the depth! * * * For the INDITER only knows the mysteries of glory, of nature, secrets of the heart and the succession of the ages. BACON.

SEC 1 ORIGIN. CLASS I ENUMERATED. MATTERS OF INTERPRETATION. EXAMPLES.

THE BIBLE, written by inspiration of GOD and for our learning, nevertheless contains things hard to be understood, which perplex and try some Christians, and things "which the ignorant and unsteadfast wrest as they do also the other SCRIPTURES, unto their own destruction" II PET 3 : 16.

Their origin is plain. BIBLE languages, distinct from one another and our own, are disused. Its expressions, images and thoughts belong to different ages, countries and persons. Its manners and customs have passed away. Its topics are various, including the history of nations and for all times. Its disclosures and doctrines refer to both worlds, and all in a brief vol. It must have been written with regard to everything known, and to every one of every age, not to have mysteries. Mysteries there are, but they are in the mind of the reader, not of the INDITER of the BOOK.

Comparing SEC 2 of CH II and SECS of CHS II–IV of PT II, it will be seen that the difficulties are due

1 *To uncertainties* of the text.

2 *Meaning* of *words* and phrases, connection of arguments, scope and authorship of particular books.

3 *Customs* and *manners* of the age in which written.

4 *Chronology*, geography and history.

5 *Apparent contradictions* of some portions.

6 *Things revealed* or commanded in the BOOK.

We will illustrate each class in order—

1 GEN 49 : 6, " Digged a wall " A V *shur*. Better read *Sar* prince—slew a prince. So Syriac (Pe*shito*) VERSION—ANGUS. Better still, " Houghed an ox " (mar *oxen*)—R V.

2 *Words* and *phrases*

a JOHN 1 : 16, "Grace for grace." "For the LAW, we have the GOSPEL." CHRYSOSTOM, BEZA, ERASMUS. Grace upon grace—abundant, immeasurable. WESLEY, OLSHAUSEN.

HEB 12 : 17, "Though he sought it diligently with tears." If *it* refers to the nearest antecedent, it means repentance, his own or father's. If to the remoter, it means the *eulogian*—blessing, which is probable. So WESLEY.

HEB 9 : 16, "Where a testament is, there must of necessity be the death of him that made it." Either where there is a will, the testator must die before it can be valid; or where there is a covenant, the victim must be slain.

I COR 11 : 10, "For this cause, ought the woman to have a sign of authority on her head, because of the angels." Sign of authority Wesley renders *veil*, which agrees with the context. Angels were believed to be present—good and evil, observing her conduct.

b *Connection of arguments*—

II PET 1: 19, "The word of prophecy made more sure." Than what? Than fables v 16. Others, than the transfiguration and voice. Better, we have the word of prophecy more confirmed by the transfiguration; rather, by the GOSPEL fulfilments. "The one as a lamp in a dark place, the other as the dawn." WESLEY.

c *Of difficulties* in the *scope* and *authorship* of books, JOB is named. It has been assigned to the time of Abraham, Moses, the Kings and later. Some ascribe it to Job, Elihu, Moses, or translated by him. Some think it is real history, others allegory. Most however agree that its *scope* is patience, to show affliction consistent with GOD'S love, to illustrate his sovereignty, and perhaps to comfort the Hebrews in Egypt or the captivity. Its place is probably GEN 12.

OBS—On the *sequel* to this poem—42 : 7-17, in prose, which the SPIRIT has left recorded for the faith and hope of the "perfect"— GOD'S chosen, tempted and tried, "him that overcometh," we feel like adding—

1 That (as the old story of GOD'S faithfulness, and truth of SCRIPTURE), it exceeds the glory of Solomon's kingdom, is like the divine interposition in favor of the Jews in Persia during the exile, the reward and elevation of Esther and Mordecai, see ESTHER Pt III, and such lesser "triumphs of virtue" as we read in ROSA of LINDEN CASTLE and BASKET of FLOWERS.

2 The sufferings, faith, patience of the "sorrowful man"—of what we do and bear for JESUS' sake, would be of little interest without its sequel—the reward and crowning day. Give me this. Give me Job's blessedness, *that* is the *true* lesson, and which can be seen only by *faith* through the clouds of mystery and grief, till God speaks and draws the veil, and the "mystery of suffering" is all plain.

It comes to us thro the years like an inspiration, or as a golden dream, supplying proof also, that man's ideal of the divine character—his righteousness, his goodness, is the *real;* and motive also, for aspiring after, of living for it. "The LORD will fulfil the desire of them that fear him." And

"Blessed is the man that endureth temptation." (I've thought that this, in connection with "the patience of Job" 5: 11, may have been suggested to James on reading the subscription to JOB.)

3 This man had risen above all in the East, and fallen lower.—

Job means sorrowful, persecuted, is a typical personage, and a fit subject for, if not also suggestive of, Milton's *Il Penseroso.*

It was while the poisoned arrows of the Almighty were within him, and his calamity heavier than the sand of the seas (some say it lasted seven, others but one year), that "Job's comforters" (his "Dear wife" joining in), were stirred up to accuse him as being wicked, a hypocrite, exhorting to repentance, tantalizing him as God forsaken, when at the lowest, and his body wasted with the worst kind of diseases.* (I have thought that the discord of our imperfection—ignorance, self-hood etc, may be more sanctifying to some of God's tried children, and pleasing to him, than the pleasures and harmonies of the sweetest music. And that on reading this book, we may well exclaim "O the depth!" and "O how great is thy goodness!!")

* * * * And "the Lord said * * * ye have not spoken of me the thing that is right as my servant Job hath. Now therefore, take unto you seven bullocks and seven rams, and go to my servant Job * * * And my servant Job shall pray for you, for him will I accept * * * And the Lord accepted Job, and the Lord turned the captivity of Job when he prayed for his friends. And the Lord gave Job twice as much as he had before. Then came there unto him all his brethren and all his sisters and all they that had been of his acquaintance before, and did eat bread with him in his house; and they bemoaned him and comforted him concerning all the evil that the Lord had brought upon him. Every man also gave him a piece of money, and every one a ring of gold. So the Lord blessed the latter end of Job more than his beginning; and he had fourteen thousand sheep, and six thousand camels, and a thousand yoke of oxen, and a thousand she asses. He had also seven sons and three daughters. And he called the name of the first Jemima, and the name of the second Kezia, and the name of the third Keren Happuch. And in all the land were no women so fair as the daughters of Job * * * And after this, Job lived an hundred and forty years, and saw his sons, and son's sons, even four generations. So Job died, being old and full of days."

* Satan had so construed the temptation, as to make it appear that God was punishing him for his sins.

What a day that must have been in Idumea, when the night of Job's sorrow ended in his justification, and of the "ways of God with man!" As by magic, when he offered—now as a prince and priest again, and with added lustre, and at his instance was restored soul and body, his body made "fresher than a child's" 33: 35. When his friends returned, with their congratulations and *kesitahs*—$2.50 (?), and over 22,000 live stock (all temporal good thrown in, as of little value in comparison to the "loving favor" of God and man, to one who has just "come fort has gold" 23: 10), raising up as from the dead those ten sons and daughters. And O what daughters, as their name also implies—days upon days, Cassia, Horn of plenty. And O how proud Job must have been of such "girls!"

d *Difficulties* in both *connection* and *words*—

One of the most difficult words is the particle *iva*. The question is whether it means *in order that*, only; or also, *with the result that*. If the former, then the connective expresses the purpose or end for which a thing is done. If the latter be one sense sometimes, then it may express the consequence without intention on the agent's part. Authorities differ. The first (*telic* sense), is the one generally given.

3 *Customs*—

ECCLS 11: 1, "Cast thy bread upon the waters, for thou shalt find it after many days." "Give to those in affliction." "Be liberal while you can." Rather, "act in gifts and effects as he who sows rice on the waters and mud—the rice ground being inundated from seed time till near harvest. The Targum understands it to mean, give bread to poor sailors. So the VULGATE and my OLD BIBLE. CLARKE.

4 *Chronology and history*—

GEN 4: 17, Cain "builded a city," and it has been asked who inhabited it? Ans. 500 A. M., there were by calculation, many hundred thousand people. CLARKE. In ans to "where Cain got his wife," the *first* marriages were lawful to next of kin—brothers and sisters.

Difficulties in chronology and numbers as said, have arisen from false readings, similarity in (Heb) letters, different modes of reckoning etc.

Matthew reckons the line of our LORD from Abraham (being to the Jews), through Joseph 1: 1, 2—"Jesus Christ the son of David, the son of Abraham." Luke gives it in the reverse order 3: 23, and through Mary "JESUS * * * being the son (as was supposed), of Joseph, the son of Heli" (Mary's father), tracing it back to GOD, the FATHER of all.

Some give more than others. In such cases the fuller account includes the shorter, and this does not contradict the longer.

In Matthew and Luke's account of JESUS till 30 yrs of age, there is scarce one verse in common. They differ, yet without contradiction. MATT 8 speaks of two, MARK 5 and LUKE 8, of one demoniac.

a The same thing is sometimes ascribed to different persons.

MATT 8: 5, 6, says the centurion came to JESUS about his servant. LUKE 7: 2, 3, that the "elders" came. MATT 20: 20, that the mother of Zebedee's children asked preferment for her sons, but MARK 10: 35, that James and John asked.—"The centurion, feeling unworthy, seems to have gone back and sent the elders. Salome was mouth for her two sons. The above is a form of speech common in the SCRIPTURES." WESLEY.

As the order is not always chronological, but facts often given in groups so to speak, study is needful to get the natural order.

Mark and Luke are generally chronological. Matthew gives facts and parables in groups, sometimes in order of time, as in the temptation c 4, where it is indicated by "then." Luke's order c 4, is different, though not affirmed; hence connected by "and."

GEN 1: 27, says "male and female created he them." 2: 21-2, the *order* and *means* of giving the woman are described. So the order of Is 38: 21-2 (Hezekiah's sickness and recovery), is in II KGS 20: 7, 8, and his thanksgiving and sacrifice (the duty of *all*, and so consistent, on deliverance from trouble),* comes next to "Berodach Baladan" v 12.

b When there is a discrepancy between the original and the reference, it may be a false reading, or have another explanation—

MARK 2: 25-6, "When Abiathar was high priest." But Ahimelech I SAM 21: 1, 2, was priest. Not a false reading, for Abiathar was present at Nob, and soon after, high priest.

MATT 23: 35, "Zachariah son of Barachiah," is Jehoiada II CHRON 24: 21. Both names mean whom JEHOVAH cares for or

* Ps 50: 14, 15.

blesses. So II Chron 26, Uzziah—strength of Jehovah, is Azariah—whom Jehovah helps II Kgs 14.

Acts 7: 16, "tomb that Abraham bought." Jacob bought it Gen 33: 19, Josh 24: 32, but was buried in Hebron, Joseph in Sychem. Jacob bought at Sychem, Abraham at Hebron. "Abraham is for Jacob, probably from error in transcription." Robinson, Clarke, Whedon. Bp Pearce supposes Luke wrote "*which he bought,*" a transcriber inadvertently inserting Abraham.

Wesley interprets thus; Stephen, running through the history, does not stop (nor was it necessary, being so well known, and supplied in the mind of the hearer) to recite particulars. He contracts into one, two sepulchres, places and purchases, so as in the first to name the buyer (Abraham), omitting the seller; and in the second, to name the seller (Hamor), and not the buyer. Abraham bought * * of Heth, Jacob was buried there; Jacob of Hamor, Joseph was buried there. He contracts the two purchases into one. This concise style was common among the Hebrews. See Wesley's note for fuller explanation.

Obs. Josephus says, the other 11 patriarchs were brought out of Egypt and buried in Hebron. But as the Scriptures are silent on this, Stephen (and Luke also here), are as good authority at least, as he, assigning to Shechem. Bp Pearce. Jewish writers agree that the patriarchs were all buried in Canaan, but none say in Hebron. As Sychem belonged to the Samaritans, this would be a reason for the Jews omitting to name the spot. Lightfoot.

Sometimes a reference supplies a fact omitted in the original.

"His feet they hurt with fetters" Ps 105 : 18. "More blessed to give than to receive." Acts 20 : 35. "Then he appeared to James" 1 Cor 15 : 7. Marriage of Salmon and Rahab Matt 1 : 5. So Jude 9, 14, Rev 2 : 14.

c Most of the *difficulties* in Scripture history have yielded additional evidence of its truth—

Luke 2: 2—"This was the first enrolment made when Quirinius was Governor of Syria." Saturninus or Varrus (his successor), was proconsul, and Publius Sulpicius Quirinius was "$ἡγεμων$" abt 12 yrs after, when the second enrolment was made and tax paid.

History says that Augustus had ordered a census 3 yrs B C, and sent Quirinius (who was in his good graces), into "the East" as imperial commissioner, to act with the governor (it is thought), about this business. Luke's words favor this explanation. Robinson, Lardner, Whedon. They also allude to a (the) second census.

Or Luke may be rendered "This enrolment took place *before* Quirinius was governor of Syria." GRESWELL, THOLUCK, CLARKE.

The *fact* is, a census was ordered as above, but the tax was not paid till 8 A. D., when Quirinius was president of Syria. ANGUS. Judea was included in Syria. Judas made insurrection on account of the tax ACTS 5: 37, and was destroyed by Quirinius.

See PALEY's EVS PT II c 6. On accordance of sacred and profane records, LARDNER is best.

5 *Apparent contradictions*—

a Sometimes the words are to be explained figuratively.

"Ye *will not* come." "No man *can* come to me, except the FATHER * * draw him" JOHN 5: 40, 6: 44. The first as compared with other passages, implies that those who hear the GOSPEL are bound to believe. They are so depraved, they will not believe and are condemned. The second says, they cannot come. Is it for lack of power the literal, or of will, the figurative sense? Both are Scriptural. Ahijah *could not* see. Joseph's brethren *could not* speak peaceably to him. How *can* ye being evil, speak good?—where the *dominion* of habit or propensity, is implied. It is to this CHRIST refers, and being in the will, it is sin.

b Restrict or *explain* some portions by others—

Divorce LUKE 16: 18, MARK 10: 11, 12, is forbidden absolutely. MATT 5: 32, 19: 9, it is allowed for adultery. In I COR 7: 15, we learn that the believing husband or wife is free when the unbelieving one determines to separate. Restrict and explain thus GEN 13: 7, 23: 17, 18, ACTS 7: 5, the last two enlightening the first, showing that the promise of the *whole* land to Abraham, was future and spiritual.

c Sometimes the same terms are used in different senses—

"A man is justified by faith apart from the works of the LAW" ROM 3: 28. "By works a man is justified and not only by faith" JAS 2: 24. Paul speaks of the justification of the *ungodly*, Jas of the justification of the *godly*. The one of justification in GOD's sight, the other in the sight of man. Paul of faith and its effects, Jas of mere assent.

So I COR 10: 33, "Even as I also please all men." GAL 1: 10 * * * "If I were still pleasing men, I should not be the servant of CHRIST." PROV 26: 4, "Answer not a fool according to his folly," v 5, "Answer a fool according to his folly."

d Sometimes the same act is ascribed to different persons—

CHRIST intercedes ROM 8: 34, HEB 7: 25, as does the SPIRIT ROM 8: 26-7, the one in heaven, the other in our hearts. CHRIST is ADVOCATE (mar COMFORTER) I JOHN 2 : 1. So is the SPIRIT JOHN 16 : 7. The one within, the other above. But a spiritual mind, with strong common sense, will often see the sense of the WORD clearer than the teacher can show.

6 AFTER the above difficulties have been solved, there are others in *things revealed* or commanded. It is in objections founded on these, that men most indulge. This last involves most of the hard things in revelation.

a Many under this head, are matters of interpretation only.

"I do (mar *have*), set my bow in the cloud" GEN 9 : 13, after the deluge, "And GOD said Let there be lights" 1 : 14—spoken of the sun, moon and stars, on the fourth day. Hebraists affirm of the first, that it existed before, but was now first used as the sign of the covenant. So CLARKE. Whether the heavenly bodies were created on the first or fourth day, much learning so far, has not settled. If on the first day, then "made two great lights" 1 : 16, means (as most Hebrew scholars think), they were first *used* on the fourth day to give light etc.

LEV 27 : 28-9, is said to authorize human sacrifices, as also JUD 11 : 34—Jephthah's daughter. Such sacrifices are forbidden DEUT 12 : 30-1, Ps 106 : 37-8, * *·* "They sacrificed their sons and their daughters unto demons." No devoted thing could be sacrificed. As to Jephthah, he saw his vow was rash. If kept literally, his act is not justified.

Those prayers, execrations and acts found fault with as vindictive, are inspired denunciations and predictive of GOD's judgments on them that rise up against him, or persecute his people, and ring with warning to sinners.

Exs. Ps 10 : 15, "Break thou the arm of the wicked" etc.
" 55 : 15, "Let death come * * * and let them go down alive into the pit"—*sheol.*
" 58 : 6, "Break their teeth, O GOD, in their mouth."
" 92 : 11, "Mine eye also hath seen my desire on mine enemies" etc.
" 109 : 6-20, "Set thou a wicked man over him" etc.

This prayer is ingeniously explained by Clarke as being the evil words of David's (and CHRIST's here), enemies, and not his own. This looks like a travesty on inspiration, or apologizing for GOD.

There are in the life of some of GOD's true and tried ones as in David's, circumstances when similar cries are extorted against CHRIST's enemies and theirs.*

Had Korah, with Dathan and Abiram not risen up against him, Moses would not have cried to GOD and "the earth opened her mouth and swallowed them up," nor "fire came forth from the LORD and devoured the 250 men who offered incense" NUMB 16 : 32, 35 But for Saul's failure, Samuel would not have had to hew "Agag in pieces before the LORD in Gilgal" I SAM 15 : 33.

I COR 5 : 5—"To deliver such a one unto satan for the destruction of the flesh." I TIM 1 : 20—"Hymenæus and Alexander, whom I delivered unto satan."

It seems from such SCRIPTURES, CHRIST had given his apostles power to deliver to satan, incorrigible offenders, to be tortured with diseases and terrors, body and mind (a warning to all), unto death, unless prevented by repentance. CLARKE, WESLEY.

Germane to this is I COR 16 : 22—"Let him be *anathema*," and punishment of Ananias, Sapphira and Elymas. But it is wicked and vain to copy such acts, and take authority to anathematize them who differ from her faith, as Rome does.

Of actions said to be ridiculous or immoral, some were symbolical or in vision only. Is 20 : 3, "Walking naked and barefoot"—without the upper garment. JER 13 : 4, 6, "Take the girdle * * * go to Euphrates" was in vision or given for illustration. LOWTH, CLARKE. EZEK 4—"Take thee a tile" and lying on thy left side 390 days etc, read as literal CLARKE. HOS 1 : 2, "Take unto thee a wife of whoredoms," i e, of the daughters of Israel. So CLARKE.

Right interpretation will clear the above class of difficulties.

SEC 2. CLASS 2. DIFFICULTIES ENUMERATED. DIFFICULTIES IN THE SENSE, USE AND LESSONS.

There are said to be

* As the cry of the SPIRIT in their heart.

1 Contrarieties between the OLD and N TESTAMENTS and teachings of CHRIST and his apostles.
2 *Things impossible* in the creation, and tracing man to a common origin.
3 *In some* of the miracles, history of the fall, of Balaam, and demoniacal possessions.
4 *Things wrong* in O T saints.
5 *Extraordinary* commands to Abraham and the Israelites.
6 *Mystery in some* of institutions of Moses, and cruelty toward idolaters.
7 *Quotations* out of the OLD in the N T in unnatural senses.
8 *Mystery in some* of the doctrines of the GOSPEL as a remedial system.
9 *In brief*, that such things are inconsistent with the object of a revelation.

We now take up the subject of this chapter, to show as GOD may help, that SCRIPTURE difficulties are not only not inconsistent with inspiration, so clearly proven CHS III–V, but are in keeping with it, and may be used as confirmatory marks, and so for our furtherance and joy of faith. We begin with the last—9.

That there are perplexing things in the BIBLE, we own. But are they inconsistent, or do they hinder its object?

From GEN to REVELATION, every doctrine and duty, the creation and redemption, is so simple and full, that the "wayfaring men, yea fools, shall not err therein" Is 35: 8.

The will of GOD and man's duty, are written as with a sunbeam. The spirituality of GOD and acceptable worship JOHN 4: 24—"GOD is a Spirit" (marg GOD is SPIRIT), repentance and remission of sins through CHRIST LUKE 24: 47; "And in none other is there salvation" ACTS 4: 12. Duty of all to repent and believe MARK 1: 15— "The time is fulfilled. ACTS 17: 30, * * * "But now he commandeth men that they should all everywhere repent." Life through the SON, death through unbelief JOHN 3; necessity of holiness HEB 12: 14—"The sanctification without which no man shall see the Lord." Aid of the

Spirit in saving our souls Rom 8: 26 * * * "the Spirit also helpeth our infirmity." In every age the end of revelation as the repository of saving truth, has been answered and its usefulness not hindered.

Compare the creed of the meanest Jew in relation to God and law, with that of the wisest heathen—Socrates, Confucius or Zoroaster, and the result is in the Jew's favor. Or the first Tusculan disputation of Cicero with any Christian treatise on immortality and the resurrection, and mark the difference. The heathen falters at every step, and dreads the conclusions his own reasoning leads to, while the views of the Christian are already settled; his chief difficulty being to *impress* his own and others' hearts with the truth. Through the Word, the vilest may be cleansed from all sin, and be made wise unto salvation.

But do not these difficulties weaken the authority, and affect the evidence of the Bible? Can it be so binding where much is concealed?

It is answered, in nature there are similar difficulties. Bp. Butler has shown in his inimitable way, that revelation is a republication of natural religion, having like mysteries in common, and that in natural religion, providence and every known law of man's duty, there are complexities as well as in the Bible. Analogy Pt II c I. There is an obscurity and deficiency of evidence, a mysteriousness of arrangement and treatment, that bespeak our life to be a warfare—a life of faith and discipline. In truth, these objections apply less to revelation than to and in our daily experience. Such objections if allowed, rob God of authority and man of motives to virtue.——Inasmuch as customs and language change, unless given to every nation and age, revelation cannot be free from difficulty. Customs and terms once familiar and facts once known, are obsolete or forgotten. The connection between them and other facts is lost, like some arts and things in science, known only to them of yore.

As rivers have snags, shoals, cataracts and turns in their course to the sea, so the life of every mortal has its trials.

And the words of the colored pilot on the Mississippi, in answer to one who asked if he knew where the snags were, are applicable here:—that it was not his business to know where the snags *are*, but where they are *not*. "If thou art wise, thou art wise for thyself" Prov 9 : 12, also comes in here. It is an evil eye that sees faults in the Author of nature or his work. The single eye and honest heart will not find the stone of stumbling and rock of offence in the Word.

3 But the very difficulties of Scripture, philological and historical, afford internal evidence of genuineness and authority. No one now doubts that the books were given in successive ages and in different tongues * * * Let us read the Credibility of Lardner, or Paley's Horæ Paulinæ, or Horæ Apostolica and Horæ Evangelicæ of Birks on the apparent discrepancies and real agreement of profane and sacred history between the Epistles and Acts, or different Gospels, and we will see that the differences create an internal evidence even greater than the external. It is the apparent discrepancy between the writers, their independence of one another in everything but truth, that forms the argument. Thus is shown that the very differences are essential to the perfection of the whole.

There has been also in keeping with the Book of God, a gradual, progressive solution of these difficulties, supplying fresh evidence to every age, proving its evidence, like its teachings, is for all time.

From the philologic and historic, we pass to the doctrinal difficulties—the mysteries of godliness and iniquity, the hard things in revelation, and veiled or dimly disclosed future. How patent it is everywhere that man is fallen—his heart depraved, his intellect darkened! Also, before observation and experience, his ideas are wrong. A revelation to his taste, even according to his ideal of virtue, would bear marks of an origin lower than heaven, like its author, as already noticed. We are finite. It is not reason that the infinite Mind, in communicating spiritual and eternal things, would accommodate to the ignorance and prejudices of a mortal, (considering his sin and misery are of his own choosing, or self procured), or be free from obscurities. There are such "revelations," as the bibles of India, Al Koran, Book of Mormon. But a revelation professing to come from omniscient WISDOM without difficulties, would be tainted with suspicion. OBJ 8.

Add to this, these difficulties have dignified **every kind of learning.** The study of modern classic literature began with that of the BIBLE. And ever since, true religion and learning are linked together, thus making learning the handmaid of the GOSPEL. "Divorce learning from religion, you dig the grave of liberty, and orators may prepare to preach her funeral sermon." BP AMES.

As the BIBLE is the repertory of intellectual wealth, so its truths are the source of intellectual power. The GOSPEL kindled, if it did not create, Milton's poetic might. It is the energy which, after years of musing and devotion, years of mysterious muttering and deep omen, sent forth its pyramid of flame in Old England, and poured its lava tide of gold and gems, fetched deep from classic and patriarchal times, adown the russet steep of Puritan theology.

This was the secret of Cowper and Pollok's heavenly muse, of Watts', the Wesleys' and Montgomery's inspiration. But why enumerate? What is modern science but one monument of the GOSPEL's quickening power?

Three hundred yrs ago, the classics were revived; but three hundred yrs ago, the GOSPEL was restored.

Digging in Pompeii, Leo and Lorenzo found the candelabra in which the classic fires had burned, but long ago become extinct. Such models of classic lore and morals as Plato, Horace and Livy— their faith and philosophy, had passed away, or only adorned the shelf of the antiquary. When lo! in the crypt of the convent, Luther, Zwingli and Melancthon discovered a light, and lifting the gravestone, found that GOSPEL the Papist had buried. There, the lamp of truth had burned on through the ages—a "lamp shining in a dark place," unquenchable in its own immortality.

Jupiter, Minerva and Apollo were dead, or grey with eld; their idols had gone to the moles and bats; but the ALPHA and OMEGA lives on, the FOUNTAIN of life. The classic lamps are filled again, and from this fount, this Pierian Spring, Bacon, Locke, Newton and all the good and great of modern times, have drunk their inspiration. The WORD OF GOD is the Promethean fire that ignites the dead truths, and reanimates the souls and bodies of dead men. LITY ATTRACTIONS, HAMILTON.

If they raise doubts and fears in some Christians' minds, is not this an evidence that the BOOK is divine? This life in every relation is a probation. We are where habitual reliance on GOD is duty, necessity, interest. And the maxim "Sleepless vigilance is the price of liberty," is as true in every one's experience seeking after the truth, as it is of "liberty." Also, the AUTHOR of nature being the AUTHOR of revelation also, analogy teaches us not to expect in the one, what is not in the other. And some would be wiser, if they would copy the example of the pilot above alluded to.

Whether revelation could have come to us free from such things, is not *our* "business" to discuss.

Instead of answering the objections in detail, mark and apply the following—

1 *Interpret* SCRIPTURE as written in the language of man, but conveying the thoughts of GOD. So far as like other books—in the words of man, explain by similar laws. But so far as different (see c VI SECS 2 and 3 especially), and much having a double sense, and "written to the succession of ages," a plenary, spiritual sense must be given. The ceremonial law, e g, only *prefigured* the coming and death of CHRIST as its "end" ROM 10:4. So the promise to Abraham is not in words *clearly* pointing out MESSIAH. But the NEW (which is the key to O T mysteries chiefly), tells us CHRIST is meant, suggesting also the exceeding breadth of GOD'S LAW OBJ 7.

2 *As* doctrines must be taken in accordance with the tenor of SCRIPTURE, so no difficulty can be admitted inconsistent with inspiration. To compare the miracles of Moses with the prodigies of Livy, Ezekiel with Æschylus, or teachings of CHRIST with Plato as some do, is fallacious reasoning. To say the miracles, reasoning, imagery are incredible or forced, is to remove difficulties on principles which set aside the authority of God. Admitting inspiration, their solution must leave that glorious attribute un-

touched. Most of the objections—2, 3, 9, are therefore inconsistent with either faith or piety.

3 *Study* SCRIPTURE as a WHOLE, having one mind and purpose running through it from first to last. All the light the first throws on the last, or last reflects on the first, may be used to illustrate, explain, defend.

This law does for its truths what the kindred rule, analogy of faith, does for words and parallel passages. Take "Whosoever hath not, from him shall be taken away even that which he hath" MATT 13: 12, apart from the context, and we are uncertain of the sense. By comparing with 25: 29, MARK 4: 25, LUKE 8: 18, all is plain. Again, the sacrifice and murder of Abel *in themselves*, seem not more important than of any other good man. But viewed according to the mind of the SPIRIT, the story assumes a vast importance and dignity. Among other lessons, it teaches 1, The damnable nature of sin—requiring vicarious sacrifice, expressive of demerit and conscious guilt. 2, The animal, as typical of the LAMB of GOD. 3, The enmity ever existing between the seed of the woman and "serpent."

Explained in this way, the doctrines, ordinances and examples of SCRIPTURE have become lessons in the church's life, individually and collectively, through the ages all along.

4 *Study* it not only *connectedly*, but in its *true* connection. The foregoing implies this. If the ten plagues of Egypt be regarded only as a means of delivering a people from bondage, they might seem severe, some even absurd. But read them as the SPIRIT intends—as manifestations of the power, justice, goodness of GOD in behalf of his own against the wicked, for liberty against slavery and against idolatry (his judgments being inflicted on "all the gods of Egypt" Ex 12: 12), the account is fruitful in lessons of faith and patience, long-suffering and faithfulness of GOD.

As to Israel, so to the church to the end of time; while its *memorial*, is a fair type of him whose blood is the pledge of a greater salvation than that of the Hebrews—"our passover * * * even CHRIST" I COR 5: 7.

Or if idolatry be regarded as a mental error only, or

Israel as any other nation, its punishment will seem hard. Really, it was on the apostate Israelite who had taken JEHOVAH as his king; and in a theocracy, it was treason; and one object was, to purge and keep the people from the sin of the age. Thus the barren fig tree MATT 21, and destruction of the swine c 8, suggest important lessons.

So in the life and character of our LORD, much that is said of him, will seem contradictory and inconsistent, if not read in its true connection. To think of him as either GOD or man only, causes confusion. Combine both views—unite in him the divine and human nature, and there is perfect harmony. And we see

> "JESUS, in whom the GODHEAD's rays
> Beam forth with mildest majesty."

To find fault with ancient saints as inconsistent with inspiration, implies a *false theory*. **If it be a revelation of GOD and man, and from GOD to man, the picture is as real as the end is practical, and every mouth is stopped.**

Let us notice the deception of Jacob GEN 27 : 33–5, and its lessons. His pre-eminence had been foretold before his birth. Isaac and Rebecca knew about GOD's choice—"the elder shall serve the younger" 25 : 23. In spite of this, Isaac made a favorite of Esau, who had married a heathen woman. Jacob had so little faith in the promise, that he removed his brother's priority by purchase; Esau in a day of trouble, was tempted to sell, and Jacob to get, the birthright for "a mess of meat." Rebecca, with no **more faith** in GOD, put up her favorite to get the blessing by fraud.

The guilt and folly of such partiality soon brought forth its fruit. The parents' weakness was punished by the alienation of their children. Esau's recklessness cost him his birthright. Rebecca seems to have become dependent on the son she had wronged. Her favorite, she never looked on more. He was exiled, and fled from his brother to Padan-aram, to hard labor, and be wronged by Laban, his mother's brother. Leah, the one he did not love, was honored as the mother of the chosen tribe. And thenceforward, in the deception, jealousies and divisions of his children, his life was imbittered.

And though the promise was fulfilled at last, Jacob received no blessing from it. Instead of his mother's son bowing down to him, he bowed to Esau, after that dark night of wrestling with the "man" at Penuel (due to his wrong to his brother), and at last, became dependent on his children down in Egypt!

The punishment was, like the lesson, complete. It may be said, nevertheless, that Jacob inherited the promise. True, for the "gifts and the calling of GOD are without repentance" ROM 11 : 29, his choice in *such cases* being not on personal merit, but for reasons he sees fit to conceal. It may be said, the blessing was obtained dishonorably. And this is true. But the objection applies to providential dealings as much as to SCRIPTURE. Man's sin is being constantly overruled for GOD's glory, and neither is our responsibility nor the holiness of GOD affected by the arrangement. A revelation without such incidents, would not be just to GOD nor true to man.

OBS. 1 *The choice* of Jacob (the younger, contrary to nature and precedent), is a clear case of "unconditional" election. See on election PT III. c I. SEC 1, II. c VII. CON. Here is a sphere in which the will of GOD must be absolute, excluding man's agency. Rebecca's failure, due to lack of faith in GOD (?), implies also her failure to observe this rule.

It is noticeable that this is the first case used by Paul in that matchless argument ROMS 9–11, illustrative of the divine sovereignty, in accounting for the stumbling and rejection of the Jews, and deserves quoting here, as the inspired comment on this doctrine. "Neither because they are Abraham's seed are they all children; But, in Isaac shall thy seed be called. That is * * * the children of the promise are accounted for a seed. * * * But Rebecca, having conceived by one, even by our father Isaac—for the children being not yet born, neither having done anything good or bad, that the *purpose* of GOD *according election* might stand, not of works, but of him that calleth, it was said unto her, The elder shall serve the younger. Even as it is written, Jacob have I loved, but Esau have I hated. * * * Is there unrighteousness with GOD? GOD forbid. For he saith to Moses, I will have mercy on whom I will have mercy. * * So then, it is not *of him that willeth,* nor *of him that runneth,* but of

God that hath mercy" 9: 7-17. Then follows the *"conditional"* choice c 10, 11—" According to the election of grace."

2 We have in the account of Isaac's family GEN 25-33, in connection with Jacob's life, an illustration of the old story of man's failure and GOD's faithfulness, as well as his sovereignty. "GOD is not mocked." The law of cause and effect in the spiritual world, is as certain and operative as in the natural GAL 6: 7. The BIBLE outlines (some of) the facts simply, adding significantly, with reference to what is suggested and its lessons, " If thou art wise, thou art wise for thyself" PROV 9: 12.

3 EVEN if Isaac's choice were on the ground of weakness, Rebecca's arts are inexcusable. Whether parent or son, or *who* was most guilty, we are not told. The house was divided against itself, and through Isaac and Rebecca's example, the sons were made Ishmaelites to all generations. Had Isaac been permitted to "bless" Esau, who had right of primogeniture, GOD would have brought about the prediction 25: 23, in his own way and time, without adding the "sorrow therewith."

4 As *said*, one's ability to overcome the world may not be greater than his weakest point. The besetting sin, is the point of greatest danger. The consciousness—the ring of victory, can be felt only in a heart, one with that of CHRIST, where faith can have an unlimited action.

Man has a complex nature, inheriting through his paternity also, virtues and vices of different kinds and degrees.. This suggests the grounds or occasions subjectively, of temptation and danger in our probation, as it may also, the means of " successful war "-fare. He who conquers the world must first "kill the dragon."

> The kingdoms of the world are thine,
>   If thou hast faith thyself to lose;
> But they who seek the *me* and *mine*,
>   The universal good refuse.
>
> The master of his own desire,
>   The victor over selfish claims,
> Doth by that death of self, aspire
>   To universal ends and aims. T. C. UPHAM.

5 *This again, suggests* reasons why so few rise to distinction in CHRIST's kingdom, or realize above glimpses, the " beauty of the LORD " Ps 27: 4, or " secret of the LORD" 25: 14 ; or the promises given 31: 19, 20, 34: 12-14—" in the land of the living." We love to contemplate those examples whose praise, like a perfume, has come down through the centuries with renewed and increasing fragrance. See EXAMPLES PT III. How gracious is the life picture

—character and experience of Abraham to our mind, as compared with his younger grandson!

6 *In all ages*, there have been in the "book of life" above (though not found in the BIBLE), names of as "good report" as the "elders"—those given in the 11 c of HEBS. That Kempis, Wycliffe, Luther, Huss, Jerome of Prague; Madame Guyon, Fenelon, the Wesleys; Mary, George and Alfred Cookman, Bp Hamline, John Dempster; Dr. and Phœbe Palmer, J. S. Inskip, "Juniata," Spurgeon, may rank with those who adorn the pages of SCRIPTURE. And our African Bishop Taylor and the author of the BRIGHT SIDE OF LIBBY and

> "All hail the power of Jesus' name,
> We are building two a day,"

with Paul and the apostles.—Does the reader desire a name alongside of those whom GOD has so honored, both in the BIBLE and out of it? and like them

> "Through the ocean tide of years,"

to shine more and more as "the day is drawing nigh?" Such an aspiration, not in the spirit of James and John (read the connection Matt 20), GOD says he will fulfil Ps 145: 19. We have aimed to point the way (as taught in the WORD), throughout this book, in this connection, and especially under PROMS and EXS. Compare MARK 9: 23, "All things possible," MATT 9: 29, "According to your faith," as the means through which Paul's list HEB 11, obtained *their* "good report."

> Earth's transitory things decay,
> Its pomps, its pleasures pass away;
> But the sweet memory of the good
> Survives in the vicissitude. SIR J. BOWRING.

As GOD is one, so his WORD and world are all of a piece, having a vital connection, as Bp Butler shows. Miracles and mysteries abound in nature and revelation—in the natural and spiritual realms; and it is owing to the order of antecedence and sequence simply—their daily recurrence, that things do not surprise, as in the rising and setting sun, day and night.

Light and power are inexplicable. Gravitation, a name for that which holds and keeps the heavenly bodies in their orbits to a hair's breadth, in such unvarying harmony from age to age, can only be explained as the hand of the CREATOR. Laws of nature so called, philosophers must own to be really the mode of the AGENT'S acting, as being in contact with every particle of matter in the universe. Earthquakes, volcanoes, the "mysterious comet," are strange phenomena in geology and astronomy.

The divine prescience, as not interfering with man's agency—will and choice, has perplexed some. The doctrine of one uncreated self-existent, **eternal BEING**, the incarnation—union of the divine and human nature; crucifixion, resurrection and ascension of JESUS CHRIST, and apostacy of the Jews, are incomprehensible. And that "MYSTERY" of the ages—"BABYLON THE GREAT, THE MOTHER OF THE HARLOTS AND OF THE ABOMINATIONS OF THE EARTH" REV 17: 5, believed to be the "man of sin" II THESS 2: 3 (mar "lawless one"),—the "beast" in his rise and progress; why the "wicked prosper" and the good suffer—wrong over right for 6000 yrs ; why antichrist should prevail against the Waldenses, Albigenses and Huguenots, to set back (?) the kingdom and coming of our LORD, are things in the spiritual world, which try the faith and patience of the saints. But in the face of these difficulties, faith has sung on—

> Right is right, since GOD is GOD,
> And right the day must win;
> To doubt would be disloyalty,
> To falter would be sin. FABER.

Man's body even, is a microcosm—little world, and **full** of mysteries. The connection between mind and matter—the volition and movement of the hand or foot e g, or pulsation **of the heart in** unconscious sleep, reason **can** never explain.

OBS. It is proper to notice **here as** a suggestive, humbling lesson, that it is only as the mind and body are regenerated, that man knows how to take care of his own person even! But from infancy to age, he goes on, neglecting or breaking the ordinances of GOD and laws of his well being, suffering the consequences, ignorant alike of the cause or cure. While the other creatures, called "Dumb," "lower animals" etc, as the cat and dog, know their MAKER's will, what is for their health and cure. But man is the most helpless and dependent of GOD's **creatures.** Objectors do not take into account that our apostacy is the cause of our ignorance in divine things, and we will add, of much of natural law also. See INTRODUCTORY and PT III c V.

As said, it is not GOD's way to give us much ready to hand. We ought to distrust our own reason in things beyond our experience and observation, especially in spiritual realities—metaphysical* subjects. The more we learn of the works and ways of GOD, the more the "light of the knowledge of * * * GOD in the face of JESUS CHRIST" illumes and sanctifies us, the more humble and docile we feel. Blessed are they who see GOD in all, and have learned to walk as on enchanted—holy ground!

Of SCRIPTURE DIFFICULTIES, the origin of evil is perhaps, the most perplexing. The genesis, existence and agency of the old serpent the devil, (in connection with the fall, and foreknowledge of GOD), his power and continuance in hindering and destroying the work and purpose of GOD in the world, (which in turn has given rise to the two views called OPTIMISM—that all is for the best, and PESSIMISM—that all is for the worst), are subjects that must remain in the archives of divinity, laid up in reversion for us it may be, till the time when "I shall know, even as also I have been known." I COR 13: 12.

You gaze upon Mont Blanc. Those heights were not made for mortal feet to tread. Only angels can breathe that ethereal, or venture to explore the deep and high things of GOD. For us, those heights were only meant to gaze upon and adore. That is where the BIBLE touches heaven. INF PROOFS p 161.

Finally, with him who wrote his letters after returning from the third heavens, we may exclaim, "O the depth of the riches, both of the wisdom and the knowledge of GOD! How unsearchable are his judgments, and his ways past tracing out!" ROM 11: 33.

* *Meta* above and *phusis* nature, attributed to Aristotle.

CHAPTER V.

THE JEWS FROM THE EXILE TO CHRIST, TAKEN FROM THEIR SCRIPTURES AND HISTORY.*

SEC 1

THE EXILE, PROPHETS AND BOOKS IN ORDER, BELONGING TO THIS PERIOD.

NOTE.—The ten tribes never returned to **their** land or GOD. Their identity is lost forever—becoming soon amalgamated it is thought, with the **heathen**. Their sad fate like their end, is veiled in mystery. Not **forsaken of** their GOD, till they with "whorish hearts" had long forsaken him, their punishment was not greater than their sin.—Our tears of sorrow fall on this tablet of their memory. See the account with causes recited II KGS. 17.

"Oh that my people had hearkened unto me,
And Israel had walked in my ways!
I should soon have subdued their enemies.
* * * * * * * *
But their time should have endured forever,
He should have fed them also with the finest of the wheat,
And with honey out of the rock, should have satisfied thee."
Ps. 81 A. V.

THE EXILE—606–536.—And the LORD sent against him (Jehoiakim), bands of the Chaldeans, Syrians, Moabites and of the children of Ammon, and he sent them against Judah to destroy it according to the word of the LORD * * * by the prophets II KGS 24: 2, II CHRON 36: 5–8.—With this second shock by Nebuchadnezzar (the first is noticed II KGS 24: 1), the captivity began, when 3023 JER 52: 28, among others, with Daniel c 1, were taken to Babylon.

The following books, **in** connection with **history,** supply information during the 70 years—

JEREMIAH 628–585, LAMS 588, HABAKKUK 612–598,
DANIEL 606–534, EZEKIEL 595–574, OBADIAH 588–583.

* USHER's Chronology.

From which it appears that Jeremiah had been blowing the trumpet in Zion and sounding the alarm 22, and Hab 6 yrs, before the gathering storm of GOD's displeasure—the judgment of Judah and Benjamin, like the "crack of doom," came. Also, that he was cotemporaneous with Habakkuk, Daniel 22, Ezekiel 11 and Obadiah 3 yrs.

He was "the son of Hilkiah of the priests" in Anathoth, his native place. From his excuse 1: 6—"I am a child," he must have been very young when GOD called him, in the 13th yr of Josiah, 629. Owing to persecution and plots against his life, even of his brethren and Father's house 12: 6, 11: 21, probably at the call of GOD, he left Anathoth and came to Jerusalem. Here and in Judea he labored for 43 years, till after the assassination of Gedaliah (whom Nebuchadnezzar had made governor), by Ishmael at Mizpah. Then he was taken by Johanan, who led the discontented and fearful of the Jews to Tahpanhes Egypt c 40, where tradition says, he was stoned to death, a year or so after the "city was broken up." Here 571, the colony was destroyed by the sword and famine by Nebuchadnezzar (after his 13 yrs' siege of Tyre EZEK 29), who set his pavilion on the very spot Jeremiah had told them he would 43: 9-13, 44: 27.

Naturally mild and susceptible, inclined to mourn in secret over the increasing wickedness (especially of those in high places), and impending ruin of his country, he nevertheless, at the call of GOD, stood forth as his champion for the right—his prophet for the times, in the face of reproach, threats, imprisonment and death. As illustrative of the first see 9: 1—"O that my head were waters," and of his courage 1: 18—"Behold! I have made thee this day a defenced city, and an iron pillar * * * against the kings of Judah, against the princes thereof, against the priests" and false prophets.

His style in elegance and sublimity, though inferior to Isaiah (who is the favorite and standard of comparison), is in places very elevated; e g 50-1, on the approaching judgment of Babylon by Cyrus, is in lofty, poetic strains.

He is more large and diffuse than Isaiah, full of pathetic allusions to his own feelings and state of the **Jews**.

A large part of this book seems to have been compiled by some careless hand—the MSS put together without regard to chronological order, as 20-37. In these 17 chs, many things in the reign of Zedekiah are before Jehoiakim, and vice versa. Also, of events in the same reign, the last come first and the first last.

From the style, internal evidence and v 31 to the end, it appears that c 52 closing, is by another hand.

DANIEL

"Judge of GOD," was of those carried to "the land of Shinar" (first deportation) in the 3rd year of Jehoiakim 606, c 1. He was probably of the house of David. The scene of his wonderful life—toil, trials and triumphs, during this gloomy period (over which GOD has in a sense drawn the curtain), is pathetically alluded to Ps 137—"By the rivers of Babylon, there we sat down; yea, we wept when we remembered Zion. Upon the willows in the midst thereof, we hanged up our harps," which Toplady has sung to the *Christian* experience in

> Your harps, ye trembling saints.

He was instructed like **Moses in** Egypt, in the learning of the Chaldeans. While yet a "youth," his name was proverbial for his wisdom—"Wiser than Daniel" EZEK 28: 3, and he is named with Noah and Job 14: 14, 18, 20. He outstripped all his companions, was soon made governor, also chief of the *magians*. Nebuchadnezzar honored him with the first place in his kingdom. During the king's seven years' madness, he is thought to have been viceroy. Three times he records it revealed to him as one "Greatly beloved" of heaven. Josephus says, after death his memory became immortal. He is famous among orientals to this day. His extraordinary gifts he ascribes to God.

His predictions are clearer and more circumstantial than of others, so that greater light seems to have been given him. They have a distinctness like history, are an important part of SCRIPTURE evidence. So much so, that from the days of Porphyry,* the only resource of infidelity, has been to assume that they were written after the events transpired.

God preserved him through the 70 years, to see the return, of which he knew from Jeremiah.—It was while the last night of Babylon was still fresh in his mind c 9, 538, he set his "face unto the Lord God, to seek by prayer and supplication, with fasting, sackcloth and ashes," to have the purpose fulfilled; thus leaving us an important example.

He lived through the reign of six kings (including Nabopolassar)—Nebuchadnezzar, Evil Merodach (Jer 52: 31), Belshazzar, Darius and Cyrus.

He was cotemporaneous with Jeremiah 22 yrs, Ezekiel 11, and Obadiah. It is a pleasing thought, the silence of Scripture not against it, that Jeremiah, Daniel and Ezekiel met, embraced and communed with one another in Judea, Babylonia—Shushan 8: 2, ("Daniel's ordinary residence"), and by the Chebar, as they doubtless held intercourse through messengers.

From 2: 4 * * * "O king, live forever!" to c 7, is in Chaldee, the rest Heb. The first 6 chs are historical, the rest prophetic.

His visions and revelations were wonderful. That of the metallic image c 2 603, representing the four great kingdoms—Babylonian, Medo-Persian, Grecian, Roman, succeeded by the last, prefigured by the "stone," becoming a "great mountain" and filling "the whole earth"—Christ and *his kingdom.*

The vision of the 4 great beasts out of the sea, 555, c 7, is a continuation. The little horn from among the 10 out of the head of the fourth beast, which "put down (or absorbed) three kings," who shall speak * * * against and "wear out the saints of the most high" and "think to change the times and the law" and continues "a time, times and a half"—1260 yrs, most agree, points out the pope or papal power.

The vision of the ram and he-goat c 8, 553, with "notable horn" again, the Medo-Persian and Grecian kingdoms, beginning with Cyrus (or Darius the Median) and Alexander. The "little horn" here—"king of fierce countenance" v 23, which cast down of the "host" and "stars," "took away the offering and place of his sanctuary" etc, writers ancient and modern refer to Antiochus proxi-

* The "ablest opponent of Christianity"—3rd cy.

mately, then the Roman power. The 2300 "evenings and mornings" (Heb)—may be literal—6 yrs 110 ds. If so, we have revealed the time from his first coming upon the Jews, till the sanctuary was "cleansed" SEC 3

c 9, 538, opens our view upon the way and means of the Restoration and times of MESSIAH so clear, that the world was looking for him when he came. Daniel's suit was about the return, and Gabriel v 24-7 in the "seventy weeks of Daniel," showed him more—1 That in seven weeks from "the going forth of the commandment" (by **Artaxerxes** Ez 7 : 8-11), Jerusalem "with street and moat," would be rebuilt. 2 That in 62 weeks more, MESSIAH would come (in his ministry). 3 That in the midst—'half of the week "—3½ yrs, he would be cut off—Thus Ezra and Nehemiah were 49 yrs finishing their great work. In 434 more—483, CHRIST came, and 7 added—490—the seventy weeks, " to anoint the most holy."

c 10 This vision (third of Cyrus 534), of mysterious import, seems also to be about things pertaining to the Restoration. From v 13 it is likely that Cyrus resisted his inspirations "**one** and twenty days," in some matter, and for causes not come down to us.

c 11 538, Is a comment on c 8, the inspired history or view perspective of GOD's people (after Persia and Greece), under Egypt and Syria. The seer's eye is directed to these **two** chief of Alexander's four kingdoms, because under them in turn, their land between. Also many Jews dwelt in those two countries.

v 2 The "three kings" after Cyrus, are Cambyses, Smerdis (Ahasuerus and Artaxerxes Ez 4), the "fourth," "far richer," Xerxes. Herodotus who lived then, says he had 5,500,000 men and 1207 ships.

3 The "mighty king" is Alexander.

4 "His kingdom shall be * * * divided toward the four winds * * * not to his posterity, but for others."

In 15 yrs Alexander's posterity was cut off, including his wives Satira, Roxana, and mother Olympias, who were murdered. "Blood calls for blood."

5 "King of the south "—Ptolemy (son of) Lagus. "One of his princes" shall be " strong above him "—Seleucus Nicator. He obtained the **dominion from** Antioch to India. SEC 3.

HIS SONS—Antiochus I 280, Ants II Theos 261, Seleucus II 246, Seleucus III 226, Ants III Gt 223, Seleucus IV 187, Ants IV Epiphanes 175.

PTOLEMIES—P Lagus 323, P Philadelphus 285, P Euergetes 247, P Philopater 222, P Epiphanes 205, P Philometer 181, P Physcon 146, P Lathyrus 116.

6 " And at the end of years," after being at war. " The daughter of the king of the south shall come "—Bernice, daughter of P Philadelphus, was given to Antiochus II, for which he was to put away his wife **Laodice** and the children, and end the war. He

recalled Laodice, who murdered him and Bernice, and set Seleucus II on the throne.

7, 8 "But out of a shoot from her roots, shall one stand up in his place"—P Euergetes, to avenge his sister. He took from Seleucus from Mt Taurus to India, 40,000 talents of silver, "precious vessels of silver and gold," spoils, with 2500 of "their gods" back with him to Egypt.

9. "He (Seleucus), shall come into * * * the south," but "return," his fleet damaged by storm and army defeated. Note opposite reading in A V, and so interpretation.

10, 11 "And his sons (Sels and Ant III), shall war" against P Philopater. First, Seleucus till poisoned, and then Antiochus continued. But his "multitude"—68,000 men and 102 elephants, was defeated at Raphia.

12 Ptolemy was "lifted up" by his success. "If he had improved it, he might have overrun all Syria."

13 "The king of the north shall return * * * at the end of the times"—14 yrs after (P Epiphanes being a minor), "with a great army."

14 And "many shall stand up against the king of the south." Philip of Macedon. "Also the children of the violent among thy people." Apostate Jews, traitors, etc. "But they shall fall." Scopas was sent into Coelosyria, also took Jerusalem and Judea back to Egypt.

15 "So the king of the north shall come." Antiochus defeated Scopas on the Jordan, took the rest of his army in Sidon, carrying all before him.

16 "He shall stand in the glorious land." He regained Judea and showed the Jews favor because they sided with him.

17. "He shall set his face to come" into Egypt, but changed his plan, and gave Ptolemy "the daughter of woman to corrupt her" —his own daughter Cleopatra, who was very beautiful and accomplished, to be a snare to him. But she acted not "for him," but revealed to her husband her father's intentions.

18 "After this shall he turn his face unto the isles." Disappointed, he next with 300 ships, scoured the Mediterranean, taking Rhodes, Colophon, Samos, Euboea etc. "But a prince * * * shall cause his reproach to turn upon him." In his invasion of Greece, Scipio Asiaticus overthrew his army 82,000, at Magnesia, holding him in 15,000 talents and his son Antiochus IV, as security. He escaped to Antioch. Then in his trouble, marched into the East about the tribute, and to plunder the temple of Jupiter Belus at Elymais.

19 "He shall stumble and fall, and not be found," seems to allude to the circumstances of his death, which are uncertain.

He reigned 36 yrs. "was distinguished for his faults and fortunes, as well as his successes and failures."

20 "Then shall stand up * * * one (raiser of taxes A V), that shall cause an exactor to pass through the glory of the kingdom"—the temple. Seleucus IV sent Heliodorus his treasurer, to rob the temple for the tribute, but he was "prevented by an angel." Within few days "destroyed." Heliodorus poisoned **Seleucus to get the throne.**

21 "A contemptible (A V vile) person"—Antiochus, "to whom they had not given the honor of the kingdom." He was not the heir. He obtained "the kingdom by flatteries"—dissimulation, gifts.

He flattered the Romans, Eumenes of Pergamos, the Syrians, who flattered him with the title *Epiphanes.*

OBS How false, how fair! Whom God calls contemptible, vile, the world calls "illustrious."

He was every man's companion. Was in the shops, prattling with the workmen. In the taverns, eating and drinking with the worst fellows, singing debauched songs. POLYBIUS.

22-3 They (his competitors), were "swept away from **before him,**" by Eumenes and Attalus. "Also the prince of the covenant"—Onias. In straits for the tribute, he displaced the good Onias and put **his** brother Jason in for 360 talents, then Meneláus his brother bought it for 300 more 174. *He*, to raise the tax, robbed the temple through Lysimachus his brother, and bribed Andronicus **governor of** Antioch, to murder Onias.

It was Jason who built the *Xystus*—gymnasium, **for obscene sports** of the Greeks, and the *Plæstra.*

24 "He shall scatter among them prey, and spoil, and substance" —at shows, by gifts, spoils in war etc. He paid his soldiers in advance, to insure their services.

In profuseness of gifts he abounded above all before him I MAC. **He** would scatter money in the streets for the people.

"He shall devise his devices—"

25 By cunning and dishonorable means, **he got the mastery of P** Philometer's "mighty army."

26 "Yea, they that eat of his meat shall **destroy him.**" He corrupted Ptolemy's servants **to** betray him.

27 Both "shall speak lies at one table." At Memphis they had conferences at table. Antiochus professing good will, to continue to his nephew the throne, now that the Alexandrians had declared for his brother Physcon. Vile hypocrisy! While Ptolemy professed gratitude to his uncle, but determining to unite with his brother against him. The lies did "not prosper."

About this time, Jason drove Menelaus **into the castle of Jerusa**lem, and put his adversaries to the sword.

28 "Then shall he **return** into his **land.**" And hearing what

Jason had done, and that the Jews rejoiced at the report of his death, "His heart shall be against the holy covenant, and he shall do his pleasure" A V exploits. He took Jerusalem by storm, slew 40000, sold as many into slavery, despoiled the house literally of its furniture, took 1800 talents of "gold," caused the daily sacrifice to cease, sacrificed a **sow on** the altar, on which **one** had been raised to Jupiter, and sprinkled of her broth throughout the holy of holies 170. Com 8: 9–14.

29 "At the time appointed he shall **return**." Finding the brothers had united, he threw off the mask, and taking Memphis, he marched for Alexandria.

"But it shall not be in the latter" as "in the former."

30 "For ships of Kittim" Rome, "shall come against him." When 7 m from the city, legates from the senate met **and warned** him to desist. On his replying that he would "consult his friends," Popilius, with his staff, drew a circle around him **in the sand, and** not to pass it without a definite answer. Antiochus **changed color** and returned, grieving and groaning (v 30), says **Polybius, Livy,** Justin.

And he shall "have indignation against **the holy covenant, and** do his pleasure * * * and have regard to them **that forsake the holy covenant**"—Menelaus, apostates, traitors I and II MAC, JOS.

He sent Apollonius 167, to massacre all the males, **take the women and children for slaves, on** the Sabbath, when **the Jews would not** fight. The streets again flowed with blood. Some concealed themselves, others got to the mountains. The copies of the LAW were burned, the Sabbath, circumcision etc, abolished. Women were driven through the streets with their children tied about their necks, and thrown from the walls and towers. The temple was dedicated to Jupiter Olympius, his statue put in it, and Jerusalem left desolate. It was decreed that all should conform to the faith of the king. Athenæus was sent to enforce the decree. See more SEC 3.

OBS 1 How apostate must a people be to be thus abandoned to the enemies of GOD and theirs! 2 And how desperate and sanguinary the struggle SEC 3, to recover their prestige—civil and religious liberties, such as now remained to them!

31 Set up "the abomination that maketh desolate." Referred to MATT 24: 15.

32 "The people that know their GOD, shall be strong and do exploits;" as Matthias and his sons SEC 3. Also the aged, pious Eleazar, Salomona and her seven sons, whom neither rewards nor sufferings could move.

33 "Shall fall by * * * flame." Some were roasted alive.

34 "Shall be holpen with a little help." In their decadence, the SPIRIT speaks of the deliverance thro the Maccabees as *little*, man, as great. In consideration of the blood, treasure etc it **cost**, it was little, as also GOD was about to reject them **wholly** and **visibly, for** rejecting his MESSIAH.

35 "The king shall do * * * his will," and "magnify himself above every god," and speak against "the GOD of gods."

To 36 is about Antiochus. From 35 most agree, is about him proximately; then prospectively, about the Romans and Papacy.

OBS The name of Antiochus is immortal as a prodigy of wickedness, a typical antichrist.

The connection suggests that he inherited a feeble moral sense or instincts, with a large share of self-love, joined to lust of power—glory of this world etc.

Such tendencies, such a disposition, may **account** for such a life. He sacrificed honor and conscience, using any or every means to **gain** his ends. Led on and influenced by others, he like Pharaoh, **hardened** his heart (he may have been atheistic v 37), even to speak and fight against the GOD of gods.

c 12 The prophetic sense of this is in dark, symbolic words, "and sealed till the time of the end" i e, till fulfilled.

Daniel's predictions reach from the Persian empire to the resurrection. And throughout the series, as from an observatory, we are still more impressed with the SCRIPTURE teaching of GOD'S providence and sovereignty over **the nations,** so boldly iterated to a heathen king in the night of the exile—"that the heavens do rule," and three times **"that the MOST** HIGH ruleth **in the** kingdom of **men"** c 4.

Daniel **it is** believed, had showed Cyrus the prophecies **of** Isaiah where 44 : 28, 45 c, is foretold the part he was to play in the Restoration, where GOD calls him "my shepherd" etc; and used his influence at the court **to** have it brought about. And we love to think **of him also, as** aiding the first colony under Zerubbabel.

CONNECTION

"**Now in the fifth** month, **on the seventh day of** the month * * *

THE EXILE—LAMENTATIONS.

came Nebuzaradan * * * and burnt the house of the LORD and the king's house, and all the houses of Jerusalem, even every great house burned he with fire * * * and broke down the walls of Jerusalem ('on the tenth day' JER 52 : 12—'Saturday Aug 27,' II KGS 25 : 8–10), and carried the people to Babylon." II CHRON 36 : 19.

Thus, with their temple (burned same day and mo as the Herodian), and city, ended the kingdom of Judah 588 *

LAMENTATIONS †

This inimitable poem by Jeremiah, is introduced in this connection, to give a better idea of the awfulness of the event it commemorates, as recorded above. It is an everlasting monument of the destruction of Judah and Jerusalem (not on the death of Josiah), and ability and piety of its author.

The first 4 chs are in acrostic form—every one of its 22 verses beginning with one of the 22 letters of the Heb alphabet. c 3 however has 66 vs (shorter than the other 4), and the alphabet therefore, thrice repeated. c 5 (not acrostic.) From 18, 20 vs, it would seem this was added later. CLARKE.

"Every letter of this elegy seems written with a tear, every word, the sound of a broken heart; its author compacted of sorrows, disciplined to grief from infancy, breathing in sighs and speaking in groans."

How pathetic for example, is the opening! Jerusalem is personified as a widow in mourning, sitting solitary amid the desolation round about, lamenting—"All ye that pass by, behold and see if there be any sorrow like unto my sorrow!"

The lesson is, that their sorrows were due to their rebellion and wickedness. To teach the Jews neither to "regard lightly the chastening of the LORD, nor faint," but turn to him, confessing their sin, and punishment less than deserved; themselves wicked, God righteous; and only trust and hope

---

* From II KGS 25 · 1, it appears EZEKIEL 24 : 1, 2, had revealed to him the very *day* Nebuchadnezzar " pitched against" Jerusalem.

† Near Golgotha is Jeremiah's cave, where tradition says he wrote this BOOK.

in him for deliverance, who would recompense also their persecutors. 4 : 21-2.

OBS. Under the doctrine of "recompense," Edom affords an impressive example. Compare 4: 21-2 above with Obadiah, repeated Ps 137,—

"Remember, O LORD, against the children of Edom
The day of Jerusalem,
Who said Rase it, rase it,
Even to the foundations thereof!"

These prayers and curses were near together.
Israel had no worse enemy. Edom was boastful, had his dwelling in the rock—*sela*; trusted in his own wisdom and strength— "Though thou mount on high as the eagle, and make thy nest among the stars, yet will I bring thee down." OBAD 3, 4.
Joel, Amos, Is, from 810-698, and Ezekiel tell of the old hatred nursed from the time of Esau and the birthright. It was the "violence done to thy brother Jacob" OBAD 10, "in the day of Jerusalem," which filled the cup of their guilt and punishment.

"As thou hast done, it shall be done to thee" OBAD 15.

Is 34, OBAD and EZEK 25: 12-17, are wholly about Edom—"The year of recompense in the controversy of Zion." Is 34, is against Mount Seir, Bozrah and Teman, her chief cities.—Nebuchadnezzar— "the hammer of the whole earth" JER 50: 23, was sent 583, to answer *proximately*, these prayers and predictions. But it is only in the light of the above 3 chs, compared with c IV SEC 3 PROPHECY, that the lesson can have its full effect.

But Israel had just been led away captive, and the land desolate. Therefore, lest Edom should glory over his brother's chastisement, the prophets add, that *Israel* should rise again, and possess Edom also, which was fulfilled 129, B C, when J Hircanus subdued the remnant, who then became Jews.

The captivity was first foretold Is 39, 712, after Hezekiah had showed the treasures of his kingdom to the ambassadors of Merodach Baladan II CHRON 32: 31

The predictions of the event describe the reasons and purposes of Providence. Though judicial, it was also for correction, to purge out their backsliding and idolatry (the last it did effectually). They (in Isaiah, Jeremiah and Ezekiel mostly), speak also of the duration, issue, change of mind and course of events, bringing about the Restoration.

THE EXILE—EZEKIEL.

CONNECTION

"And them that escaped from the sword, carried he away to Babylon, and they were servants to him and his sons until the reign of the kingdom of Persia.* To fulfil the word of the Lord by the mouth of Jeremiah (29: 10, 597,—'After seventy years * * * I will visit you * * * in causing you to return'), until the land had enjoyed her Sabbaths; for as long as she lay desolate, she kept sabbath, to fulfil threescore and ten years" II CHRON 36.

* * * * * * * *

THE DISPERSION.

NEXT to the punishment for crucifying their King, this was the greatest calamity the Jews ever suffered. They now became the "tail," were "tossed to and fro among all the kingdoms," fulfilling the curses of DEUTERONOMY 28. —With Zedekiah, ended their king and kingdom, never to be restored till they shall accept CHRIST the SON of David for their head.

The distress and consternation of the godly, whose lot was cast in these dark times—better imagined than described, is recorded in the LAMENTATIONS.

But in all this we are to see GOD, ordering in man's failure, for the furtherance of his *own* purposes. Through the dispersion, a better (?) knowledge of JEHOVAH and his LAW was given the heathen Also, in preparing the way for the coming of MESSIAH, by taking away some things in which consisted the glory of the Jewish dispensation.

OBS. While this, and more may be true, how much better for mankind would it have been, for the Jews to have kept their LAW! For then, CHRIST, who is the *end* and *completion* of the LAW, could have come in a glorious manner, and with glorious results, from every point of view.

EZEKIEL

"God will prevail," was of those (2nd deportation) II KGS 24: 14, II CHRON 36: 10, taken with Jehoiachin (Jeconiah and Coniah Jer 28, 37), and planted in Mesopotamia (Chaldea) 1: 3, about 200 m N of Babylon.

* "In that night was Belshazzar * * * slain, and Darius the Median took the kingdom," DAN 5: 30-1, 538. Cyrus set Darius (his maternal uncle) on the throne, and succeeded him 536-529.

His place is in the last 11 yrs of Jeremiah and first 11 of Daniel, beginning in the fifth year of their captivity. He was of the sacerdotal race. His mission was to the exiles at *Tel Abib* by the Chebar 3: 15.

In the portion (6 yrs), before the destruction of Jerusalem, he calls the Jews to repentance, telling them that trust in Pharaoh Hophra 29: 6, JER 37: 5, was vain, for their city and temple would be burned. After that, the exiles are consoled with promises of return to their land and worship, and coming of MESSIAH, closing 40–8, with symbolic representations of a new city and temple. The waters issuing from under the temple 47: 1, it is agreed, prefigure the GOSPEL

"In Ezekiel, we see inspiration acting on a mind of the firmest texture, absorbing all the powers of the soul and body. He ever thinks and feels as the *prophet*, in contrast with Jeremiah, whose history and feelings are interwoven throughout his writings" ANGUS.

His style is bold, dashing, vehement, tragical, diction not always refined or elegant. He amplifies, and is more minute than others, yet more obscure. His visions, allegories, images, though understood it may be at the time, are (many) now inexplicable, in which the Jews also, agree. GOD's chariot c 1, Gog and Magog 38–9, and 40–8, are of this class.

"In Ezekiel we admire and wonder, but are not impressed as in Isaiah. Here is the sacred awe and silence, interrupted only by the seraph's cry 6: 3. In Ezekiel, the sight and noise of wheels and wings confound us."

SEC 2 FROM THE RESTORATION TO MALACHI 139 YRS. CLOSE OF THE CANON.

"WHEN the LORD turned again the captivity of Zion, we were like unto them that dream" Ps 126.

> They come, they come; thine exiled bands
>   Where'er they rest or roam,
> Have heard thy voice in distant lands,
>   And hasten to their home. MONTGOMERY.

THE return is celebrated by the prophets as a remarkable display of GOD's providence. (Mark how the hearts of Cyrus, Darius and Artaxerxes were inspired to favor it.) And like the Exodus of their forefathers from Egypt, it is used as prefiguring our redemption by CHRIST, and journey to the heavenly Canaan Is 51 : 11, 35 c. And Zerubbabel, grandson of Jeconiah, and progenitor of our LORD, who led the first band (as also Joshua ZECH 4–6), is spoken of as a type of CHRIST; and the commotions attending his first and second coming, are represented by the shaking of the "heavens and earth," and destruction of earthly kingdoms HAG 2 : 20–3, comp ZECH 3.

About 50,000 returned under the decree of Cyrus (distance via Arabia Deserta abt 600 m), besides those who came with Ezra about 1800 "males" c 8, and the two (or three) companies brought by Nehemiah. (For some think from 2 : 6 in connection with 7 : 1, 2, he went back after finishing the wall, before the return mentioned 13 : 6, 12 yrs after. But the "time" 2 : 6, may have been extended.

Although most cast their lot among the heathen (being mixed with, or settled among them), other companies we believe, from time to time, in considerable numbers, joined their brethren to rebuild and occupy the towns and cities, every one to his inheritance, so far as the records preserved would show.—If the "males" of Ezra brought their families with them, there must have been several thousand— "about 6000" ANGUS. See also ZECH 2 : 6.

The RESTORATION was a means of preserving the germs of spiritual religion, in connection with its typical forms, against CHRIST's coming.

Again, the prescience and certainty of prophecy is seen, as to the land. Unlike that of the 10 tribes, it was not trodden down of the heathen, but kept Sabbath, the fear of GOD as the "cherubim and flame of a sword" guarded it. For it was known to the heathen, it was to be reoccupied.

JUDEA

Was subjected to Persia as a "province" Ez 2 : 1, NEH 7 : 6, from 536 till 331, paying "tribute, custom or toll" Ez 4 : 13, but having their own governor and high priest. After the conquest of Persia by Alexander at Arbela in Assyria that year, it fell to the Grecians. SEC 3.

AS THIS PEOPLE were, in their church, state, life and

land (as we have shown), typical and for " our examples," this portion of their history is interesting and profitable to us.

1 *As further proving that the* SCRIPTURES *were, and are to-day, in active, unchangeable force.*

2 *As illustrating the divine providence and* GOD's *moral government.*

Thus the **Jews** from the return till CHRIST (as **before and for 1800 yrs past**), afford evidence external and internal, of the **truth of** revelation—that GOD governs this world by rewards **and** punishments; that "the curse of the LORD is in the house of the wicked, but he blesseth **the** habitation of the righteous," which also applies **as well to** the *land.* See HAGGAI.

That " history repeats **itself,"** has its best illustration in this people, and it is just as **true** that it has no *significance*, but for the GOD in the history.

This section, so pregnant with warning **and** counsel, is found chiefly in the remaining 6 books of the O T; EZRA, ESTHER and NEHEMIAH especially

For the best light on this subject, see PRIDEAUX' CONNECTION on EZRA, ESTHER and NEHEMIAH, CLARKE's Com.

THE PEOPLE

Smelled—bore back the taint of Babylon **and Bel,*** as **soon showed itself by their** affinities for the Canaanites in the land, though first **noticed on Ezra's** coming 9 : 2—" The holy seed have mingled **themselves** (in more ways than ' falling in love ' with their daughters and widows), with the peoples of the lands * * * the princes and rulers have been chief **in** this **trespass."**

Notice Ezra's sorrow, humiliation, fasting and prayer 9 : 3 to the end. Then the divorce cases—113 *named*, including **priests c 10. For we believe** many are *not* named ; besides those who chose rather to be " cut off" from Israel, than their " wives." And some had more than one, we think.†

* *Belus* **their supreme** tutelary god **Is** 46 : 1, JER 50 : 2.
† Of **the exiles, some** returned **in** marital relations with the heathen.

THE PEOPLE.

So among the first things noticed under Nehemiah, while yet on the wall, "There arose a great cry of the people and of their wives against their brethren." Some had mortgaged their houses and lands, to get bread by reason of the dearth. Some had borrowed money to pay the king's tribute. Some had sold their children, and could not redeem them, because other men held their houses and vineyards 5 : 1–5.

About 12 yrs after (13 : 6), he found Eliashib the high priest "allied unto Tobiah the Ammonite," and had prepared for him a chamber in "the house of GOD," during Nehemiah's absence in Persia. Also the portions of the Levites, singers (and priests), had not been given, so that they had "fled" to provide for their own, and the house of GOD was neglected. He found some "treading winepresses on the Sabbath, and bringing in sheaves and lading asses." "There dwelt men of Tyre also therein, who brought in fish and all manner of ware and sold on the Sabbath." "Then I contended with the nobles * * * What evil thing is this that ye do and profane the Sabbath?" To others, who were locked out, but came and "lodged without Jerusalem once or twice" he said, "If ye do so again, I will lay hands on you" v. 15–21.

OBS. Had such a spirit been in the Christian's *tirshatha*, Sunday visitors would also have been locked out of our Columbian Exposition in 1893.

"Also, saw I the Jews that had married women of Ashdod, Ammon and Moab" * * * And I "cursed them, and smote certain of them, and plucked off their hair" etc.

OBS. We are struck with the spirit and power of Nehemiah in punishing offenders and righting wrongs. It was the same SPIRIT that moved Elijah, Josiah, and our LORD, who with a "scourge of cords," drove out of the temple them that bought and sold therein.

2 As to his prayers against his, and the enemies of GOD, read in the light of those times, they are in accord with the LAW, its sanctions and penalties. They are inspired, agreeable to justice, violate not the law of mercy and love. SEE on this, Pt III c IV Sec 1.

As to their knowledge of the LAW, when Ezra had prepared a fair copy Neh 8, in the vernacular* (the Heb ceased to be a *spoken* language during the exile), he read it to them in Heb, in the "broad place"—square or plaza, while their scribes caused the people to understand the sense. And "all the people wept when they heard the words of the LAW"—being convicted of transgressing it (many thro ignorance), and fear of punishment. This compared with vs 14, 17, and places in following chs, suggests that some of the ordinances had fallen into disuse, and by others, forgotten. The feast of tabernacles was renewed—for "since the days of Joshua the son of Nun, had not the children of Israel done so"—in such a religious manner. v 17. See Ez 3 : 4.

As the reading progressed from day to day, they found more sins, as "strangers," to separate from, c 9. We notice the full confessional prayer of the priests, in historic order, from the beginning 9 : 4 to end of the ch, followed by a formal renewing and signing of the covenant, to keep their LAW thenceforward 9–10 c

How solemn and suggestive is this confession, and *how affecting* is the allusion to their condition as under the heathen!

This revival 91 yrs after the return, is the first noticed, subsequent to Josiah.

It is through such incidental notices, the reader may get as fair a view of the moral state of "the children of the captivity," as can be portrayed. We think some had *teraphim*† in their houses, as some Christians have now, in *other forms.*

In the light of such disclosures, we also get an idea of what the morals of the heathen were, among whom Israel's lot was henceforth cast.—"Say not thou, What is the cause that the former days were better than these?" ECCL 7 : 10.

THE TEMPLE.

After the foundation was laid Ez 3 : 10, 535, and the Samaritans' offer refused c 4, see PT II c V Sec 1, they weakened the hands of the builders, hiring "counsellors

---

* To this we trace the origin of the Chaldee *Targums.*
† Household gods.

THE SECOND TEMPLE.

against them to frustrate their purpose, all the days of Cyrus" (died 529). And in the reign of Ahasuerus (Cambyses, son of Cyrus 7 yrs 5 mos), they wrote "an accusation against" them v 6. And in the days of Artaxerxes v 7 (Smerdis the *Magian*, a usurper 7 mos), "wrote Rehum the chancellor and Shimshai the scribe." And obtaining their end fully, "went in haste to Jerusalem * * * and made them cease by force and power" v 23. (Blood was no doubt shed), till the "second year of Darius" (son of) *Hystaspes* v 24, 520.

Pending the letter of Tattenai (governor), and Shethar-Bozenai to Darius 5: 1, Haggai, then Zechariah (2 mos after 1: 1), arose and encouraged Zerubbabel and Joshua to resume the work. Here these 2 BOOKS begin, and after Darius' answer c 6, they "prospered through the prophesying of Haggai and Zech" v 14, and the house was finished and dedicated to Jehovah "according to the commandment of the GOD of Israel, and * * * decree of Cyrus, and Darius and Artaxerxes"* v 14-16, with joy, "in the sixth year of Darius"—515.

This temple was 60 cubits broad and 60 high. Solomon's, 30 by 20, and 30 cubits high.

It is with feelings of sadness, we record that the glory had departed with the first temple. It had been despoiled of the ark, containing the pot of manna and Aaron's rod that budded, the fire from heaven, Shekinah, spirit of prophecy, Urim and Thummim, and other signs of spiritual life. *This* was to wax old, until left "desolate" forever, when their MESSIAH, rejected *in* it, "departed" the last time MATT 23: 38.†

OBS. We admire Tattenai, Shethar Bozenai and Darius, in contrast with Rehum, Shimshai and Smerdis. And notice how GOD overruled the envy and hate of enemies in the Jews' favor, and granting like Cyrus, a very liberal decree.

The Suez canal by Pharaoh Necoh ("the lame") 610, was reopened 508.

* Surnamed *Longimanus*—long handed—reaching to his knees. He commissioned Ezra and Nehemiah with new privileges Ez 7, NEH 2.

† The sound of hammer, axe and tool, was doubtless heard in building *this* I KGS 6: 7.

Herodotus born 484.
Reads his history at the Olympic games 445.
Socrates, wisest of Grecian philosophers, b 470.
Plato his pupil, b 427.
Æsop b 620.

Ezra 457

BORN in exile, was grandson of Seraiah the high priest, who was of the captives slain at Riblah in Hamath II Kgs 25: 21.

Though not coming till 78 yrs after the return, with him began the Reformation which Nehemiah with him, completed.

He was a very holy man, and learned in the LAW, which Artaxerxes notices.

He set out on the first of the first month, *Nisan*, and arrived at Jerusalem first of the fifth month 7: 9. He had made his boast in GOD, not asking soldiers of the king, but fasted and prayed, and *so* came through the "enemy and lier in wait" c 8, bringing the treasures for the temple; the gold and silver alone estimated at "£1,080,600" 8: 26-7, from the king and people, in all of which Esther and Mordecai's offices doubtless, contributed largely.

THE BOOK

Divides itself into 2 parts—
I About the Restoration and rebuilding of the temple. 1-6.
II Is about Ezra's coming, the king's commission, and notices of his work—1 year 7-10.

OBS. Haman's plot was 4 yrs after this.
Ezra speaks of himself as the author (chiefly) 7: 27-8, 8: 1, 24-9, 9: 5.
From 4: 8 to 6: 18, 7: 1-27, is in Chaldee.
Ezra is said to have edited out of existing MSS, a corrected text; 1 of the LAW. 2 PROPHETS. 3 *Hagiographa*—the CANON to his day. JESUS quotes it LUKE 24: 44.
OBS. In this, the Jews say he had the aid of the GT SYNAGOGUE, including Daniel, Shadrach, Meshach and Abednego!
Also, to have added what was necessary to complete them, as the death of Moses etc DEUT 34, PROV 25, last 2 vs of II CHRON. Many interpolations are credited to him and Simon the Just.
The Jews regard him as a second Moses, that he lived also 120 yrs, that as Moses gave, so Ezra restored their LAW.

THE TRADITIONS.

OBS. If in Josiah and Hilkiah's time, the PENT was so scarce II KGS 22: 8 (though from II CHRON 34: 14 the, or *an* autograph copy of Moses may be meant), we may guess how it was after the exile.

Some think Ezra returned to Persia, as best accounting for the "great affliction and reproach; the wall of Jerusalem" broken down etc, as reported at Shushan 12 yrs later, by Hanani to his brother Nehemiah—1: 3.

TRADITIONS OF THE ELDERS MATT 15: 2.

With the written LAW (they teach), GOD gave Moses the interpretation, which is their *oral law*. This is styled CONSTITUTIONS OF MOSES FROM SINAI.

When he came from the mount to his tent, he delivered the first to Aaron, then the oral Then to Eleazar and Ithamar, next to the 70 elders, and left. Aaron then repeated it to all and left; next Eleazar and Ithamar, then the 70 elders to all. They then went into the congregation and rehearsed it to all.

In the fortieth year, from the 1–6th day of the 1st mo, Moses called and rehearsed it to all, giving 13 copies of the written LAW, 1 to every tribe, and 1 to be in the tabernacle; and after repeating the oral part to Joshua, died.

Joshua gave it to the elders, who transmitted it to the prophets, on till Jeremiah, who gave it to Baruch, he to Ezra, he to the GT SYNAGOGUE, the last was Simon the Just, on to Hillel; Hillel to Simeon (who took Jesus in his arms), Simeon to Gamaliel (Paul's teacher), on to R Judah the Holy, who wrote all in the *Mishna*.

The *truth* is, after Simon the Just 300, arose the *Mishnical* doctors, who had to do with the traditions, which *they* say Ezra and the GT SYN received or allowed. Those who followed, added their imaginings; so that, as a snow ball, the farther it rolls the bigger it grows, the larger and more numerous these grew. Till in the 2nd cy R Judah, head of the school at Tiberias, compiled all in 6 rolls of 63 parts. This is their *Mishna*—repetition.

Their chiefs in Judea and Babylon, later, added *their* comments, which are called *Gemara*—completion. So *Mishna* is text, and *Gemara*, the comment. And these together constitute their Talmuds, the Jerusalem Talmud dating from 3–5th cy, the Babylonish, in the 6th.

The LAW is quite justled out of their Talmuds, yet in them the Jews believe as given from Sinai, preferring them even above or to their LAW, thus "making void the word of GOD" by their tradition MARK 7: 13.—They are their Alcoran, with like delusion and imposture as Mohammed. For the rest see Sec 4.

HAGGAI.

HAGGAI 520

"The work of the house of God" (through opposition of enemies, interrupted 14 yrs), had ceased till the second year of Darius Ez 4, and the people had turned attention to their own houses, lands and flocks, saying "It is not the time * * * for the Lord's house to be built."

It was at this juncture, "came the word of the Lord by Haggai" to Zerubbabel and Joshua 1: 1.

The book contains four messages in about 4 months, so brief that it is thought to be only a summary of the original, an observation which may also apply to the twelve lesser prophets.

1 The first of the 6th mo of the second year of Darius, he reproves and stirs up the leaders to rebuild, promising the divine favor c 1.

2, 24 days after, Zerubbabel and Joshua resume, assured that "I am with you, saith the Lord."

3 Their zeal cooling down, the 21st of the seventh month, he tells them that the Lord is with them, and that the glory of this house should be greater than of the former 2: 1-9.

4 The 24th of the ninth month, he reproves the priests, and reminds them how it had gone ill with all from the foundation of the house till now, promising as a sign (though now in June), a fruitful year for their good work 15-19.

4 The same day he tells Zerubbabel, who was of David's line, a type and progenitor of our Lord through both Joseph and Mary Matt 1: 12, Luke 3: 27, of God's care amidst the shaking of the "heavens and earth," and overthrow of kingdoms 2: 20-3.

Obs. These may refer proximately to the taking of Babylon (which had rebelled), by Darius, near the time the temple was finished, after a siege of 20 mos. Zech 2: 6.

2 "Lord of hosts," peculiar to the last three prophets, suggests that this cognomen may have come into use more, in connection with the dispersion.

On the Land

As *typical*, and 1 As a *proof of* Scripture. 2 Of God's providence and *government* (see people), alluded to Pt II c VI, Jerusalem, a volume might be written.

This land, a "good land," "Which the Lord thy God careth for * * * from the beginning of the year to the end" Deut 11: 12, had, in the time it lay desolate, undergone great geological changes; also in its physical geography, early and latter rains etc.

On the agreement and sympathy of nature—connection and relation of the natural and spiritual world with GOD'S LAW—the fertility and productions of the soil, with the moral state of those who occupy it, Haggai shall speak. Connect with MAL 3 : 11, 100 years later.

They had sown much and brought in little; they ate and drank, but had not enough; clothed themselves, but none warm; earned money to put in a bag with holes; had looked for much and it came to little. I did blow upon it. Why? Because of mine house that lieth waste * * * and the heaven was stayed from dew, and the earth from her fruit. I called for a drought (see NEH 5 : 3), upon the land * * * and on the labor of the hands 1 : 6-11. * * * "From before a stone was laid upon a stone in the temple of the LORD, through all that time, when one came to a heap of 20 measures there were but ten; to draw out 50 vessels of wine, there were but 20. I smote you with blasting, and mildew, and hail, yet ye turned not to me" 2 : 15-17.

The above, like lightning gleams, gives us an idea of how it was with the land from the return, and on till CHRIST. The near, assignable reason in Haggai, is the temple; in Malachi, robbing GOD etc. See also under PEOPLE.

The SPIRIT, true to experience, gives us also a picture of human nature to our times. Wedded to his sin and its numerous progeny, man does not know to rise to a holy state; and for want of GOD, in the rage and fever to fill the aching void in the soul, seeks gratification in the *creature* as the *summum bonum*—sowing much, eating and drinking, clothing, earning, looking for much, but with results as above given.

There were a few, as Haggai, Ezra and Nehemiah, like the happy man II SAM 6 : 10-12, I CHRON 13 : 14, on whom the blessing of the LORD rested, and all his house. Even the dog, cat and fowls showed their keep, in contrast with their neighbors.

It is the smile of GOD that makes a land rejoice; his displeasure, that causes sterility and drought. And the curse is removed in proportion as the kingdom of GOD is restored Is 35. Also, it is sin—the infraction of GOD's LAW and laws of our well being—ordinances of GOD, that gives edge and pang to the ills of life, as the effects of a torrid summer, or chill in winter to our bodies, forsooth.

The markets of Jerusalem showed what kind of tenant, tillage and owner had field and flock. Much of the fruit, vegetables and meat, presented a sorry appearance, as in Philadelphia market to day. Frost bitten, sun smitten—so deteriorated in quality (as also quantity), and medical properties, as not to supply body and brain with that nourishment and vigor the CREATOR intended.

"If ye be willing and obedient, ye shall eat the *good* of the *land*" Is 1 : 19.

The sinner only destroys and consumes. It is the Christian who is the conservator and producer.

We instance in one of the forms only—the *ab*-use of grain etc, raised for the still, which product in turn goes to impoverish and destroy the bodies and souls of men ; suggesting also the time, labor and money of man and beast, wasted—turned from its legitimate purpose.

The curse everywhere, is still heavy on the land.

The locust, cankerworm, caterpillar, palmerworm JOEL 2: 25, dearth, destroying East wind, sent by GOD to consume the productions of Palestine, were types of the wicked. All who break, or fail even, to observe the ordinances of the CREATOR—in both revealed and natural law, the land is represented as groaning under their burden, calling to heaven to avenge its wrongs old and new, and pour out the curse on its abusers still!

So related is the moral world to this, that like as the Selenium cell in the Lick telescope is sensitive to light, so the transgression of a law of love or order here, though only in thought or feeling, is announced in heaven!

"Whoso is wise and will observe these things, even they shall understand the loving kindness of the LORD" Ps 107 : 43 A V.

ZECHARIAH

Grandson of Iddo the "prophet," returned with Zerubbabel NEH 12: 16.

Next to Isaiah, he has the most frequent allusions in the N T to MESSIAH, and is the most symbolical and obscure, though the imagery and allusions were, we believe, understood at the time. Himself even asks the angel their meaning.

The book is in three parts, (after the warnings 1 : 1–6.)

I The first consists of 9 visions—1 : 7–6 c. The first showing that although 70 yrs since the 9th of Zedekiah (temple burned in his 11th yr), and the whole earth at rest, the Jews were still in trouble. How long? is asked, and the answer promises the restoration of the temple, city etc. The man with the measuring line 2: 1, may mean Nehemiah. 2: 6—"Ho! ho! flee from the land of the north " is in allusion to Darius taking Babylon, calling to the Jews still there, to come out and return to Judea.

The fifth c 4,—the golden candlestick fed by two olive trees, shows how the SPIRIT in Zerubbabel and Joshua—the " two anointed ones," should finish the temple.

II 7–8, Is about the fasts which some from Babylon ask about, observed in the exile on account of the temple, death of Gedaliah etc, now that the second temple was being finished. Zechariah answers that GOD had not sanctioned them, but to return to him, do the weightier matters of the LAW, followed by promises etc.

III The authorship of 9–14 is uncertain. The 1st 8 chs are Zechariah's. 9–11 Is of things before the captivity of Judah or the 10 tribes. The style is like Jeremiah's, rather Hosea's age and manner—800–775. 11 : 12, 13, are quoted MATT 27 : 9, 10, as from Jeremiah.

12–14 Are one prophecy. Part III is so different from I, II, that it might be viewed as a 13th book. As a book, Zechariah is more disconnected than any other. CLARKE.

OBS. Is there an error of copyists? Ezra or Zechariah know, but we will not recall their *manes* to tell us.

ESTHER 464–52.

Is probably an extract from the " records of the Chronicles of Ahasuerus," i e of Persia 6 : 1. This may account for retaining the word *Purim*, things of Ahasuerus' kingdom, as names of his ministers—" seven wise men " 1 : 14, Haman's sons; also Jews in the third person, Esther as " the queen," Mordecai as " the Jew " etc.

As the Chaldee has five times as much, and Vulgate and Greek 13 vs more to c 10, and 6 chs additional, so the Heb may have been larger at first.

The feast of *Purim** observed from its inception, and the favor it received of the Jews from the first, are proofs of its authority.

Though the *name* of GOD is not in the book, his hand is seen from first to last, anticipating and overruling e g, in Haman's plot; taking " the wise in their craftiness," causing the wrath of man to praise him, in preserving his own; and for the good, even of the heathen.

* Lots—13th of *Adar*, 12th mo, fixed on by Haman through divination, and observed by the Jews as the fast of Esther. The 14th and 15th, the feast of *Purim*. These are the *bacchanals* of the Jews.

234 FROM THE RESTORATION—NEHEMIAH.

ESTHER is in Oriental style, has the charm of romance, its truths stranger than fiction. In this picture, we worship the wisdom, justice, goodness of GOD. Had Haman's plot succeeded, the seed of Abraham even in Judea, would have perished, and with them, the church of GOD.

Mordecai's faith looms up

"In hope against all human hope"

with the occasion—above the decree—"laws of the Persians and Medes," which alter not, using his adopted niece rather for her honor, than as the *necessary* means of rescue 4: 14.

ESTHER affords us glimpses of Israel in Persia 72 yrs after the return. Haman's plot (if 453), was 4 yrs after Ezra's coming. We may imagine the state of mind in the "province," and rejoicing over their miraculous deliverance.

OBS. More than its historic interest even, its lessons of faith in GOD, above any human emergency, give this book an important place in our BIBLE.

NEHEMIAH 445.

"I am doing a great work, so that I cannot come down." Nehemiah to Sanballat, when he sent for him to meet in the plains of Ono 6: 3.

He who succeeded Ezra in the government of Judea, was Nehemiah, the son of Hachaliah. He was probably of the royal or priestly line, for he says, "I was cup-bearer to the king," an office of great honor, influence and profit, which he may have owed to Esther or Mordecai. It may also account for his being able of his own purse, to set that example of self-denial and devotion in providing for his own—"brethren" and retinue of servants for so many years; and at the governor's mansion (comp 2: 8), "keep open house" with such expensive magnificence and hospitality, entertaining besides the 150 rulers, priests etc, those who came from the provinces on affairs of state—persons of quality etc.

This book was written or compiled by Nehemiah 1–7, 12: 27–43, 13 c. ANGUS.* Compiled out of his journal or memorandum, by another hand. CLARKE. With Ezra, it composed at first but one book.

The occasion of his coming, he tells us 1: 1–3— * * * "In the month Chislev (9th), in the twentieth year

---

* So WHEDON.

FROM THE RESTORATION—NEHEMIAH.

(of Arts) as I was in Shushan (the royal winter headquarters), that Hanani * * * and certain men out of Judah came * * * And they said unto me, 'The remnant that are left * * * are in great affliction and reproach,' the wall of Jerusalem also is broken down and gates thereof are burned with fire."

OBS. Had not the walls been repaired? If so, they were down through violence, the heathen anxious to keep Israel down—"the under dog."

On hearing this, he was overcome; wept, mourned and fasted 1:4. After 4 mos thus waiting on GOD, and the cause of his sadness revealed to the king, he obtained " letters " from him, ("the queen also sitting by him " 2: 6), granting all he desired, and a military escort. He came to restore the city of his " father's sepulchres" 2:5.

OBS. Like Ezra, he asked largely, and received.

On delivering the letters to the *satraps* beyond the river (Jordan), Sanballat and Tobiah were " grieved exceedingly." Three days after his arrival, he made exploration of the walls by night. Then laid before the rulers his object and authority. "And they said, Let us rise up and build " 2:18. When Sanballat, Tobiah and Geshem heard of this, " they laughed us to scorn, and despised us, and said, Will ye rebel against the king?" 19, 20 v. c 3, is a program of names, and parts assigned to the builders, many working over against their own house.

c 4 Is the story of one of the greatest works under the greatest difficulties, on record. The wall is "joined together unto half the height thereof" v 6. Sanballat and Tobiah oppose. Then conspire with the Arabians, Ammonites and Ashdodites to destroy the Jews and city. We are deeply impressed with their leader and his little band, like lambs environed by gaunt wolves. They wrought day and night with weapons in one hand, some standing on guard, while he nor his servants put off their clothes—working, praying, fighting their way to victory.

By faith, Nehemiah built the walls of Jerusalem.

Next 5: 14-18. After the " great cry " previously noticed and correcting, he adds * * * " From the twentieth year even unto the two and thirtieth year of Artaxerxes, I and my brethren have not eaten the bread of the governor. But the former governors that were before me, were chargeable unto the people, and took of them bread and wine, besides forty shekels of silver. Yea, even their servants bare rule over the people. But so did not I, because of the fear of God," and the " bondage." "Yea, also I continued in the work of this wall, neither bought we any land * * * all my servants were gathered thither unto the work. Moreover, there were at my table of the Jews and the rulers 150 men, besides those that came unto us from among the heathen. * * * Now that which was prepared for one day was one ox and six choice sheep, and also fowls. * * * And once in ten days, store of all sorts of wine."

c 6 When SANBALLAT and Co hear the wall is up, (though the doors not yet in the gates), they were much cast down, perceiving the work was of GOD, and changed their plan, and sent to Nehemiah to meet them in the plains of Ono, (to get him out of their way), even to the fourth time. Then an *open* letter (a great insult), accusing him of rebellion, and to report to the king. Shemaiah in the interest of Sanballat, used *his* arts to get him take refuge in the temple, to disgrace him, give Sanballat a chance to proclaim his rule at an end, etc. Traitors, false prophets, yea

"All the swarming hosts of hell,"

including a woman—Noadiah, were roused up against one man for Jerusalem's sake!

OBS. 1. As Zion was the seat and radiating point of CHRIST's kingdom, it was reason that satan in his incarnate legions should be up. "His goods," till JESUS in the person of his servant came, "were in peace."

2. So when JESUS began *his* work, the evil spirits—there *before*, were made *manifest*.

3. But for the failure of the many, such restitution of toil and suffering would not have been required.

"So the wall was finished in the twenty and fifth of Elul (12th mo), in fifty and two days" v 15—"with street and moat, even in troublous times" DAN 9: 25, 143 yrs after it was broken down.

Next 7: 1-4, Hanani is appointed mayor, and Hananiah with him, in charge over the city. The rest of the ch is about revising the genealogy of Ezra c 2—adding such as had come up, and expunging those now extinct, which may account for the difference in the registers, explained PT II. c V.—MODES *of reckoning*. Order of time in the latter part of the book, does not seem to be strictly observed.

The ostensible object of his coming being completed, Nehemiah turns his attention to further measures for the public weal, to organize and settle church and state upon a permanent basis 8–10. Accordingly, the reading of the LAW, feast of tabs (read the confession of their sin 9 : 4 to end), renewing of the covenant, with name of the rulers sealing on behalf of the people, and both enter into a curse to walk in GOD's law. 1, To be separate from strangers. 2 Keep the Sabbath. 3 Pay the temple tax. 4 Render the tithes and first fruits—sins " commonly practiced," comes in order.

OBS. It is believed that the PENTATEUCH was now begun to be read in the "cities," and that this antedated the synagogue, which at first may have been in a simpler form, as a tent.

2 This multiplication of their temples may have been with this people, like Church Extension is with Christians, and Methodists may think of Kynett and McCabe as their Ezra and Nehemiah therein.

11 : 1, 2, Having fortified the city, and set his servants to keep watch and ward on the walls and towers, open and shut the gates (according to custom) at sunrise and sunset, finding "the city wide and large, but the people were few therein, and the houses were not builded" 7 : 1–4, lots were cast, to bring one in ten of the people to settle in it; the grateful citizens blessing those especially who "willingly offered." Thus Jerusalem began to fill again, and regain of its former magnificence.

5–36, Is a patronymic table of heads of families—priests, Levites etc, and numbers. Comp I CHRONS 9, which seems to be the one on their return, and the discrepancies may be reconciled by the rule under c 7. *Nethinim*—servants, JOSH 9 : 21, descendants of the Gibeonites.

12 : 1–26, Is a table of the priests and Levites who "went up with Zerubbabel" to the time of Nehemiah and Ezra. The high priests v 10, 11, are given—Joshua, Joiakim, Eliashib, Jonathan, Jaddua, to "the reign of Darius" v 22—335. SEC 3.

27–43, Is about the dedication of the wall, which (at earliest convenience), was celebrated with great publicity; the people summoned from far and near, "villages" having been built about the city for them. Two companies of the "princes," one headed by Ezra, the other followed by Nehemiah, in solemn procession, with trumpets, cymbals—"musical instruments of David"

MARCH AROUND JERUSALEM

in opposite directions, meeting in the gate of the guard v 39, opposite the temple, and in the temple; offering great sacrifices, and the women and children rejoicing, "so that the **joy of** Jerusalem was heard even afar off." It was a national jubile

Thus was their capital given into GOD's keeping.

OBS. The heathen dedicated their walls and cities to the gods.

C 13 Is about the profanation of **the** temple by Eliashib, tithes withheld, Sabbath breaking, **and** other sins many had fallen into during Nehemiah's absence in Persia—(1 **yr** CLARKE, 5 yrs PRIDEAUX), and their correction; closing with—

"Remember me, O my GOD for good!" an ejaculation he often uses.

He continued about 36 **years, and this is the last of the** historical books.

Nehemiah presents us with a character and personality as unique as his work is radical, among SCRIPTURE examples. In some respects, we associate him with Josiah and J. Maccabeus. In the attributes and qualities of manhood or true greatness—faith, courage, patriotism, consecration, zeal, love for Zion, blazing out in his record from first to last, he ranks with the first of his nation, as the Jews testify. He resigned royalty, wealth, ease, for a life of toil and persecution, to restore the hope of a fallen nation, and of the world.

MALACHI

Is the latest O T voice **come down to** us, and is as said PT II PROPHECY, lifted up **against an** increasingly profane and sensuous worship, with **foregleams** clearer of MESSIAH —his character and work.

Though without a clue to time (unless we associate "governor" 1: 8 with Nehemiah), it came after the service of the second temple had been established 3: 10.

C 1 Begins, reminding Israel that GOD had chosen him before Esau, charging him with ingratitude. The priests are charged with offering to GOD the blind, lame and sick; as ungodly, ignorant of their LAW 2: 7; causing many to stumble; and therefore "I have made you contemptible and base before all the people" v 9. If "like people like priest" HOS 4: 9 be true, the uninspired "like priest like people," is equally true.

2: 10-17 Is about the abuse of the law of marriage—marrying

"the daughter of a strange god" v 11. Some it seems, put away their wives when past the flower of their age, to get younger ones!

C 3 Is about "My messenger" and the "LORD," MESSIAH and his work—"as a refiner and purifyer of silver"—purifying the sons of Levi by his doctrine, judgment, mercy.

V 7-15 Is about the sin common to Christians also—robbing GOD in tithes and offerings. If brought into the storehouse, GOD would **pour out his blessing**, rebuking also the "devourer"—locust, hail, **mildew** etc.—The curse is here again noticed as upon field, flock and vineyard, for their behavior.

16-18 Is a touching allusion to the manner and estate of GOD'S true and tried ones in corrupt times—"Then they that feared the LORD, spake one with another" etc.

C 4 Is JEHOVAH'S valedictory—"The SUN of righteousness" to arise, Elijah for the sign preceding, and admonishing to remember the LAW till he come.

As to the long silence, like the dark before the dawn, calm before storm, 1 Revelation (the O T) was complete. Of the SCRIPTURES—will of GOD, light as to the coming ONE, the people had had enough. 2 So GOD (as his way is), leaves them to serve in their own way, to prove them.

MALACHI as from a last observatory, affords us a parting glimpse of this nation's after life, as suggestive as it is *predictive*, both prospective and retrospective. The impression is a dark, sad one, and talismanic of the curses of DEUT. 28, as in their varying fortunes it now remains briefly to narrate. The materials are found mostly in I, II MACCS and JOSEPHUS, an "Epitome" of which is in CLARKE VOL IV, after MAL.

SEC 3. THE JEWS FROM MALACHI TILL CHRIST. CIVIL HISTORY.

AFTER Nehemiah, Judea was made subject to the *satrapy* of Syria, the rulers of which committed the affairs of state as well as church, to the high priest. Thus the sacerdotal function became an office under the heathen. This union of the civil and spiritual power made the office thenceforward an object of ambition, and occasion of strife and murder, in the family of Aaron. For example Bagosas 366, displaced Jonathan in favor of his brother Joshua, who was killed in the inner temple by Jonathan, which in turn Bagosas avenged, imposing also a heavier tribute on the Jews.

KINGS OF PERSIA—Xerxes DAN 11: 2, 484, Artaxerxes Long 465, Xerxes II 425, Darius II Nothus 424, Artaxerxes Mnemon 405, Artaxerxes Ochus 381, Darius Codomanus 335–1.

HIGH PRIESTS NEH 12: 10 Joshua, Joiakim, Eliashib, Joiada 413, Johanan (Jonathan) 374, Jaddua 341.

UNDER ALEXANDER AND THE PTOLEMIES 331–198.

CONNECTION

DAN 8: 1-7 In the third year of Belshazzar * * * as I was in Shushan the palace, by the river Ulai, I saw and behold! a ram with two horns * * * And behold! a he goat came from the west, * * * and ran upon him and cast him down and trampled upon him.

After the victories on the Granicus and at Issus over Darius' generals in Asia Minor 334-3, and taking Tyre after a 7 mos siege, Alexander went to punish the Jews, because they still adhered to Persia. But it is related that Jaddua and the princes (after fasting, prayer and being directed in a vision), in solemn procession in their robes of office, met the conqueror as he approached Jerusalem; whereupon he bowed and saluted them, declaring that he had seen a vision at Dio in Macedonia, just such a sight, assuring him of the conquest of Persia.

Jaddua conducted him into the city and showed him the predictions of Daniel concerning him Alexander was so pleased with his reception, that he not only spared the capital, but continued to the people their laws, religion, and exemption from tribute on the Sabbatic year. Many Jews enlisted in his army.

Samaria he put under his favorite Andromachus, who on being burned to death in his house in that city, was avenged by the people being deprived of their rights, some banished, a colony of Greeks planted there, and the rest given to the Jews.

After his romantic expedition into, and dispossessing Darius of Egypt, he founded Alexandria, which became the capital of lower Egypt, placing many Jews there.

Then, after sacking Gaza, he overthrew the Persian empire at Arbela.

OBS. Nothing could exceed the valor and fury of the Grecian phalanxes, or rapidity, extent and splendor of the conquests of the king of Macedon. "With 50,000 he ran upon 700,000 at Arbela, killing 300,000, with loss of only 500" WORCESTER.

Alexander was born at Pella in Macedonia 356, and died at Babylon 324.

H PRIESTS   Onias 321, Simon the Just 300, Eleazar 292, Onias II 251, Onias III 195.

CONNECTION DAN 11 c SEC 1.

ON the division of Alexander's kingdom, Judea fell to his successors in Egypt. Under the first two, the Jews (with the Egyptians), were at their greatest prosperity. On account of many removing thither, and the royal favor, the new city became a place of very great importance to them. They were granted their rights, religion and privileges of citizenship.

Their welfare was also promoted by Simon the Just 300-292. He fortified and repaired Jerusalem and the temple, made a reservoir "in compass as a sea," was the last of the GT SYN, completed the Canon. It was under the care of his brother Eleazar, the SEPT was prepared.

Ptolemy Euergetes found Onias "old, weak, covetous," and the tribute unpaid for many years. On demand, backed by an army, the king's wrath was pacified by Joseph, Onias' nephew, who acted as receiver general for the tax.

Under P. Philopater, their affairs grew worse. For he, after his victory at Raphia DAN 11: 11, in a tour through his dominions, ventured into the holy of holies, was seized with a horror and carried out On his return, being in a rage, he deprived the Jews of their rights, stigmatized them with the ivy leaf in honor of his god Bacchus, and required them to renounce their faith. He then gathered them into the Hippodrome to be destroyed by 500 elephants. But the enraged animals rushed upon the spectators, killing *them*. This so changed his heart, that he reversed his decrees against them. However, about 40,000

16

perished in Alexandria, and **900** apostatized. **WORCESTER.**

UNDER THE SELEUCIDÆ—KINGS OF SYRIA 198–63.

ON the death of Alexander, Seleucus one of his generals, overthrew Antigonus another of his generals at Ipsus, thus getting his kingdom in Asia, and founded that of Syria or Syro-Media, which lasted from **312–63.** The kings were called *Seleucidæ.*

OBS He was a great general and popular sovereign, won 23 battles, founded 16 cities including Antioch, and Laodicea, the former of which became the capital, a great, splendid city. It was called the "Queen of the East," and "Eye of the Christian Church." "**The** disciples were called Christians first in Antioch" ACTS 11: 26.

Judea, lying between **Egypt** and **Syria, was** much affected by the frequent **wars** agitating **the** two nations, aggravated by the increasing wickedness of **the** people.

It changed masters when Antiochus drove Scopas out **198.**

The reader will connect with and supply from **Dan 11 c (sec 1),** the interval here from 198—to Maccs 166, including the persecution of Antiochus, anticipated there.

Matthias, a priest of the Asmonean family, with his sons John, Simon, Judas, Eleazar and Jonathan, now fled to Modin in Dan. Apelles was sent to enforce the act of conformity. Matthias slew the first Jew who approached the altar, then the king's commissioner, then retired to the mountains; whence, with a **band of followers, including the sect** of the Assideans, he took the field, encouraging his sons to "stand up for the LAW." He made it lawful to fight on the Sabbath in self defence, (for the enemy **had** taken advantage of **this weakness** of the Jews, to do them much harm) He marched around the country, cutting off apostates and heathen, and restoring the worship, till called from labor to rest 166, at a great age.

Judas now took the army, with his bro Simon, "a man of remarkable prudence," the others assisting.

After defeating Apollonius **and** killing him, finding his sword, he from that time fought with it. Then after defeating Seron governor of Cœlo-syria, after calling upon GOD with his 3000 men, he overthrew more than 50,000 of his enemies, regained and entered Jerusalem on the Sabbath day, with great thanksgiving and devotion 163.

He next with 10,000, defeated Timotheus and Bacchides with 65,000.

During the respite which followed, he restored and dedicated the temple, the 25 of Kislev 163, (Compare here DAN 8 : 14,—"two thousand three hundred evenings and mornings" with the new moon of Dec. About the 18th of Dec CLARKE.) It was to be ever observed as the feast of dedication. JOHN 10 : 22, A D 28, it fell on Nov 29 STRONG.

The motto on Judas' banner was *Mi Camoka Baelim Jehovah* EX 15 : 11—"Who is like unto thee, O LORD, among the gods?" From the initials M C B I, came Maccabee, which became the surname of the family, and of all who joined their cause. Though some say from *makkab* hammer, in allusion to Judas' valor in beating his foes.

Antiochus now threatened to exterminate the Jews, and make Jerusalem their common sepulchre. But GOD interposed. He was first seized with pains in his bowels, his parts became ulcerated and alive with vermin, so that he was nauseous to himself and all about him. In his extremity, owning his sickness as from God, he vowed to make restitution for all the wrongs he had done to his people, if he would help him. But he died, raving mad at Tabæ Persia, his body consumed with abominable ulcers.

OBS Did he not, like the Herods and Paine, have a foretaste of the torments of hell, while in the body?

While Judas was besieging Acra in Jerusalem, Antiochus V marched 130,000 men, 300 chariots and 32 elephants to its relief. In the battle, his brother Eleazar was killed by an elephant he had stabbed. Judas retired into the temple, and the enemy was suddenly called back to Antioch.

Menelaus was suffocated by Lysias, in a tower with ashes thrown by a wheel (a Persian punishment), and Alcimus an apostate, a wicked man, put in his place.

Lysias, in league with other nations, now renewed the merciless war, in the progress of which Judas, after unparalleled fighting, fell at Azotus, covered with wounds and glory, while contending with 800, against the hosts of Bacchides and Alcimus.

OBS Judas ranks with the greatest patriots and heroes of that nation, and is worthy a name in that list " who through faith * * * waxed mighty in war, turned to flight armies of aliens " Heb 11. See the story in MACCABEES.

He was laid to rest at Modin, the ancestral burial ground, amid the lamentations of a sorrowing people 161.

Jonathan succeeded, but was overpowered, and his band scattered in Tekoa on a Sabbath day. Alcimus died suddenly of palsy, and Demetrius received orders from Rome to desist from vexing the Jews. Notwithstanding, the malcontents engaged Bacchides to return. But they were so artfully dealt with by Jonathan and Simon, that Bacchides made peace, restoring his prisoners.

Jonathan now repaired the walls and temple, punished apostates and made several reforms. And at the instance of Alexander, took the priesthood "now vacant seven years" CLARKE.

OBS Jason, Menelaus and Alcimus were high priests 174–161. Though Jos says Judas acted as high priest his last three years.

Onias son of Onias III, who had fled from Antiochus, obtained a grant of P Philometer and Cleopatra 149, to build a temple at Leontopolis, *Nomus* of Helipolis, Egypt, like the one in Jerusalem. He professed Is 19: 19–24, had predicted such a house and priesthood in that place. The LORD did not prosper his work, and the house was afterward shut up.

H PRIESTS Jonathan 161, Simon 144, John Hircanus 135, Aristobulus 107, Alexander Jannæus 106, J Hircanus 79, Aristobulus 70. Last 2 by turns 70–40, Antigonus 40, Ananel 35, changed for Aristobulus.

THE MACCABEES. 245

Annas made high priest by Quirinius 8 A D, deposed 14. Then followed Ismael, Eleazar, Simon then Joseph—Caiaphas 26, but deposed 35. ROBINSON.

KINGS OF SYRIA—Ants V 162, Demetrius Soter 160, Alexander Balas 150, Demetrius I 146, Ants VI Theos 144, Tryphon 143, Ants VII 139, Demetrius II 130, Alexander Zabina 127, Ants VIII 123, Ants IX 111, Ants VIII, IX 108, Philip and Ants X 93, Demetrius Eucerus 92, Tigranes of Armenia 83, Ants XI 69.

These eighteen kings averaged 4½ yrs, not one so far as we know, dying a natural death.

The first got the crown from his cousin Ants V by statecraft and murdered him.

Alexander a pretended son of Antiochus, slew Demetrius.

And was displaced by P. Philometer for Demetrius I, his head cut off in Arabia and sent to Philometer.

Ants VI was murdered privately by Tryphon a courtier, usurper and assassin.

Tryphon's reign was so insecure and disputed, that he killed *himself*.

Demetrius was defeated and murdered by his brother Ants VII, who lost his life and army 400,000, in Parthia, "throats cut in one night."

Demetrius II was defeated and murdered by Alexander Zabina, a pretender.

P Physcon gave the crown to Ants VII and put Zabina to death.

The above we give in the decadence of Syria,
1 To show how literally the SCRIPTURES have been fulfilled even outside the church.
2 As a striking example of children inheriting the iniquity of their fathers—Ants IV e g. The taint of his sin was transmitted downward—its guilt and punishment. "The seed of the wicked shall be cut off" Ps 37.
3 Reveal the increasing darkness before the dawn.

Jonathan and his two sons, after being deceived by, and got into the power of Tryphon, were murdered. Simon his brother was assassinated with his sons by Ptolemy his son-in-law, a usurper, to gain the priesthood.

J Hircanus shook off the Syrian yoke, and with his sons Aristobulus and Antigonus, destroyed the cities and temple of the Samaritans, subdued Idumea and the Edomites to the faith and made alliance with Rome He was a mighty prince, and enlarged the bounds of Judea. Was a Pharisee, but was drawn over to the Sadducees, and made it a penal offence to observe the doctrines of his first faith.

Aristobulus was the first to assume the *title* of king. He starved his mother to death in prison, shut up all his brethren, save Antigonus whom he killed, and died unhappy.

Alexander Jannæus was much engaged in war with P Lathyrus and the neighboring nations during his 27 yrs, with varying fortunes. He died of ague while besieging Ragaba in Gerasena. His record is stained with cruelties, as giving up the people and city of Gaza to the fury of his soldiers, and crucifying 800 of his rebel subjects in the presence of his wives and concubines at a feast, after killing their wives and children before their face.

Alexandra his widow, made Hircanus ruler. She favored the Pharisees, and with such arts, that they acknowledged her as queen dowager, and flattered her dead husband with many encomiums. The Pharisees now recalled the exiles, revoking the laws against them, and avenging themselves on the Sadducees. Aristobulus his brother, in a battle at Jericho, supplanted Hircanus.

Antipater moved Hircanus to appeal to Aretas of Arabia. As a result of the strife, Pompey took Jerusalem, destroyed the fortifications, restored Hircanus, taking away the crown, and uniting Judea with Syria to Rome 63.

"Gabinius governor of Syria, removed the civil power from the Sanhedrim into five courts, according to the number of provinces which he divided the land into" CLARKE.

Antipater procurator of Judea, made his sons Phasael and Herod, governors of Jerusalem and Galilee.

Malicus who was next to Antipater, bribed Hircanus' butler to murder his friend Antipater, to get next to Hircanus. Herod murdered Malicus at Tyre. Phasael and Herod quelled the faction this caused in the city, and matters were compromised by Hircanus giving his granddaughter Mariamne to Herod. Phasael and Herod, through Mark Anthony, were now made tetrarchs of Judea.

Antigonus son of Aristobulus, for 1000 talents and promise of 800 of the fairest women in the land, engaged the Parthians, who took Jerusalem without resistance, put Phasael and Hircanus in chains (Herod escaping), and set Antigonus on the throne. Phasael dashed his brains out in prison, and Hircanus' ears were cut off to disqualify him for office, and by the Parthians left at Seleucia.

Through favor of M Anthony, Herod in 7 days obtained the sovereignty of Judea. In the war which followed, he gained the cities, but through the treachery of some, Jerusalem remained to Antigonus. Gaining from Anthony all that he desired, he soon took the capital, but bought off his soldiers from destroying the inhabitants and sacking the city. Antigonus was sent to Anthony who was bribed to murder him—that with him should end the line of Asmonean princes—from 166-37.

UNDER THE MACCABEES 166-37.

Though the Jews were freed to a greater degree from the Syrian yoke, and enlarged their borders toward Syria, Phœnicia, Arabia, and possessed Idumea, it was at the cost of continual wars and internal dissensions.

With the decline of Egypt and Syria, and rise of the "fourth beast" DAN 7: 7, they changed masters, and became tributary to Rome, and lost their prestige wholly with the loss of their capital and "king."

* * * * * *

Herod began his reign with executing the members of the Sanhedrim, save Hillel and Shammai, and made Ananel, born of the priests in Babylon, high priest; but was persuaded by relations, to change to Aristobulus, younger brother of his beloved Mariamne 35. And as some paid regard to Hircanus, he was recalled, and by false accusation, murdered.

Alexandra Mariamne's mother, plotted to make Aristobulus king also, which ended in his death 29. Both mother-in-law and his wife were next cut off 28, then his sons Alexander and Aristobulus, for expressing pity for their mother.

Such cruelties caused Herod remorse, which also affected his body. His trouble was increased by the conspiracy of his eldest son Antipater by Doris, whom he murdered, at which Octavianus * exclaimed, It were better to be Herod's hog than his son!

To keep in with the emperor, he built Sebaste (Gr for Augustus), and Cæsarea 25; then a theatre and amphitheatre in Jerusalem, set the Roman eagle over the gate of the temple, and reared a gorgeous fane of white marble, all idolatrously to Augustus.

He tortured to death ten men who conspired to kill him in the theatre. To ingratiate himself with the Jews, he began to rebuild the temple, which after 520 yrs, like their covenant, was "nigh unto vanishing away." HEB 8: 13.

* * * * * *

It was in the 27th year of the reign of Cæsar Augustus (from 27 B C to 16 A D), LUKE 2: 1, and 36th yr of Herod's reign, when the temple of Janus was closed in token of universal peace, that the

SAVIOR OF THE WORLD WAS BORN.

SEC 4 STATE OF THE JEWS, MORAL AND RELIGIOUS IN THIS PERIOD.

" Darkness shall cover the earth, and gross darkness the people" Is 60: 2.

"The times of this ignorance therefore, GOD overlooked" ACTS 17: 30.

FROM what has been said (of the rulers chiefly), we get an idea of this nation's spiritual life, which will be further suggested by notice of the sects which arose along, which in turn, will enlighten N T allusions to them.

From their connection with the heathen, especially from the coming of the Grecian language 331, supplanting the Aramean, came also their ideas and philosophy SEE c I SEC 3. This will in part account for the admixture of their

---

* Caius Cæsar Octavianus Augustus.

absurdities with the pure Hebrew faith e g, as in the teachings of the leading three sects, in common with those of the Stoics, Epicureans and Pythagoreans.

OBS. In the adoption of the oral law—"precepts of men," then heathen faiths added to their own—comparing Moses and the prophets with Socrates and Plato even, we have in Judea an example of the tendencies of human nature everywhere—its affinities for error—doctrines even of devils, that "the heart is deceitful above all things, and it is desperately sick." Like the sin cursed soil, impregnated with the germ seed and root of every evil growth—"thorns also and thistles"—every "plant which my heavenly FATHER planted not."

2 Also, of the supremacy of "the mind" over "the flesh"—the rational and spiritual man over the carnal. Of GOD, truth, good, over satan, lies, evil. As being conscious of sin and misery, and seeking after the truth—restored union and happiness enjoyed with GOD in Eden.

3 Also, that as man—"the world through its wisdom knew not GOD," so of his inability to "come to the knowledge of the truth," and need of the RESTORER of the "old paths," "the SUN of righteousness."

THE PHARISEES

Were lineal with the Assideans—*Chasidim*—holy, saints, named SEC 3, noticed first by Jos Bk XIII, in the time of Jonathan 160-144. The name is from *parush*—separated or expounders.

That they took the name as being more holy than others, or manner of interpreting—unfolding the WORD, as opposed to the Sadducees who took the literal sense, is at variance with trustworthy, ancient authors. MCCLINTOCK and STRONG.

OBS. *Perushim* may have been given in reproach, as the *odium* of it must have come from the *self*-righteous, hypocritical portion, class caste being no part of a sincere, catholic spirit.

As primary in their faith, were Levitical purity, tithing and separation from the heathen. The LAW required separation.

On the first two see MARK 7: 1-4—"washing of hands" etc, MATT 23: 23-6—tithing "mint," LUKE 18: 12—"I give tithes of all that I get." On the 3rd LUKE 7—Simon and the woman, Acts 10: 28—Peter to Cornelius. Was Peter a Pharisee? " They had many observances not found in the LAW " Jos.

They believed the SCRIPTURES, in a resurrection, angel and spirit. Though fatalists, they allowed some freedom— " They do not deny freedom to act as one thinks fit, seeing GOD has given a temperament, whereby what he wills is done, yet so that man may act virtuously or viciously." Jos.

OBS. To *us*, this is ambiguous psychology. Josephus makes them confound or mix GOD and man's sphere of action. On the connection of divine prescience with man's freedom, see PT II c VIII. But whether our views of freedom be more Scriptural than theirs, who will decide?

They believed in *metempsychosis*—transmigration of souls JOHN 9: 2.

That GOD's people "are an elect race, a royal priesthood, a holy nation, a people for GOD's own possession " I PET 2 : 9—that we all alike, are called unto these blessings.

OBS. What GOSPEL, millennial light, do such doctrines suggest!

They ate after a priestly manner—sacramentally.

They represented the national faith, orthodox Judaism, the democratic party, i e, were the favorite sect.

As interpreters of the LAW, they excelled, and men believed them to be favored of GOD. Jos.

"The Scribes and Pharisees sit on Moses' seat" JESUS.

They constituted a school rather than sect. WHEATLEY.

Were "over 6000," many being of the priestly class.— But this may not include all, as there were several orders besides the two leading schools of Hillel and Shammai. And the two *Talmuds* speak of seven kinds or classes. They would not swear allegiance to Rome.

From being the reformers, how degenerated in 200 years must they have been, to merit the seven woes from JESUS! MATT 23.

In them we are struck with the anomalous, incongruous elements of reform and conservatism, progress and Puritanism, sincerity and hypocrisy.—Of them were some of Abraham's noblest scions, as Simeon, Nicodemus, Joseph of Arimathea, Gamaliel, Paul who was "of the straitest sect" ACTS 26 : 5, and many of CHRIST'S apostles and followers.

IN CON While in some, religion **was** the expression of honest but misguided zeal ROM 10 : 2, in others

>   Taught by self and satan how to paint
>   Their tomb, their nature white

a punctilious devotion to lifeless ritualistic, ceremonial observances— "dead works," with dead faith—straining " out the gnat but swallowing the camel," had engendered spiritual pride, hypocrisy, fanaticism.

As casuists **and** politicians, they remind **us of the Jesuits. Over** weak rulers, especially women, they had great **influence**—"Alexandra ruled others, the Pharisees ruled her."

So abused does the mind become through error—"precepts of men," that its very light is darkness. So this people were offended —caused to stumble **at** him who kept their perfect LAW, whose every word was **truth,** and **became his** bitterest enemies. While in turn, they made **themselves obnoxious** to his correction, reproofs, and even "judgment **of hell**" MATT **23 :** 33. While at times their inconsistencies and pretensions were held up or exposed to ridicule or contempt in seeming irony and sarcasm—"I came not to call the *righteous.*" The man who had not on a wedding garment—CHRIST'S righteousness, is the Pharisee. **Also** "Righteous persons " and Pharisee's prayer. On their traditions see SEC 3.

SEE LIFE AND TIMES OF JESUS—EDERSHEIM.

THE SCRIBES were the editors and expounders of the LAW, hence called doctors LUKE 5 : 17, and lawyers MATT 22 : 35. **They** were **mostly** Pharisees and often **named with** them.

The *Masorites*—traditionists (i e their scribes), counted the words and letters of **every** book, unusual construction and forms, and note things more curious than wise ; **as**

The middle letter **of the** LAW **LEV** 11 : 42, middle words 10 : 13. Of the PSALMS, the middle letter is 80 : 14, middle v 78 : 36.

These letters were written, and still printed in an unusual size **or** position, and said **to** have a deep, spiritual meaning. Also how often every letter **and** word in every book of the Bible is found.

THE SADDUCEES

Are from Sadoc pupil of Antigonus Sochæus, **about the**

time of P Philadelphus. So *Talmuds* and Maimonides (b 1135, Cordova Spain); or *tsedek* righteousness

They regarded with suspicion, revelations later than Moses, and traditions not divine.

And not regarding the spiritual import, nor development of truth in the PENT, a divine providence, and making GOD as indifferent—as an idle spectator of the affairs of the world, they almost set aside the authority of revelation. They " say that there is no resurrection, neither angel nor spirit" ACTS 23.

They were rationalists—the Materialists, deists of that day.

While the Pharisees believed too much, these believed too little.

They believed in free will, denied fate, and with the Epicureans, that man is rewarded according to his work here. That prosperity and adversity are signs of GOD's favor and disfavor.

Such a faith produced dispositions cold and repulsive Jos.

They were mostly of the rich, aristocratic class, believed in a life of enjoyment—" Let us eat and drink, for to morrow we die " I COR 15.

Caiaphas (and Jos says Herod), was of them. If so, we note the supremacy of truth and conscience over an error his *head* had adopted, in Matt 14: 2—John " risen from the dead."

After the 1st cy, they disappear from history.

THE ESSENES

Probably owe their origin to Egypt, are noticed by Jos 160-144, were " about 4000."

Though " unqualified fatalists," they believed in man's agency, immortality, that the SCRIPTURES have a deep, spiritual purpose, to be discovered by prayer, study, meditation.

At first they were the expression of a tendency—(as not finding in the other sects that higher life experience the heart craves), than organization, and came into repute as the exponents of **our** spiritual **nature** in quest of reunion with GOD.—They trusted **to be the** progenitors, or like John, forerunners of MESSIAH. JOS.

They did **not marry, though** approved **it in others;** adopted children **to** educate **in** their faith, **did not keep servants.**

"They lived among the people," unlike the monks. JOS. Like the Christians ACTS 4 : 32, they had all things common. No rich, no **poor.** Those who joined, must pass over **their** worldly **goods** to the order, be on probation a year, then two more preparatory to full membership.

They showed greater love **for** one **another** than others did.

The spirit of **prophecy** lingered among **them,** as in Menahem, who **told Herod** when a boy, that he would **be** king, about his character, acts and long reign. Jos.

They were simple, self denying, fasted * and prayed much, had "a time for everything and everything in its time." They took **food** similarly with the Pharisees, and **for health, and as a means of grace.**

OBS. So do some Christians (as did the Wesleys and Fletcher), who have been taught by the MASTER. Taking of food is as much an ordinance of GOD as the LORD'S Supper. How few understand this!

Thus, living the "tranquil and quiet **life"** I TIM 2, **they** outlived others, some over 100 yrs.

Like **the** Pythagoreans in some things, they remind us **also of the** "quietists" and followers of Geo. Fox, **and were a** type of monasticism in all ages.

John Baptist may have been of them rather **than of the others.** Comp MATT 3 : 4, 7, LUKE 1 : 80.

When **persecuted even unto** death, they **showed** the true martyr spirit.

For more, and peculiarities in doctrines, manner of life, see JOS, who gives them praise ab all others VOL II, BK II.

Though not formally noticed in the N T, CHRIST seems to allude to them MATT 19 : 12—"eunuchs for the kingdom of heaven's sake."

In history they are known as *Therapeutæ*—soul physicians.

* The Jews fasted Monday and Thursday.

THE HERODIANS were chiefly Sadducees by profession, though a political rather than religious body. ANGUS. They derived their name from the Herod family, and were in the interest of Cæsar. MATT 22: 15–22.

THE GALILÆANS were akin to the Pharisees in doctrine. ANGUS. They came from Judas, who in the days of the enrolment ACTS 5: 37, taught that it was not lawful to be subject to the Romans. The Pharisees tried to identify CHRIST and his apostles with them LUKE 23: 5, 6, ACTS 2: 7. They were of a turbulent spirit. Pilate was provoked to kill some LUKE 13: 1, while sacrificing at the temple.

THE SAMARITANS are spoken of by our LORD MATT 10: 5, 6, as different from Israel and the gentiles.

Of spurious descent and despised by their neighbors, they naturally entertained more liberal views of MESSIAH'S kingdom than the Jews.

After the destruction of their temple 129, they have been decreasing till 140–150 only remain. They still point to DEUT 18: 15, GEN 12: 3, 22: 18, etc, as the promise of CHRIST'S coming.

After CHRIST, three sects arose, two of which by Simon Magus and his pupil Menander, survived for centuries.

For the rest see PT II. c V. Samaria.

CHAPTER VI.

LETTER I.

ADVENT AND NATIVITY OF CHRIST.

TO MY DEAR MOTHER,
    GRACE AND PEACE

"The voice of one that crieth, Prepare * * * the way of the LORD." Is 40: 3.

"He shall be called the SON of GOD." GABRIEL to MARY.

WE have shown how the LAW and purpose of GOD to make of Israel a holy and mighty people, was a failure, and that the church and state were without life or power. Man from the first, has proved false to GOD.

The prophecies of MESSIAH and signs of his coming as said, were growing clearer and being fulfilled. Many

NATIVITY OF JESUS CHRIST.

pseudo CHRISTS had come through the ages past. The world had been looking for the PROMISE for 4000 years. Eve it is thought, believed her first born to be the "seed of the woman." But Cain turned out to be a murderer.

His person, work, etc, had been foretold—"Unto us a child is born * * * a son is given." Isaiah gives account of his birth, character, sufferings, death, atonement, glory (and by inference) resurrection, reign. 53 c. He was to be "a shoot out of the stock of Jesse," "grow up before him as a tender plant" * * * "a man of sorrows and acquainted with grief"—mar sickness. "And with his stripes we are healed."

NAMES AND TITLES. He is called the seed of the woman, seed of Abraham, STAR out of Jacob, that PROPHET, a priest, KING of Israel, MESSIAH, SON of GOD, the MIGHTY GOD, EVERLASTING FATHER, PRINCE of PEACE, SON of David, "My servant," the BRANCH, the LORD etc.

As our PROPHET, he is the AUTHOR and expounder of GOD'S LAW. He was foretold also as the restorer of the old paths, the lost knowledge of the true GOD—

"He comes, from thickest films of vice
To clear the mental ray."

The earth was to "be full of the knowledge of the LORD as the waters cover the sea" Is 11: 9. Isaiah, than whom no prophet seems to have had brighter visions of MESSIAH, is also the most descriptive of him. For example in c 35 inanimate nature is personified as seeing and owning her LORD, and breaks forth into singing—

"The wilderness and the solitary place shall be glad,
And the desert shall rejoice and blossom as the rose."

As our HIGH PRIEST, he was to atone by death for our sins, satisfy the LAW and divine justice; and after, ever live to make intercession for us at GOD'S right hand. As our KING, to rule and reign over us, by first destroying our enemies—our sins, and reigning in our heart.

The Jews desired a temporal prince and earthly glory. CHRIST is spiritual. "My kingdom is not of this world."

"Rejoice greatly, O daughter of Zion. * * * Behold! thy KING cometh unto thee * * * riding upon an ass"— ass' colt. ZECH 9: 9. Notice how the SPIRIT paraphrases this SCRIPTURE MATT 21: 5, in the day of fulfilment— "Tell ye the daughter of Zion, behold thy King cometh." And paradoxical though it seem, he was to be "A stone of stumbling and rock of offence to both the houses of Israel" Is 8: 14. * * * "But he that believeth, shall not make haste" 28: 16,—rendered "shall not be put to shame" ROM 9: 33. (It is instructive to note how Paul connects and applies the opposite doctrines in these two SCRIPTURES in this reference.)

There had been long silence since the last of the seers. Malachi (who was cotemporaneous with, or just after Nehemiah), had said, "Behold! I send my messenger. * * * And the LORD whom ye seek, shall suddenly come to his temple," which Montgomery touchingly alludes to in ver 4th of

Angels from the realms of glory.

It is in grace as in nature, there is a calm before a storm. "The DESIRE of nations," by Jew and gentile, was looked for. * * * The angel Gabriel now reveals to Zacharias (and naming), the birth of John—"Elijah" of Malachi, and "voice" of Isaiah. And in the "sixth month" this same archangel was sent to Nazareth to make the "annunciation" to a virgin named Mary. Nine months after, he returns to tell some shepherds of the SAVIOR's birth in the "city of David." And suddenly, a flock of angels broke the stillness of the night with the new, ravishing song —

"Glory to GOD in the highest!"

Between one and two years after MATT 2: 7, 16, his "star in the east" brought the *magi* to Bethlehem, with royal gifts to worship him, not now in a manger, but "the house" GOD had meantime provided by Zacharias or others.

Obs. In the murder of the "innocents" which followed, Herod having a son under 2 yrs old, slew it also. Clarke.

Our "Incarnation" hymns are among the loftiest and most pathetic of the poetic muse—

> Say, shall we yield him in costly devotion,
> Odors of Edom and offerings divine?
> * * * * *
> Richer by far is the *heart's adoration*,
> Dearer to God are the prayers of the poor Heber

In con. I have joy in the Lord, that we both are come in the course of these lessons, to "The beginning of the gospel." O give thanks unto the Lord! and join in asking him for grace to write and read aright, in the mystery of the coming and kingdom of our Lord, upon which this is introductory.

> The tide of time shall never
> His government remove.

Farewell Dear M. Jesus reigns.
Philada 5, 22, '88.   From "John."

II.

Life of Jesus till he "Began to Teach."

Dear M.

"Unto you * * shall the Sun of righteousness arise." Mal 4: 2.

The circumstances of his birth were miraculous. The names Jesus and Immanuel, were given before his conception. Two of his biographers have given us a little about his birth and childhood only, till he "began to teach." A visit to Jerusalem and a passover at 12, and two scratches of Luke's pen, is all the light the Holy Spirit has given from 12–30, 18 yrs of his life a blank. What a book this —the unwritten part of his life, would make! As large as a quarto Bible. Its facts, more wonderful than fiction or golden fancies. There is an article on "The Childhood of Jesus" by Dr. Curry in the National Repository Apl 1878, cautiously written, and much more might be said.

From what *is* said of him Luke 2: 46-7,—"sitting in

the midst of the doctors, both hearing them and asking them questions; and all that heard him were amazed at his understanding and his answers," we infer that he knew more at 12 than the doctors, even Gamaliel, who was of that number, and may have been present.

And his answer to his mother—" How is it that ye sought me? knew ye not that I must be in my FATHER's house?" suggests the state of his mind, and preparation in view of his office and work—a budding, developing state of mind—the dawning light at *least*, of conviction, as to the *hypostatic* union, his divine embassy and redeeming work.

While v 40—" And the child grew and waxed strong, filled with wisdom, and the grace of GOD was upon him " 52, " And JESUS advanced in wisdom and stature, and in favor with GOD and men," teach that he grew in body and mind not only as other boys, but that his progress was rapid, in proportion as he was without sin ; perfect in body and mind, and under the special care of his FATHER, and influence of the HOLY SPIRIT.

From v 46-7, we reason that even before a lad, while teaching (?) him in things pertaining to filial and religious duties e g, the child in turn " amazed " the parents by his " understanding and answers." By looks, words and actions, impressing them that their son was more than a mortal.

We fancy Joseph and Mary at the feet of their boy, like Mary "at the LORD's feet," both hearing and asking *him* questions. And they must often have felt reproved by his words, superior sense and holiness. He is the only *child* that could ever say, " I have more understanding than all my teachers " Ps 119.

He was quick to perceive and grasp the truth—the relations of things, the ordinances of GOD in nature and grace, and the spiritual import of the LAW. His insight of people's character and motives was clear, and he was saved from mistakes.

In this holy child, there was no affinity for the evil ways —dissipations, gratification of the senses, seen in other children. Though happy and cheerful even, he was not hilarious like them, but serious, quiet, contemplative.

As "the carpenter," what if we think of him as the little architect, amazing his relations now with a *fac-simile* of the tabernacle, or model of Solomon's temple (*both of which may have been lost*), then, giving the Jews improved plans for synagogues?

As he "advanced," we think of him as the young evangelist and missionary, going forth as the SPIRIT moved, in a widening circle "in the country, towns, villages," "doing good." Now, ministering the GOSPEL to an aged Zacharias and Elizabeth, speaking to the field hands or fishermen; then, taking part or leading in the synagogue. Anon, he hies away to John preparing himself in the wilderness of Judea, with wonderful words of light and comfort. (We do not read that he did not begin to work miracles—heal the sick, cast out devils etc.) And how happy those homes as at Bethany, lighted by his "angel visits"—favored with his presence and words!

He was much alone with his FATHER—in study, meditation, prayer and praise—the secret of power with GOD and man. In such seclusions, on such mounts, he renewed his strength, received fresh revelations of the FATHER's love, as his only and "beloved SON," and of his will; also of redemption, and preparation therefor. What Tabor communings and Pentecostal experiences JESUS had, we are not told.

It was now that he began to utter the "thoughts that breathe and words that burn," which later, shook the hills and vales of Palestine and Jerusalem, with greater effect than the "earthquake in the days of Uzziah" ZECH 14, that made "to tremble not the earth only, but also the heaven * * * that those things which are not shaken may remain" HEB 12:—

"Wonderful words of life,"

which, like a mighty glacier, began to grind and plough the very structure of society civil and religious, of Jew and gentile, into new form and life, to set up his own—a "kingdom which shall never be destroyed" Dan 2, to find its perfection in the millennium, or when he hath made "all things new"

> "And every law of sin reverse,
> That faith and love may make all one."

He was the *anatola*—"day-spring," "dawning" of that dark, cold age. How impressive is this view of our LORD's character, foregleamed by Isaiah 9 e g, and alluded to, quoted and realized Matt 4 :—

> "The land of Zebulon and the land of Naphtali
> Toward the sea, beyond Jordan,
> Galilee of the gentiles.
> The people who sat in darkness
> Saw GREAT LIGHT."

All were in expectation or wonder, some believing him to be "KING of the Jews," others the "MESSIAH," others "Elijah" etc.

IN CON. But it is only the spiritual mind that may fill out this part of the life of JESUS better than our language can. For like himself, CHRIST's manner of life is a mystery, to be understood only *by faith.* * * * "The light shineth in the darkness, and the darkness apprehended it not * * * He was in the world * * * and the world knew him not" JNO 1. Yet JESUS is

> The joy of all who dwell above,
> The joy of all below,
> To whom he manifests his love,
> And grants his name to know.   THOS KELLY.

In his introduction, John "the divine" gives us glimpses of the riches of his grace. What a *plethora* of power as the SAVIOUR of body and soul is suggested v 4—"In him was *life*, and the life was the *light* of men!"

LIGHT was a favorite subject with JESUS (himself the SUN of righteousness)—often likening himself to it.

How sublime does he appear in the temple JNO 8: 12,

in the face of the darkness of unbelief and rejection, exclaiming, "I am the light of the world!"

The simile is the more impressive, as the sun is the most expressive symbol of the GODHEAD in heaven and earth—the fountain of life and blessing to beings terrestrial. How like CHRIST it is! And like as *he* is treated, strange though it sound, most shut *it* also out of heart and home!

Like him, it is the smile of GOD on our world. In homes where sunshine receives the largest welcome, good cheer, health, happiness, *thought* are found; while the demons fear and despondency, are driven out.* FLORENCE NIGHTINGALE.

How blessed must those Christians and homes be, where JESUS receives the fullest welcome—where the GOSPEL has come with power! Those as at Bethany were happy above others, to whom the LORD came as a *transient* guest. But from his glory home, he assures us who keep his word, he will come to *abide*, bringing his FATHER (and by inference the COMFORTER), with him. Compare REV 3: 20 * * * "I will come in to him, and will sup with him and he with me."

It is a pleasing, suggestive view of our Christian life (implied in his being our example), that it is a "reappearance" of the life of our LORD—a following of CHRIST in the different relations and states through which he passed and adorned, while he "dwelt (mar tabernacled) among us."

This imitation of CHRIST, beginning at the time one is born of GOD, passes on through the infant life of JESUS (as a lamb among wolves), youth, manhood—his "regeneration" to the end. He shall share his poverty, self-denial, baptism, witness, fasting, temptation, fellowship of sufferings, conflicts, victories (JESUS never lost a battle), Gethsemane, Calvary, resurrection, ascension, GLORY.

And this following is not in spirit only, which is a refine-

* The properties and effects of sunlight are ably set forth under SUNLIGHT AND HEALTH in H H AND HOME ECONOMICS.

ment, or mystic view, and adapted to the cloister rather,* but in his outward, historic relations as well.

III.
The Gospels.

DEAR M

WHAT glory gilds the sacred page!—COWPER.

As a chart aids the traveller, so some account of these books and their writers, will help to a better understanding of them, and add interest to the things therein.

The "generation" of our LORD was copied from the tables—family records of the Jews. This people were careful about keeping the genealogies correct, partly on account of their MESSIAH. And many a Jewess of the chosen tribe, entertained fond hopes of being the mother.

These two tables are a confirmatory proof of the N T and divinity of CHRIST. Matt proves him to be the SON of David by way of Solomon, Luke through Nathan and in reverse order—"And JESUS * * * was about thirty, being the Son (as was supposed) of Joseph, the son of Heli," Mary's father 3 : 23. Mary is believed to have been a descendant also of David.

The GOSPELS are of greater value than the 23 other parts of the N T. They are like so many side lights or views of CHRIST's vicarious life, work and sufferings. Although what has come down to us be but an epitome in brief, some idea of the spirit and power of JESUS, in word and deed, is suggested in the last of John,—"Many other things which JESUS did, the which, if they should be written every one, I suppose that even the world itself would

---

* While the merits of MUSICA ECCLESIASTICA—the best of this class, are inimitable and imperishable, there are defects in it due to the time and circumstances (in a convent), in which produced. The merits of KEMPIS with his (few) faults, are discussed (with Chalmers' views) in Introductory to IMAGO CHRISTI. IMAGO is a good supplement to KEMPIS.
6, 14, 88.

not contain the books," yet (as harmonized), is it fruitful in precept and example, either expressed or suggestively, of the whole plan of our salvation. All that is in the ACTS and LETTERS, is here in embryo.

They are the breaking and sowing time of the "bare grain" of GOD's new and latest dispensation to man. The ACTS and LETTERS narrate the doings—springing and growth of the good seed—workings of the leaven after Christ's ascension and Pentecost, for over 33 yrs. The seed and germs of all the fruits of holiness JESUS' toil and sufferings procured, are in this plot—these immortal VOLS. And it is JESUS the opening eye of faith is to seek in all. And to the pure in heart, he manifests himself in the "GOSPEL glass" as nowhere else. As one has said (better than any we ever saw), "CHRIST is himself in truth, the GOSPEL * * * his coming and work, constitute the glad tidings of great joy unto all people."

THE GOSPELS IN THEIR MUTUAL RELATION.

"Mark presupposes and supplies what is omitted by Matt. Luke gives us what is omitted by Matt and Mark. John what is wanting in the other three. The first particularly points out the fulfilment of the prophecies for the conviction of the Jews. Mark wrote a short compendium, adding some remarkable circumstances omitted by Matt. Luke treats mostly of the office of CHRIST and in a historical manner. John refutes those who denied his GODHEAD. Each choosing to treat more largely of those things which most suited the time when, and persons to whom written." WESLEY INT TO THE GOSPELS.

As the FIRST is to the Jews, the writer does not dwell on their customs or topography. The lineage of JESUS he traces through their "father" down, and shows how the N T is the fulfilling of the OLD.

The SECOND it is agreed, was written for the Romans. Jewish customs and places have explanations. Narrative is preferred to discourse or doctrine, reciting the actions rather than words of CHRIST. The style is graphic, practical, suited to the energetic, business habits of the Romans. Mark strikes out abruptly—"The beginning of the GOSPEL of JESUS CHRIST," and adding a paragraph about John Baptist, passes to the TEACHER's works. Here the MASTER is revealed in his servant form, and Mark is sometimes called "servant" or "worker." Is more concise than Matt and Luke, often speaks in the present tense, introduces **persons** as speakers, is minute as to persons and localities.

LUKE writes to the **gentiles** at large. **In** this GOSPEL CHRIST appears in a **new** light, not as the "minister of the circumcision" (ROM 15: 8), his character in MATT; nor the "wonder WORKER" as he does in MARK; but as the **SAVIOR** of the *world*, traced back to **the head of the** human **family, and to GOD.** While Matthew speaks of **the 12 apostles sent to Israel, Luke** tells also of **the 70 sent as to the nations of the whole earth.**

He is more biographical **than** the others, **the** order generally chronological. The **various** additional facts related, give this book a peculiar value. **The parables** of the good Samaritan and prodigal son (only here), while they are **sharp rebukes to pride, and** encourage the humble, open to us new views of the

"Wisdom, love and power"

of the TEACHER. Jewish customs and chronology are intelligible to foreigners. The conversations of JESUS, with the incidents giving **rise,** words of **hearers,** results, and **discourses** so **full, as to** satisfy the curiosity **even** of the Grecians. The book is not supplementary but original.

In JOHN, **there** is what meets the higher speculative **tendencies in man,** correcting **the** false in Jewish and heathen **religion and** philosophy. The writer's object is stated 1: 1-18, 20: 31. It was to give the world just views of the nature, office and character of the DIVINE REDEEMER. He records those passages in our SAVIOR's life which so clearly display his power and authority; and discourses in which he speaks plainly of his nature, work and efficacy of his death. The others speak of JESUS in Galilee chiefly. *Here*, he is seen in Judea mostly. He speaks of three passovers at least, the others of one. Most is **new as** 13-17, 10, 11 chs. Records six miracles, omits most of the parables and sermon on the mount.

Thus the GOSPELS in their mutual relation. They **really** make but one, a "four-sided gospel;" **not a complete biography, but** rather memoir. But in unity and variety, **adapted** to the wants—spiritual and temporal condition of every people, in every clime and age. And in all, GOD in CHRIST is revealed as our IMMANUEL—BROTHER, FRIEND in nearest, holiest relationships.

7, 22, 88.

IV

THE EVANGELISTS IN THEIR RELATION TO THE GOSPELS.

DEAR M.

MATTHEW (wrote 37–63), is called Levi his Hebrew name, **MARK** 2: 14, LUKE 5: 27. Was of Galilee and called 9: 9, from "the place of toll," in or near Capernaum, before the sermon on the mount. He had his **MASTER** "at meat" in his house v 10, Mark 2: 15, and "many publicans and sinners" present. This was probably made occasion of parting with his old companions in sin etc. CLARKE, WESLEY. In 10: 3, he speaks of himself as the *publican*, to magnify GOD in his call to be an apostle. He wrote before the fall of **Jerusalem, in Greek** (some think in Heb) from internal evidence. And Greek was the vernacular in Palestine—books, business and common life. His aim is by a record of what JESUS did and suffered, to redeem him from reproach, disarm prejudice, and to future ages, set forth the character of MESSIAH.

MARK 48-65, who bears the Hebrew name of John, was the son of Mary, whose house in Jerusalem, seems to have been a resort for the disciples, and place of prayer. Here Peter came, out of prison ACTS 12: 12, 25. He was nephew to Barnabas; and both, Paul's companions COL 4: 10. He went with Paul and Barnabas from Jerusalem, but left at Perga in Pamphylia 13: 5, 13. **Afterwards** at Antioch, desiring to go with them on the 2nd journey, Paul "thought not good," "and there arose a sharp contention, so that they parted asunder," and Barnabas took Mark and sailed to Cyprus 15: 39. He was afterwards restored to Paul's favor, for we find him Col 4: 10, II Tim 4: 11, Phil 24, commended to the churches.

Though not an apostle, he was their friend and companion, and believed to have been a witness of much of our Lord's ministry. Early writers concur in saying that he was a fruit of Peter's ministry I Pet 5: 13, and was with him in his labors, and wrote under his direction, or as his amanuensis. Justin calls this book "the gospel of Peter." Internal evidence is in favor. Most of the acts recorded, Peter was present at, things honorable to him are omitted, while faults are freely given.

Luke 57–62, is believed to be the "beloved physician" Col 4: 14, and no doubt wrote the Acts, not earlier than 63. (The Acts cover about 33 yrs, from 30–63. Paul reached Rome in 61, and preached "two whole yrs" 28: 30, at least. Nero's persecution Tacitus says, began in 64, on occasion of his setting the city on fire. Paul and Peter some say, were martyred that year. "Paul suffered in 67." Usher. We know that it was after his release, and return from visiting his churches.) In the preface, he speaks of "the former—mar *first* treatise," while both are to "Theophilus." Antiquity assigns his nativity to Antioch. He is thought to be the one with Cleopas, going to Emmaus. It seems, from his knowledge of Greek and name *Loukas*, that he was a gentile, and from Hebrew terms, words and phrases in both books, and understanding of the Jewish religion, that he became a proselyte; but on receiving the new faith, a zealous follower of Paul Acts 16: 10, 20: 5 etc. From 28: 15, Phil 24, he was with him in his first, and from II Tim 4: 11, was at his side in his second imprisonment, to the last.

His style is both historical and classical, among other peculiarities. Also a "technical definiteness" in the miracles of healing, favors his *therapeutic* knowledge.

THE EVANGELISTS.   267

JOHN. 97 (?) Bro of James, was son of Zebedee and Salome. Theophylact says (a GR. MS ROYAL LIB. VIENNA, agreeing), that Salome was a daughter of Joseph by a former wife, making her and sons, sister and nephews to our LORD. CLARKE. His father was a fisherman of Bethsaida, having hired servants Mark 1: 20, and Salome was of them who ministered to JESUS MATT 27: 56. Having been brought up by a pious mother, he seems early to have become one of John Baptist's disciples (to whom he was cousin), and one of the two who heard John speak and followed JESUS 1: 40. JESUS surnamed James and John *Boanerges.*

John with Peter and James, was soon admitted to intimacy with the MASTER, and to be with him in the most interesting events of his life MATT 26: 37 MARK 5: 37. He was at his transfiguration and in Gethsemane.

At the supper he was "reclining on JESUS' bosom," was the one "JESUS loved." He followed JESUS into the high priest's palace, brought in Peter, was through the trial, at the crucifixion, where he was honored with that solemn, affecting charge "Behold thy mother!" and "took her to his own home" 19: 26-7. He outran Peter to the tomb, was the first who "saw and believed."——His place is with that number he beheld standing with their LEADER "on Mt Zion" REV 14, who "follow the LAMB whithersoever he goeth."

He is said to have staid in Jerusalem till the death of Mary, about 48. After Paul left "Asia," he went to Ephesus and founded churches in that region. Was banished to Patmos in the Ægean Sea by Domitian or Nero, and on this observatory, wrote the APOCALYPSE about 96. Tertullian says he was taken to Rome, thrown into a caldron of boiling oil, but came through unhurt; then sent to Patmos.

On the accession of Nerva, he returned to Ephesus, wrote his GOSPEL (the last book probably written), and fell asleep, some say over 100 yrs old, A D 100. He is the only apostle who died a natural death. In extreme age

Jerome says, he would be borne into the church, **if only to say to** his flock—"My little children, love one another."

He omits the siege of **Jerusalem, as** that event had **been long known.** He portrays the GODHEAD **and** manhood **of** JESUS to the life. None have revealed the lineaments of his humanity **with** such delicacy **and beauty, nor** the SAVIOR's **heart** like John. **Clement calls this the divine or spiritual** GOSPEL.—" It **is the** GOSPEL **of love, life and light; the** GOSPEL **of** the heart, taken **from the very heart of** CHRIST, on **which his** disciple **leaned in the supper."**

SCHAFF.

RESUMÉ

OUR task is done.

IN accordance with our plan, we have considered the claims of the BIBLE to genuineness. 1 From the original Heb and Greek MSS, Greek N T and SEPT, age and character, Heb text. PT I, c I SEC 1-5. 2 Ancient versions, various readings. The AUTHORIZED and REVISED VERSIONS II 1-4.

Under authenticity and authority III, the two TESTAMENTS—law, prophets and PSALMS; GOSPELS, ACTS, letters, REVELATION, as written by the names they bear and of divine origin. This is shown 1, From the books themselves. 2 The divinity of our LORD, the O T being confirmed chiefly and proximately by the New. While their inspiration and canonicity 1-2, is implied in, and depends on their authority. All which is further illustrated and confirmed by the two branches of evidence—external and internal IV, V. Next

The BIBLE—A revelation of GOD, man, and spiritual truth, gradual and progressive; its unity, though not systematic VI.

Next in order (introducing the exegetical portion, with rules therefor PT II c I—VIII) c 1, The necessity of care, tropical words, and above all, the spirit in which the WORD is to be studied 1-3.

II Sense of the words, connection, context, scope, comparing SCRIPTURE with SCRIPTURE.

III External helps—opinions and ideas, history, profane and ecclesiastical, chronology, natural history 1-5.

IV Manners and customs, coins and medals, time and modes of reckoning 1-3.

V, VI Biblical geography—natural and physical, towns, cities etc.

VII Allegories, symbols, types, parables.

VIII Prophecy.

Next PT III c 1, under systematic and inferential study

—Doctrines, precepts; moral and positive precepts 1–3. II Promises, examples. Then III, Quotations of the OLD in the N T. IV Origin, nature and use of SCRIPTURE difficulties—an interesting chapter.

V State of the Jews from the exile till CHRIST, including the Restoration, with notice of the 12 books—(all, from Jeremiah 628—13th of Josiah, to Mal) 1–2. Civil and moral history from Malachi to CHRIST 3–4.

"The Sabbath and port of our labors" is gained in the glorious appearing of JESUS CHRIST and his GOSPEL c VI. Here may be found two life pictures of JESUS till thirty years of age. Also, the GOSPELS his memoirs, and their authors, in their mutual relations to one another—from the most authentic sources.

ONE object or idea of the revisers of the A V, seems to have been to transmit it down as an "English Classic." And this will in part, account for the "music of its cadences and felicities of its rhythm "—" unequalled English diction;" sacrificing even *literalness* in places, to this end.

It is a *superstitious* reverence with some, comparable to that of the Jews for Moses as against their MESSIAH, or his GOSPEL (in connection with its classic feature), that will cling to the OLD VERSION in this generation.

As an illustration (not one of its "felicities"), in HOLY GHOST (not in the O T), GHOST, from *geist*, is both *unsightly* and *unmusical;* while SPIRIT (from Gr πνευμα), is beautiful, and euphonious to our ears. And yet there are some who may think us lacking in reverence for speaking thus, and seeking to have it changed (as the American company desired), and as a consequence, in our literature also.

The unprejudiced lover of truth for its own sake, cannot read SEC 4 c II especially, and the reviser's preface to the N T, without being satisfied, that we now have the best translation in the world.

And when we are told that the N T *especially* (see reviser's pref), was found faulty, we feel justified in repeating that the R V must soon displace the A V, as one of the things " which * * * is ready to vanish away;" if indeed an American version should not be called for, which might be suggested by our copious indexes even, in the "English version."

THE END.

www.ingramcontent.com/pod-product-compliance
Lightning Source LLC
Chambersburg PA
CBHW031936230426
43672CB00010B/1937